◀ PUNTO

With outstanding safety, comfort and sheer practicality, coupled with a distinctive, smooth and rounded shape, it is not surprising the Punto was voted European Car of the Year 1995. The Punto offers a choice of 7 engines ranging from 1.1 litre petrol to 1.7 litre turbo diesel. It is available in 3 and 5 door form and in 14 different colours. With such a wide range, the problem is deciding which one to choose.

FIAT COUPE ▶

Fiat's classic Italian sporting heritage has been combined with the finesse of modern automotive technology to produce the strikingly seductive, Pininfarina-designed Coupé. There's room to seat 4 adults in comfort and safety, whilst the 16v and 16v Turbo 2.0 litre engines provide breathtaking performance.

ULYSSE ▶

The Ulysse, arriving in October 1995, offers a wide range of seating options and comfortable accommodation for up to eight people. Its saloon car standards of performance, ride and handling make the Ulysse a joy to drive and a choice of both petrol and turbo diesel engines means there is a perfect power unit to suit your needs.

BARCHETTA ▶

Compact, elegant and timeless, the new Fiat Barchetta is a left hand drive two seater convertible that exudes effortless class. The 1747cc 16 valve twin cam engine delivers 130 BHP and the car will accelerate from 0-60mph in just over eight seconds, but above all the Barchetta is an open top sports car that is a joy to drive.

FIAT **RANGE**

INTERPRETATION OF THE MAP

Counties and Regions

England

The West Country
pages 1-64

London and the South
pages 65-105

East Anglia and the East Midlands
pages 110-118

The Heart of England
pages 123-140

The North West
pages 144-172

Yorkshire and the North East
pages 177-194

Wales

pages 197-204

Scotland

Southern
pages 210-213

Central
pages 216-227

Highlands & Islands
pages 230-237

Channel Islands

pages 240-244

Ireland

Northern
page 246

Republic
pages 249-262

WESTERN ISLES

HIGHLAND

GRAMPIAN

SCOTLAND

TAYSIDE

CENTRAL

FIFE

STRATHCLYDE

LOTHIAN

BORDERS

DUMFRIES
AND GALLOWAY

NORTHUMBERLAND

TYNE & WEAR

DONEGAL

LONDONDERRY

ANTRIM

NORTHERN
IRELAND

TYRONE

DURHAM

CLEVELAND

FERMANAGH

ARMAGH

DOWN

CUMBRIA

SLIGO

MONAGHAN

ISLE
OF MAN

NORTH YORKSHIRE

MAYO

LEITRIM

CAVAN

LANCASHIRE

WEST
YORKSHIRE

HUMBERSIDE

ROSCOMMON

LONGFORD

LOUTH

MEATH

GREATER
MANCHESTER

SOUTH
YORKSHIRE

REPUBLIC
OF IRELAND

WESTMEATH

DUBLIN

MERSEYSIDE

GALWAY

OFFALY

CHESHIRE

DERBYSHIRE

NOTTS.

LINCOLNSHIRE

KILDARE

CLWYD

GWYNEDD

ENGLAND

CLARE

LAOIS

WICKLOW

STAFFS.

NORFOLK

TIPPERARY

CARLOW

KILKENNY

WEXFORD

SHROPSHIRE

LEICESTERSHIRE

LIMERICK

POWYS

WEST
MIDLANDS

NORTHANTS.

CAMBRIDGESHIRE

SUFFOLK

KERRY

WATERFORD

WALES

HEREFORD
AND
WORCESTER

WARKS.

BEDS.

CORK

DYFED

GLOUCESTERSHIRE

BUCKS.

HERTS

ESSEX

WEST
GLAM.

MID
GLAM.

GWENT

OXFORDSHIRE

GREATER
LONDON

SOUTH
GLAM.

AVON

BERKSHIRE

SURREY

KENT

WILTSHIRE

SOMERSET

HAMPSHIRE

WEST
SUSSEX

EAST
SUSSEX

DEVON

DORSET

ISLE
OF
WIGHT

CORNWALL

CHANNEL
ISLANDS

© Crown Copyright

© GEOprojects (UK) Ltd

Introduction

Welcome to the 57th edition of SIGNPOST.

There have been some changes since our last edition. After 22 years, the ownership of the title has reverted to the maternal grandson of the founder, W G ("Mac") McMinnies. Malcolm Orr-Ewing's company, Priory Publications Ltd, specialises in international annual travel guides.The past owner of Signpost, Christopher Carney-Smith (pictured below) continues as a consultant and we have appointed Alistair Hankey, until recently a director of the British Tourist Authority, as our new editor.

The layout of the edition has also changed as you will notice. Each full page property now has a coloured map to assist travellers. These should be used in conjunction with normal maps and atlases and are designed to guide readers 'over the last five miles' to the door of their chosen hotel. The *Bargain Breaks*, previously a separate secton, have been re-absorbed into the main hotel entries. Another innovation is the re-inclusion of Ireland in the guide, for the first time since 1982. Once again we have featured *Diary of Events* and a *Selected Local Attractions* lists for each region.

For the 1996 edition, we have also included for the first time some 35 *Budget Hotels*. These are establishments for business travellers and others on a set budget. Many do not have the same range of facilities as the traditional *Signpost* profile hotel but all have been visited by one of our inspectors and are considered to offer good value for money within their price range and area. These hotels and guest houses normally come at the beginning or end of a regional section and are usually represented with half pages without maps.

New publisher Malcolm Orr-Ewing (left) with Christopher Carney-Smith, consultant (centre) and Alistair Hankey, editor, right in front of the Bibury Court Hotel, Gloucestershire.

GUIDE TO PREMIER HOTELS
IN GREAT BRITAIN AND IRELAND

57TH EDITION

1996

 PRIORY
PUBLICATIONS LTD

Syresham, Brackley, Northants NN13 5HH, UK
Tel: (+44) 1280 850 603. Fax: (+44) 1280 850 576

ISBN **1 871985 21 8**

Editor: Alistair Hankey; **Cartographer**: Neill ffrench-Blake
© Priory Publications Ltd 1996

Printed by Ebenezer Baylis & Son Ltd, London Road, Worcester WR5 2JH

Trade distribution in UK by W Foulsham & Co Ltd
The Publishing House, Bennetts Close.
Cippenham, Berks SL1 5AP
Telephone: 01753 526789; Fax: 01753 535003

Signpost is published in the USA under the title *Premier Hotels of Great Britain & Ireland*

Signpost is now available electronically on the Internet under the web site:
http://www.SIGNPOST.com

Front cover: *Stapleford Park, Melton Mowbray, Leicestershire.* *Rear cover*: *The Royal Hotel, Jersey.*

CONTENTS

WHEREVER YOU'RE
TRAVELLING,
WHY NOT TRAVEL THERE IN
STYLE
WITH
FIAT

FIAT BRAVO AND FIAT BRAVA ▼ ▶

All aspects of the stylish new Fiat Bravo and Fiat Brava have been built to combine driver enjoyment with the highest standards of safety. The 3dr Bravo with its flowing yet aggressive lines epitomises the natural flair and exuberance of Italian designers while the Fiat Brava combines the elegance of Italian design with the rationality and roominess

of a class leading 5 door. From the lively 1.4 12v to the exhilarating 1.8 16v, all of the Fiat Bravos and Fiat Bravas are equally at home driving in the city or cruising on the open roads. All models come with driver's airbag, seat belt pre-tensioners, energy absorbing steering wheel with collapsable column and a third brake light fitted as standard.

TEMPRA SW ▲

The Tempra's exceptionally solid construction and distinctive styling incorporates a huge load area with a split folding rear seat available on all models. The wide and flexible range includes petrol and turbo diesel saloon and stylish Station Wagon versions, offering up to 54.7 cu ft of load space.

CINQUECENTO SPORTING ▲

The Cinquecento Sporting is the latest version of a star performer. It's the ultimate city car with excellent open road performance. The Sporting, voted Best Budget Car 1995 by What Car magazine, offers tremendous fun, packed into a stylish little car.

Top: Signpost hotel inspector Olof White (left) with proprietors John and Tove Taylor and their son George and Sally Harvey outside Buckland-Tout-Saints Hotel, Goveton, Devon.
Below: Signpost inspector Sue Long with Richard Prideaux-Brune, proprietor of Plumber Manor, Sturminster Newton, Dorset.

Above: Signpost inspector Tricia Doyle with Martin Price, co-proprietor, at the Hare and Hounds Hotel, Tetbury, Glos.
Below: Signpost inspector Susie Horsley (right) with Maree Langford, Head Receptionist (left), and Ruth Brown, General Manager (centre), at the Bay Tree Hotel, Burford, Oxfordshire.

Above: *(left to right) Signpost editor and London hotels inspector Alistair Hankey, Chef de Cuisine Jean-Marie Zimmermann, Master Sommelier Barrie Larvin and Michael Sharp, General Manager, outside Selsdon Park Hotel, Sanderstead, Surrey.* **Below:** *The new headquarters of Signpost in Northamptonshire.*

xi

How to use Signpost

1. All hotels are listed in two separate indices:

a) on pages 272-279 in county order within their regional areas (as indicated on the map on page v)

b) on pages 280-282 by alphabetical name.

2. The book is divided into sections containing hotels in **England, Wales , Scotland, Channel Islands** and **Ireland**. Each country is divided into regions, then counties, and the nearest town or village to each hotel appears alphabetically at the top of the page. For example, in the West Country *Falmouth Beach Resort Hotel* in Cornwall is on page 5 and *Blunsdon House*, Near Swindon, Wiltshire, is on page 64, the last page in the West Country regional section.

3. The type of licence held by each hotel is indicated by:
   F = Full
   R = Restaurant
   R & R = Restaurant and Residential

Please use the two pages at the rear of the book to send us both your *Confidential Reports* and *Recommendations for New Hotel Inclusion* in Signpost, the Premier Hotel Guide for the British Isles.

THE WEST COUNTRY SELECTED LOCAL ATTRACTIONS

■ Historic Houses, Gardens & Parks

AVON
Clevedon Court, Clevedon
Sally Lunn's House, Bath

CORNWALL
Cotehele House, St. Dominick, Saltash
Glendurgan Garden, Mawnam Smith, Falmouth
Kit Hill Country Park, Callington
Lanhydrock House, Bodmin
Mount Edgcombe House & Park, Torpoint
Trebah Garden, Mawnam Smith, Falmouth
Trelissick Garden, Truro
Trengwainton Garden, Penzance
Trerice, Newquay

DEVON
Arlington Court, Barnstaple
Bicton Park & Gardens, East Budleigh
Overbecks Museum & Garden, Salcombe
Rosemoor Garden - Royal Horticultural Society's
  Garden, Great Torrington
Saltram House, Plympton
Ugbrooke House & Park, Newton Abbot

DORSET
Athelhampton House & Gardens, Puddletown,
  Dorchester
Forde Abbey & Gardens, Chard
Hardy's Cottage Garden, Higher Bockampton,
  Dorchester
Kingston Lacey House, Nr. Wimborne

SOMERSET
Barrington Court Gardens, Barrington, llminster
Clapton Court Gardens
Fyne Court, Broomfield, Bridgwater
Hestercombe Gardens, Fitzpaine, Taunton
Lytes Cary Manor, Charlton Mackrell, Somerton
Montacute House
Tintinhull House Garden, Nr. Yeovil

WILTS
Avebury Manor
Corsham Court
Dyrham Park, Dryham, Chippenham
Great Chalfield Manor, Melksham
Hazelbury Manor Gardens, Box, Corsham
If ord Mamor Gardens, Bradford-on-Avon
Lackham Gardens & Agricultural Museum, Lacock,
  Chippenham
Lacock Abbey
Mompesson House, Salisbury
Stourhead House & Gardens, Stourton, Nr. Mere
Westwood Mamor

■ Walks & Nature Trails

AVON
The Cotswold Way, first part from Chipping Campden
West Mendip Way, starts at Uphill following the crest of
  the Mendip Hills

CORNWALL
The Camel Trail, runs along the River Camel from
  Padstow to Poley's Bridge
The North Cornwall Heritage Coast

DEVON
Dartmoor National Park Guided Walks
The Tarka Trail

DORSET
Brit Valley Walk
The Dorset Coast Path
Hardy's Dorset Walk

SOMERSET
Exmoor National Park Country Walks
West Somerset Mineral Railway, from Watchet to Washford

WILTSHIRE
Discover the Villages Trail
The Imber Range Perimeter Path

■ Historical Sites &Museums

AVON
Bristol City Museum & Art Gallery
Harveys Wine Museum, Bristol
Museum of Costumes, Bath
Pump Room, Bath
Roman Baths Museum, Bath

CORNWALL
Launceston Castle
Restormel Castle, Lothwithiel
St. Catherine's Castle, Fowey
St. Mawes Castle
St. Michael's Mount, Marazion
Tintagel Castle

DEVON
Buckfast Abbey, Buckfastleigh
Buckland Abbey, Yelverton
Castle Drogo, Drewsteignton, Exeter
Compton Castle, Marldon, Paignton
Dartmouth Castle
Okehampton Castle
Powderham Castle, Kenton, Nr. Exeter
Royal Albert Memorial Museum, Exeter
Watermouth Castle, Berrynarbor, llfracombe

DORSET
Corfe Castle
Dorset County Museum, Dorchester
Maiden Castle, Dorchester
Portland Castle
Sherborne Castle

SOMERSET
Cleeve Abbey, Washford, Watchet
Dunster Castle
Glastonbury Abbey
Nunney Castle
Taunton Cider Mill
Wells Cathedral

THE WEST COUNTRY - SELECTED LOCAL ATTRACTIONS/DIARY OF EVENTS

WILTSHIRE
Avebury Stone Circles, Nr. Marlborough
Great Western Railway Museum, Swindon
Longleat House, Warminster
Museum & Art Gallery, Swindon
Old Wardour Castle, Tisbury, Salisbury
Salisbury Cathedral
Stonehenge, Amesbury, Salisbury

■ **Entertainment Venues**

AVON
Bristol Zoological Gardens

CORNWALL
Cornish Seal Sanctuary, Gweek, Helston
Flambards Victoria Village Theme Park, Helston
Land's End, Penzance
Newquay Zoo
Paradise Park, Hayle
World in Miniature, Truro

DEVON
City Museum & Art Gallery, Plymouth
Combe Martin Wildlife & Dinosaur Park

DEVON (continued)
Dartmoor Wild Life Park & West Country Falconry
 Centre, Sparkwell, Plymouth
Kents Cavern Showcaves, Torquay
Paignton & Dartmouth Steam Railway, Paignton
Paignton Zoological & Botanical Gardens
Plymouth Dome, Plymouth
Riviera Centre, Torquay
Torquay Museum

DORSET
Brownsea Island, Poole
Lyme Regis Marine Aquarium
Weymouth Sea Lite Park, Lodmoor Country Park,
 Weymouth

SOMERSET
Cheddar Showcaves, Cheddar Gorge
Haynes Motor Museum Sparkford, Yeovil
The Tropical Bird Gardens, Rode
West Somerset Railway, Minehead
Wookey Hole Caves & Papermill

WILTSHIRE
Lions of Longleat Safari Park, Warminster

THE WEST COUNTRY DIARY OF EVENTS 1996

April 1 to
May 31

CORNWALL 'S GARDENS FESTIVAL
Various Gardens, Truro, Comwall.

April 7

BOURNEMOUTH EASTER PARADE
From Boscombe Pier to Bournemouth Pier

April 30-May 3

OLD CUSTOM HOBBY HORSE CELEBRATIONS
Minehead, Somerset

May 3-6

THE GREAT CORNWALL BALLOON FESTIVAL
Venues in St Austell, Newquay, Cornwall. Hot air balloon festival.

May 1-2

PRO/AM SURFING CHAMPIONSHIP
Fistral Beach, Newquay, Cornwall. Two day surfing champion
ship open to both professional and amateur.

May 2-5

BADMINTON HORSE TRIALS
Badminton House, Badminton, Avon.

May 3-6

ENGLISH NATIONAL SURFING CHAMPIONSHIPS
Fistral Beach, Newquay, Cornwall. 3-day surfing contest.

May 4-5

SOUTH WEST CUSTOM AND CLASSIC BIKE SHOW
Royal Bath & West Showground, Shepton Mallet, Somerset

May 5-6

WEYMOUTH INTERNATIONAL BEACH KITE FESTIVAL
Weymouth Beach, Dorset

May 8

HELSTON FLORA DAY, Helston, Cornwall

WEST COUNTRY DIARY OF EVENTS

May 16-18	DEVON COUNTY SHOW - 101st SHOW Westpoint Showground, Clyst St. Mary, Devon.
May 17-June 2	BATH INTERNATIONAL MUSIC FESTIVAL Various venues in and around Bath, Avon
May 17-June 2	SALISBURY FESTIVAL. Various venues, Salisbury, Wiltshire
May 22- September 15	THE MINACK DRAMA FESTIVAL The Minack, Porthcurno, Penzance
May 24-27	INTERNATIONAL FESTIVAL OF THE SEA Bristol Historic Harbour, The City Centre, Bristol, Avon
May 24-June 8	ENGLISH RIVIERA DANCE FESTIVAL Victoria Hotel Ballroom and Town Hall, Torquay, Devon
May 29-31	ROYAL BATH AND WEST OF ENGLAND SHOW TheRoyal Bath & West Showground, Shepton Mallet, Somerset. (West Country's Premier Agricultural Show)
June 6-8	ROYAL CORNWALL SHOW Royal Cornwall Showground, Wadebridge, Cornwall
June 16	SAILING - EUROPE I SINGLE HANDED TRANSATLANTIC RACE Royal Western Yacht Club of England, Queen Anne's Battery, Plymouth, Devon. Race starts south of Plymouth Breakwater and finishes at Newport, Rhode Island, USA
June 19	BRISTOL TO BOURNEMOUTH VINTAGE VEHICLE RUN Ashton Court Estate, Long Ashton, Bristol, Avon
June 22	PORT OF BRIXHAM INTERNATIONAL TRAWLER RACE AND QUAY FESTIVAL New Fish Quay, The Harbour, Brixham, Devon. New Quay open to the public during the day, and the festival includes stalls, live bands and displays.
June 29	THE GLASTONBURY PILGRIMAGE Glastonbury Abbey, The Abbey Gate House, Glastonbury Somer set. (Anglican Pilgrimage)
July 4-21	EXETER FESTIVAL. Various venues, Exeter, Devon.
July 6	TORBAY ANNUAL CHAMPION SWIM Meadfoot Beach, Torquay, Devon. Annual race from Torquay to Brixham and retum.
August 1-11	WORLD PROFESSIONAL SURFING CHAMPIONSHIP Fistral Beach, Newquay, Cornwall
August 2-9	INTERNATIONAL FESTIVAL OF FOLK ARTS - SIDMOUTH The Arena and other venues, Sidmouth, Devon
August 7	RAF ST MAWGAN AIR DAY RAF St Mawgan, Newquay, Cornwall.International air show with flying displays, stalls, funfair, helicopter flights etc.

WEST COUNTRY DIARY OF EVENTS

August 9-11   BRISTOL INTERNATIONAL BALLOON FIESTA
Ashton Court Estate, Long Ashton, Bristol, Avon

August 10-11   YEOVIL FESTIVAL OF TRANSPORT
Barwick Park, Dorchester Road, Yeovil, Somerset.

August 19-20   SURF LIFESAVING AND 'IRON MAN' CHAMPIONSHIP
Fistral Beach, Newquay, Cornwall

August 23-26   CORNWALL FOLK FESTIVAL
Town Hall, The Plat, Wadebridge, Cornwall.
Folk concerts, dances, ceilidhs, workshops. children's entertainment

August 23-26   GLASTONBURY CHILDREN'S FESTIVAL
Abbey Park Playground, Fisher's Hill, Glastonbury, Somerset.
20 different performances for children each day + many
participative workshops.

August 24-31   BUDE JAZZ FESTIVAL
Various venues, Bude, Cornwall

August 26-
September 2   'WAYS WITH WORDS' LITERATURE FESTIVAL
Dartington Hall Gardens, Dartington, Devon

August 29-31   PORT OF DARTMOUTH ROYAL REGATTA
Various venues, Dartmouth, Devon

September 5-8   WEST OF ENGLAND OPEN AMATEUR GOLF CHAMPIONSHIP
Burnham and Berrow Golf Club, St Christoher's Way, Burnham-
on-Sea, Somerset

September 7-8   COUNTRSIDE CAVALCADE
The Royal Bath and West Showground, Shepton Mallet, Somerset

September 10   WIDECOMBE FAIR
Old Field, Widecombe-in-the-Moor, Devon.

October 12   EXETER CARNIVAL

November 7   BRIDGWATER GUY FAWKES CARNIVAL
Town Centre, Bridgwater, Somerset

November 9   NORTH PETHERTON GUY FAWKES CARNIVAL
Town Centre, North Petherton, Somerset

November 11   WELLS GUY FAWKES CARNIVAL
Town Centre, Wells, Somerset. Illuminated carnival floats visiting
various towns in Somerset & Avon over an eleven-day period.

For further information contact:
The West Country Tourist Board
60 St. Davids Hill
Exeter, Devon EX4 4SY
Tel: 01392 76351

Southern Tourist Board
40 Chamberlayne Road
Eastleigh, Hampshire
Tel: 01703 620006

HOLLY LODGE
8 Upper Oldfield Park, Bath, Avon BA2 3JZ
Telephone: (01225) 339187/424042   Fax: (01225) 481138

Holly Lodge is a delightful town house that has been skilfully and sympathetically converted to provide the utmost comfort for guests. The décor and furnishings are superb with pastel shades predominating and many antiques. The bedrooms have every modern convenience including satellite TV, direct dial telephone, beautiful bathrooms and in fact everything one could need. The hotel received the English Tourist Board 'England for Excellence Award' for 1993. Chauffeur driven limousines, guided tours, restaurant and theatre bookings and onward accommodation can all be arranged. Bath is one of only three world heritage cities in the UK and , as well as being a tourist attraction in its own right with Regency buildings and superb shops and theatres, is an ideal centre for touring the south Cotswolds. Double room £75-85; single £48 inc. VAT. **Bargain breaks** available November to March for two nights or more.

London 104, Bristol 12, Chippenham 13, Chepstow, Devizes 19, Frome 13, Tetbury 23, Warminster 16, Wells 19

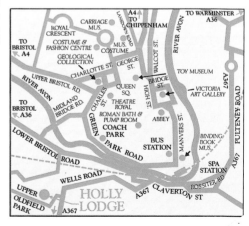

Four doubles, two twin, one single, all en suite. Colour TV with satellite and video films, direct-dial telephone, hairdryer, strictly non-smoking, airport pickup by arrangement, car parking (8), trouser press, some facilities for disabled. No restaurant.

DORIAN HOUSE
One, Upper Oldfield Park, Bath BA2 3JX
Telephone: 01225 426336
Fax: (01225) 444699

Four double, 3 double/twin, one single room, all en suite; colour TV; direct dial telephone; hairdryer; tea/coffee making facilities, car parking (8); major credit cards accepted

A warm welcome and an aura of nostalgic luxury await you at this gracious Victorian house. Enjoying magnificent views of Bath, Dorian House is a ten minute stroll to the city's historic attractions, shopping centre, railway and bus station. Bath has its own Theatre Royal, entertainment, music festivals, varied sport and a fine range of restaurants.

Owned and run by Jane and Brian Taylor, help is always available for your enquiries or to assist you to plan your time in and around Bath. Every room is individually designed and beautifully decorated. Single £42; double £58. Major credit cards accepted. Dinner available by prior arrangement. Honesty Bar.

EAGLE HOUSE HOTEL
24 Church Street, Bathford, Bath, Avon BA1 7RS
Telephone: and fax: 01225 859946.

Eagle House is a fine Georgian house by John Wood the Elder, lying in the beautiful conservation village of Bathford, three miles from Bath. The house and its 1^1/$_2$ acres or garden are set on the edge of an area of outstanding natural beauty and enjoy far reaching views. The drawing room, with its open log fire, can be made available to guests for meetings on request. There is a separate walled garden cottage for self catering. Double rooms £42-£68; singles £32-£39.50 (cooked breakfast extra). **Bargain breaks** available November to mid-March; details on request. ETB 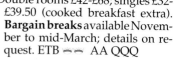 AA QQQ

Three double, two single, three family bedrooms, all en suite. Plus two bedrooms in cottage. Colour TV, direct-dial telephone, tea/coffee making facilities; hairdryers;. Cots and extra beds on request. For golf courses within four miles; riding, tennis, cycle hire and boating all nearby. Good restaurants and pubs within walking distance.

THE CROSS HANDS HOTEL
Old Sodbury, Bristol BS17 6RJ

Tel: 01454 313000; Fax: 01454 324409

Six twin rooms, nine single, nine double; all en suite. Bed and breakfast from £33.50-£89.50. Lunch available from noon-1430 from £4. Dinner 1830-2230 from £13. Colour TV + satellite, tea/coffee making facilities, hairdryer, trouser press, ample car parking, Conference facilities from 2 to 120 delegates

Fourteenth century coaching inn with a friendly historic atmosphere. Queen Elizabeth II sheltered here from a blizzard in 1981. The bedrooms are clean and comfortable and the Beaufort Restaurant is popular with locals and residents alike. Convenient for Badminton (special rates apply) and for touring Bath and the South Cotswolds.

MAYFAIR HOTEL
5 Henleaze Road, Westbury on Trym, Bristol BS9 4EX
Telephone: 01779 622008

The Mayfair Hotel is a small family run hotel with a friendly and informal atmosphere, situated in a quiet residential area close to the Downs. It is conveniently situated close to Bristol with its shops and restaurants and theatres. Not far away is Bath with all its attractions and weston-super-Mare and Cheddar Gorge are also only a short drive away. A comfortable hotel from which to visit these areas for those travelling on a limited budget. Single room from £22; double from £40.

Two twin rooms, one en suite; four single, one en suite; three double, one en suite. Colour TV and tea/coffee making facilities; car parking to rear of hotel; children welcome

TREGLOS HOTEL
Constantine Bay, Nr. Padstow, Cornwall PL28 8JH

Telephone: 01841 520727   *Fax: 01841 521163*

Treglos has been recommended by Signpost for many years. It is run as a country house hotel - the 'hotel' atmosphere being hardly apparent. It is a veritable model of elegance and luxury, standing in its own grounds overlooking the Atlantic. Personal consideration is the keynote to this splendid house, personally cared for by the owners, Ted and Barbara Barlow, their son Jim and his wife Rose, who retain loyal, cheerful and attentive staff. There are five lounges, all traditionally furnished to the highest of standards. The décor is pleasant and restful with freshly cut flowers and, in cooler weather, log fires. Upstairs is as sumptuous as down, with all the appointments expected here. In the newly refurbished dining room, Treglos has a great reputation for the excellence of the fare. A varied selection of interesting and carefully prepared dishes is offered and local seafood and vegetables are served whenever possible. All this good food is complemented by a wide selection of carefully chosen wines at moderate prices. The elegantly designed indoor swimming pool leads to open lawns and sunken gardens. Within a few hundred yards are the sandy beaches of Constantine, Treyarnon and Booby's Bay. Dinner, room and breakfast from £58.50 (single),demi-pension weekly from £320 per person including VAT. Closed mid November to early March; office open for enquiries. **Bargain breaks:** Discounts or free golf offered the last weeks in May, July and August. Discounts are also offered for non seaview rooms throughout the season. Please enquire about our special three day breaks.

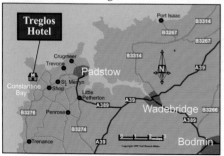

London 256, Newquay 12, Padstow 3, Falmouth 36, Truro 20

R and R licence; 44 en suite bedrooms, all with telephone, colour TV, hairdryers. Three rooms with sitting rooms (one ground floor); lift; meals to 9.30p.m.; night service; off season conferences; diets; logfires; full central heating; bridge room; snooker and pool table; indoor heated swimming pool; spa bath; sea bathing; sailing; boating; golf and tennis by arrangement with Trevose Golf Club; special rates available at Treloy, Bodmin and the new Bowood Park golf courses; sea fishing; riding nearby; surfing; four self-contained luxury flats.

THE FALMOUTH BEACH RESORT HOTEL
Gyllyngvase Beach, The Seafront, Falmouth,Cornwall TR11 4NA

Telephone: 01326 318084   Fax: 01326 319147

The problem with this hotel is choice: between room or apartment, restaurants, leisure centres, even which part of Cornwall to visit. However your comfort is assured in the luxurious surroundings of Falmouth Beach with its seaside position, warmed by the Gulf Stream, close to the old port and bustling modern town of Falmouth. The bright bedrooms, many with balconies and sea views, are furnished in soft colourings and with every facility you would need. An alternative is available in the choice of serviced or self-catering apartments nearby, ideal for those wanting independence and for young families. Refreshment choice is straight-forward and I can vouch for the superb food in the main restaurant, although the alternative of a light snack in the lively Feathers Bar was tempting. Both leisure centres with swimming pools are well geared to meet every demand and even include computerised aerobic equipment. The ever friendly staff are happy to advise on the many attractions in this most beautiful area. Single room including breakfast from £39-£50. Double room with breakfast from £62-£84.
Leisure Breaks: From £45 pppn, db&b October - March. £55 pppn, db&b April - September. Garden Holidays £60 pppn, db&b.
Land's End 50, Penzance 25, Bodmin 34, Plymouth 65, Truro 11, London 308

Full licence. 127 en suite bedrooms with radio & satellite TV; direct-dial telephone; hairdryer, trouser press, laundry service, non-smoker bedrooms, tea/ coffee making facilities; 24-hour room service; safety deposit box. Facilities for disabled. Last orders for dinner 21.00 hrs. Special diets available. Billiards/ snooker; fitness centre; indoor games room; Jacuzzi; watersports; two indoor pools; sauna. Riding, squash, fishing, golf by arrangement nearby. Full business services and five meeting rooms with capacity for 200. AV equipment. Airport pick-up; car rental. Car park-ing for 107 cars. Open all year. All major credit cards accepted.

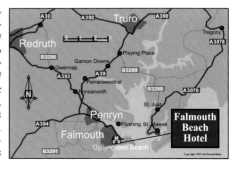

ROYAL DUCHY HOTEL
Falmouth, South Cornwall TR11 4NX
Telephone: 01326 313042   *Fax: 01326 319420*

With well kept gardens in the historic, maritime resort of Falmouth on Cornwall's famed riviera coastline, this is the ideal setting for a seafront hotel. It is just a short, level walk to the town centre and harbour, with views across Falmouth Bay to Pendennis Castle. Owned by the Brend family who own other luxurious hotels, including the Carlyon Bay Hotel, near St. Austell - see page 8, the hotel is expertly managed by Darryl Reburn. With very good furnishing and colour schemes, both bedrooms and public rooms are comfortable and relaxing, with a friendly atmosphere. The food is distinguished by its high standard and the choice of interesting dishes. It is beautifully cooked and presented, and complemented by a well chosen wine list. I can thoroughly recommend a stay at the Royal Duchy in all seasons - whether for relaxation or a more active holiday, you will always enjoy first class service. Room and breakfast from £50.00 single, £47.50 double/twin, per person, and dinner, room and breakfast from £57.50 single, £53.00 double/twin, per person. Prices include VAT. Do write for their attractive brochure. Other terms, including special summer saver tariffs and autumn and winter breaks on application. Recent ground floor luxury refurbishment.

Bargain breaks. Winter breaks from £82; Autumn breaks from £98; special June and July Breaks from £108 and special July breaks from £117. 00. All prices are per person for a minimum stay of two nights and include dinner, bed and breakfast.

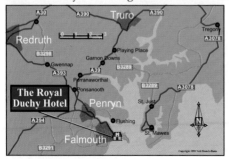

Redruth 10, Truro 11, Lizard 20, Penzance 25, Bodmin 34, London 267.

F licence; 50 en suite bedrooms (1 suite suitable for the disabled), all with direct dial telephone and satellite TV; room service; baby listening; night service; lift; last orders for dinner 9.00 p.m, bar meals; specialities; children welcome; dogs accepted at manager's discretion; conferences max. 40; small srooker/billiards table, table tennis; indoor heated swimming pool; sauna; solarium; spa pool; sea bathing; free golf to hotel residents at Carlyon Bay; sailing, boating, riding, shooting and fishing all locally; open all year; most credit cards accepted.

THE CORMORANT HOTEL
Golant by Fowey, Cornwall PL23 1LL

Telephone 01726 833426   Fax: 01726 833426

What a delightful hotel was my first reaction to The Cormorant, situated high above the waterfront in an unspoilt Cornish fishing village. This charming house makes a comfortable retreat for anyone wanting to "get away from it all", but is also close enough to Fowey and within easy driving distance of many of the beautiful treasures of Cornwall to do exactly the opposite! The setting of the Cormorant is an attraction in itself for all rooms enjoy the magnificent views over the Estuary, or you can relax by the indoor pool to get the same experience. The hotel has recently been taken over by Mr and Mrs Elworthy who have modernised the public rooms to reinforce the atmosphere of friendliness and comfort. The bedrooms too, with that view, were very pleasing - surely warm in the winter and certainly airy in the summer. The attractively decorated restaurant enjoys a well deserved name for good fare with its emphasis on fresh sea-food, which would delight a gourmet and is complemented by a full wine list. For those seeking more energetic pursuits the hotel's location ensures easy access to all the main water sporting activities including water skiing and sailing. However, I shall return again before too long simply to relax in this exquisite place. Single room including breakfast from £35.00. Double room with breakfast From £70.00.

Leisure Breaks: 3-night break offered throughout the year. Special winter bargains. Enquire at hotel.

St. Austell 7, Plymouth 28, Bodmin 9, Truro 23, London 277

Full licence. 11 en suite bedrooms with radio, colour TV. Last orders for dinner 21.00 hrs. Special diets available. Indoor pool. Car parking for 15 cars. Open all year. All major credit cards accepted.

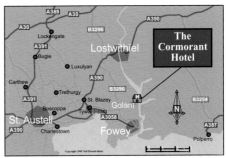

MARINA HOTEL
Esplanade, Fowey, Cornwall PL23 1HY

Telephone: 01726 833315   *Fax: 01726 832779*

Tucked quietly away on the Esplanade, the Marina Hotel commands a unique waterfront position overlooking both the River Fowey and the sea. Guests have a bird's eye view of all that goes on in the estuary including the Regatta. Moorings are available to guests, and the hotel has its own access to the water from the secluded walled garden, a haven for sun worshippers. The hotel is Georgian and period features have been retained throughout. Four of the bedrooms have sun balconies, all are en suite and have colour television and direct dial telephone. The restaurant at the Marina has wonderful views and both the table d'hôte and à la carte menus include locally caught fish and shellfish. An interesting selection of wines is available to complement each dish. A special feature of this hotel is that bargain breaks of two days or more are offered throughout the season. Proprietors, John and Carol Roberts, provide a warm welcome at this attractive small hotel and I know you will enjoy your stay. Room and breakfast from £26.00 per person, for two people sharing a double room. Weekly half board from £266.00.

Bargain breaks: Two nights for the price of one for the month of March and the last two weeks of November and first two weeks of December. Applies to accomodation only for a min. stay of two nights with two people sharing a room. Does not apply in Bank Holidays if these fall within these periods.

London 270, Plymouth 35, Bodmin 12, Truro 22, St Austell 9, Megavissey 14

R & R licence; 11 en suite bedrooms, all with direct dial telephone and TV, baby listening;   night service; last orders 8.30 p.m; special diets; dogs accepted; sea bathing; sailing/boating; golf and tennis five miles; riding, shooting two miles; fishing nearby; Visa and Mastercard accepted.

POLURRIAN HOTEL
Mullion, Lizard Peninsula, Cornwall TR12 7EN

Telephone: 01326 240421   Fax: 01326 240083

Three hundred feet above Polurrian Cove, and surrounded by wonderful National Trust coastline, the Polurrian Hotel enjoys an enviable position overlooking some of Cornwall's loveliest scenery. Steps lead down from the hotel to the sandy beach where bathing is safe and clean, or there is an alternative of indoor or outdoor heated swimming pools. In the hotel's leisure club, is a hairdressing and beauty salon, sauna and solarium, a gym for the more energetic, and light snacks can be enjoyed in the Aqua Bar. An inviting 18 hole golf course is nearby, and further sporting activities at the Polurrian include tennis. Small children can enjoy a safe-play area within the hotel's gardens, an indoor activity room, and during my visit, a conjuror! The attractive restaurant romantically overlooks the sea. The dishes are expertly cooked and presented, and seafood is a speciality. Early rising guests can help catch the latter in a local fishing boat! The bedrooms are luxurious and are all en suite, some having four-posters. The Polurrian Hotel also has its own self-catering apartments and bungalows. Do write for the brochure and enjoy a really exceptional family holiday. Dinner, room and breakfast from £42.00 plus VAT.

Bargain breaks: For a special occasion or a break from the stress of life, our Feature Breaks and Leisure Breaks in this unspoiled part of Cornwall will provide you with a memory to treasure. 3 day breaks - dinner, room and breakfast from £105 per person.

Penzance 22, Truro 26, The Lizard 4¹/₂, London 323
Full licence; 39 en suite bedrooms (5 ground floor), all with direct dial telephone and TV, room service; baby listening; night service; last orders for dinner 9. 00 p.m.; special diets; children welcome; dogs accepted; conferences max. 100; games room; snooker/billiards; outdoor and indoor heated swimming pools; leisure centre; sauna; solarium; spa pool; gymnasium; squash; tennis; sea bathing 200 yards; golf ¹/₂ mile; shooting/fishing ¹/₂ mile; sailing/boating 5 miles; hotel closed from 3rd January - 17th February inc.; all major credit cards accepted.

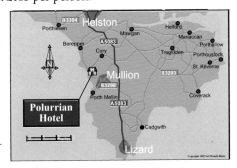

THE HEADLAND HOTEL
Fistral Beach, Newquay, Cornwall TR7 1EW

Telephone 01637 872211   Fax 01637 872212

It is rare to find a "Grand" hotel in such a spectacular position. The Headland, as its name implies, commands superb panoramic views over Fistral Beach and the Victorian charm of the hotel itself is now enhanced with every modern facility. The guests of the nineteenth century would be amazed at the variety of opportunities for an enjoyable stay here, whether as a leisure visitor or on business: there are indoor and outdoor swimming pools, two hot-air balloons to say nothing of easy access to all the conventional leisure activities such as golf and tennis. The standards of service and cuisine may well be unchanged: I found both to be of a very high quality and Mrs. Beeton would surely be pleased to see that the flair, the flavours and the willing service remain as impeccable for the modern day visitors as they always were for our Victorian predecessors. The facilities for doing business are also very comprehensive and include a variety of meeting rooms. Yet for the holidaymaker, too, with or without family, whether active or just self-indulgent, The Headland has everything to offer. Single room with breakfast from £42.00. Double room incl. breakfast from £74.00

Leisure Breaks: Special reductions in Spring and Autumn combined with activity holidays - bridge, golf, murder/mystery, walking.

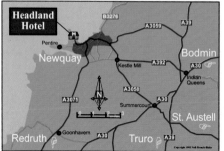

London 255, Wadebridge 16, Bodmin 20, Penzance 38, Truro 16.
Full licence. 100 en suite bedrooms with radio, colour TV, direct-dial telephone; tea/coffee making facilities; 24-hour room service; safety deposit box. Last orders for dinner 21.00 hrs. Special diets available. Billiards/snooker, croquet, fishing, golf, indoor games room, watersports; Indoor/outdoor swimming pools, tennis. Riding, squash, shooting - nearby. Full business services and 6 meeting rooms with total capacity for 250 guests. Facilities for the disabled. Car parking for 400 cars. Open February - early December. All credit cards accepted.

CARLYON BAY HOTEL
Nr. St Austell, Cornwall PL25 3RD

Telephone: 01726 812304;

Fax: 01726 814938

Carlyon Bay Hotel, which 50 years ago was called St Austell Bay Hotel, featured in the first edition of SIGNPOST in 1937 and was described then as "a perfectly equipped, splendidly conducted and entirely modern hotel....magnificent site overlooking the sands....deluxe hotel atmosphere applied with first rate cuisine and a wide choice of indoor and outdoor sports." Today it is even better for it has been charged with new ideas, energy and attractions, under the efficient and expert ownership of the Brend family. Here indeed is a place with character, luxury and an atmosphere of wellbeing. The public rooms are elegant, well furnished with pleasant décor and a lift to all floors takes you to the comfortable and well-appointed bedrooms. In the recently refurbished dining room you can be assured of delicious food that is cooked and presented with skill and imagination. The wine list is well chosen and extensive. Carlyon is a sportsman's paradise and includes a championship 18-hole golf course. But it is, above all, recommended for a superb family holiday throughout the year. Room and breakfast from £66 single, £75 double/twin per person. All prices include VAT. Other terms on application. Bargain breaks: Winter (Nov/March) from £97; Spring (March/May exc. Easter) from £147; early summer (May-July) from £151; late summer (August-September) from £157; autumn (Sept-October) from £149. All per person fro a minimum of two nights inc. room, dinner, breakfast, golf and VAT.

Bodmin 11, Truro 14, Falmouth 25, Exeter 75, Bristol 147, London 242.

F licence; 72 en suite bedrooms, all with direct dial telephone and satellite TV; room service; baby listening; night service; lift; last orders for dinner 21.00 hrs. Special diets available; bar lunches; children welcome; conferences max. 125 persons; games rooms; two snooker/billiard tables; indoor and outdoor heated swimming pools; sauna; solarium; spa pool; sea bathing; golf free to residents; two tennis courts; sailing, boating, riding, shooting and fishing all locally; open all year; all major credit cards accepted.

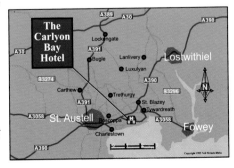

BOSKERRIS HOTEL
Carbis Bay, Nr. St. Ives, Cornwall TR26 2NQ

Telephone: 01736 795295; Freephone 0500 121491; Fax: 01736 798632

Boskerris stands in attractive gardens above the safe golden sands of Carbis Bay, with fine views across St. Ives Bay. This delightful hotel is owned and personally cared for by the Monk family, who have created a friendly, happy atmosphere. The public rooms are attractive and furnished to a high standard and together with the Cocktail Bar have extensive views over the Bay. In the dining room a carefully chosen menu is offered. The dishes are interesting, well presented and nicely served. Similar care is given in the selection of wines, which is excellent. The majority of the comfortable and well appointed bedrooms, most with private bathrooms, enjoy sea views and overlook the well kept gardens. Boskerris is an ideal centre for a wide range of activities, including a golfing package which enables you to play at 14 major golf courses in Cornwall, all within easy distances, plus the many beautiful moorland and coastal walks. Room and breakfast from £26.40 per person, or with dinner £40.00, including VAT. Other terms on application. Open Easter till November.

Bargain breaks: Low season breaks from two to four days - prices on application. Golfing packages available.

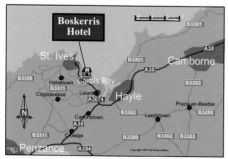

London 277, Helston 13, Penzance 8½, Redruth 14, St. Ives 1

R and R licence; 18 bedrooms (some ground floor),one apartment or suite,16 private bathrooms, remote control colour TV, direct dial telephone and tea/coffee making facilities; diets available; children welcome; drying and games rooms; heated outdoor swimming pool; putting green; golfing packages available; sea bathing, boating, surfing, rock climbing and tennis all nearby, ample car parking facilities.

THE GARRACK HOTEL

Burthallan Lane, St. Ives, Cornwall TR26 3AA

Telephone 01736 796199   *Fax 01736 798955*

The discerning traveller seeking a classic small country house hotel could hardly do better than to stay in the family-run Garrack with its spectacular views over the old town of St. Ives and the sea. It has two acres of gardens , is near a coastal footpath and its excellent leisure centre caters for every eventuality. The personal touch and friendliness of the Garrack is reflected in the main lounge with its books, magazines and board games and there are two other more formal lounges and a pleasant cocktail bar. Whilst the bedrooms in this the main house are traditional as befits the building, an extension houses additional rooms of more modern design and equally comfortable. Some rooms have four posters, others whirlpool baths. There are family rooms and a room for guests with disabilities. The hotel restaurant is justifiably renowned for its seafood, as fresh as is the other locally produced food with many of the vegetables coming from the garden and it would take several weeks to work through the wine list. The Garrack is a rarity - one of those places which it was a delight in itself to visit - and so hard to leave. Single room including breakfast from £58.00. Double room with breakfast from £42.00 p.p. **Bargain breaks** available October/November.

Penzance 10, Redruth 14, London 319, Truro 25

Full licence. 18 en suite bedrooms with TV. Direct-dial telephone, hairdryer on request. Morning tea service. Last dinner orders 20.30. Conferences up to 25 guests. Indoor whirlpool and swimming pool, sauna, solarium and fitness area. Access to fishing, riding, shooting (clay), golf, water sports, squash and tennis. Airport pick-up and car rental by arrangement. Car parking for 20 cars. Open all year. All major credit cards accepted.

TREGENNA CASTLE
St. Ives, Cornwall TR26 2DE

Telephone: 01736 795254   *Fax: 01736 796066*

Set amidst acres of private estate land in an idyllic location, Tregenna Castle was originally built as a private house in 1774. The spacious en suite bedrooms, some of which benefit from panoramic sea views across St. Ives Bay to Godrevy Lighthouse, have recently undergone refurbishment, and provide guests with comfortable accommodation in a superb setting. The hotel's Trelawney Restaurant, offers a mouth-watering selection of fresh local seafood dishes which feature on both the à la carte and table d'hôte menus. An extensive selection of world famous wines is also available to complement your meal. I would recommend this hotel, particularly for the traditional family holiday. Children are welcome, and during the high season, a full programme of entertainment and activities are provided including Outdoor Adventure Centre and indoor play room. Prices start from £30.00 per person bed and breakfast, and £45 .00 per person, for dinner, bed and breakfast, and are inclusive of VAT and service.

Bargain breaks: Special 3,4 and 7 day breaks available. Prices from £99.50 for room, bed and breakfast for 3 nights plus one free round of golf. Special interest breaks include Murder and Mystery, Golf, Culture Breaks, Glorious Garden Breaks and Activity and Racket Sporting Breaks. Please telephone the above number for full details. Christmas and New Year programmes also available.

Plymouth 50, Exeter 90, Bristol 170, London 280
F licence, 72 en suite bedrooms (4 for the disabled), 25 cottages, with direct dial telephone and TV; room service; baby listening; night service; lift; last orders for dinner 9.30p.m.; seasonal Bistro; specialities; children welcome; conferences max. 250; games room; full health and beauty suite; outdoor and indoor heated swimming pools; solarium; squash court; 18 hole golf course; three tennis courts; snooker room; croquet; putting; open all year; all major credit cards accepted.

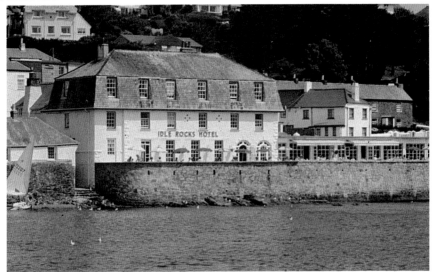

THE IDLE ROCKS HOTEL
Harbourside, St Mawes, Cornwall TR2 5AN

Telephone: 01326 270771 Freephone: 0800 243020 Fax: 01326 270062

The Idle Rocks Hotel stands in a magnificent position overlooking the picturesque port of St Mawes and the River Fal Estuary. With its mild climate and relaxed air, this charming village is the ideal place from which to tour some of England's most scenic and dramatic countryside - the Roseland Peninsula and the coastline of West Cornwall. Each bedroom at the Idle Rocks is decorated with style to a high standard and most feature outstanding views of the sea. Breakfast and dinner are served in the Water's Edge Restaurant, where fine cuisine can be enjoyed from tables overlooking the harbour. At lunchtime, the 1203 Terrace is a very popular venue with its sunny outlook and light, imaginative menu. The lounges are stylishly decorated and furnished in pastel shades and one is non-smoking. A foot ferry operates regularly between St Mawes and Falmouth or one can drive to Falmouth and nearby Truro via the King Harry Car Ferry. For further information, call the hotel for a copy of their well illustrated brochure and for details of seasonal breaks. Room, dinner and breakfast from £39 per person including VAT.

Truro 20, St. Austell 20, Plymouth 58, London 273.

F licence; 17 en suite bedrooms, all with direct dial telephone and TV; further rooms in elegant Georgian annexe and also a range of cottages around the village; all enjoy service at the Water's Edge, the hotel's Two AA Rosette restaurant. Last orders 9.15 pm. Bistro-type bar meals available at lunchtime from the 1203 Terrace. Pets accepted by prior arrangement. Sea bathing, sailing/boating, fishing, hiking; golf courses nearby; riding. Car parking facilities opposite the hotel. Open all year. All major credit cards accepted.

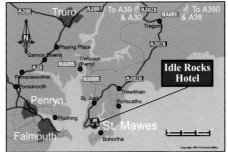

LEA HILL HOTEL
Membury, Nr Axminster, East Devon EX13 7AQ
Telephone 01404 881881

This very unusual place has its origins in the 1300's when it was a single story long-house dwelling partitioned for cattle; now it is the gem of a hotel, situated in the seclusion of an area of Outstanding Natural Beauty. Loving hands have created a work of art here and the combination of its flagstones, oaken beams, wood panelling and ingle-nook fireplaces deserves the top award for character with comfort not far behind. To relax in the spaciousness of a beautifully furnished lounge, the bar or charming sitting room is an indulgence, whilst an overnight stay in any one of the bedrooms is for hedonists: there are suites, or sumptuous bedrooms, and a luxurious double with a jacuzzi, with each having its own garden area. The ambiance of the restaurant and its beamed ceiling is restful and wholly in keeping with the other rooms and I found an interesting menu, varied and imaginative with its use of fresh produce from the hotel's garden. Lea Hill is located in peaceful countryside close to beautiful coastline and many picturesque villages: it has its own special style, character and supreme quality, so although unique is a word rarely used for hotels, in this case it is surely justified. Bed and Breakfast from £29.00 pppn in low season and from £32.00 pppn in high season.

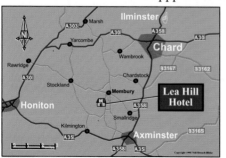

Lyme Regis 9 , Taunton 22, Yeovil 24 , Exeter 27 , London 156

Full licence. Nine en suite bedrooms with individually controlled central heating; remote control TV, radio, direct dial telephone, hairdryer, tea/coffee making facilities. Dinner from 19.30 to 20.30. Special diets available. No smoking area in public rooms - except bar. Visa, Mastercard accepted.

BLAGDON MANOR COUNTRY HOTEL
Ashwater, Devon EX21 5DF

Telephone: 01409 211224   *Fax: 01409 211634*

Blagdon Manor Country Hotel is as charming and original as the owners, Tim and Gill Casey. Most of the building dates back to the 17th century, and the whole is set amidst peaceful countryside. The fabrics and wallcoverings used in the decor of Blagdon Manor are unusual, vibrant and tasteful, with antique furniture throughout. The seven bedrooms are exquisitely decorated, with many thoughtful touches to make guests feel instantly at home. They are all en suite with bath and shower. Guests dine together "dinner party style" in the elegant and well furnished dining room. Gill Casey supervises all the cooking which is superb and plentiful, the wines have been well chosen, and nothing is too much trouble for your hosts. The pretty sitting room is very comfortable, as is the library, and there is also a bar and delightful billiard room. Blagdon Manor is ideally situated on the border of two counties in the heart of the West Country, and lends itself to varied journeys from the moors to the coast, encompassing many areas of natural beauty and historic interest. To find Blagdon Manor, leave Launceston on the A388 Holsworthy road. Pass both Chapman's Well and the first sign to Ashwater. Turn right at the second Ashwater sign then first right at the Blagdon signpost. The hotel is then a few hundred yards further on, on the right. Room and breakfast from £45.00, dinner, room and breakfast from £62.00. Prices are per person and include VAT. **Bargain Breaks:** Spring, Autumn and Winter Breaks. Weekend house parties. Please call for further details.

Launceston 8, Bideford 25, Exeter 43, London 218
R&R licence; 7 en suite bedrooms (1 four-poster room), all with TV; dinner served at 8.00 p.m.; hotel not suitable for children; dogs accepted by prior arrangement; conferences max. 14 (7 couples); bar; billiard room; library; croquet; practice ground for golfers; riding and fishing nearby; shooting in season; two golf courses within 10 miles; open all year; most credit cards accepted.

DOWNREW HOUSE
Bishops Tawton, Nr. Barnstaple, North Devon EX32 ODY

Telephone: 01271 42497/46673   Fax: 01271 23947

Downrew is a small Queen Anne Country House with lodge three miles south of Barnstaple, off the A377, on the slopes of Codden Hill. The original building dates from 1640 and was enlarged in 1705. It stands in 12 acres of meadowland and well kept gardens and has its own 5-hole 9 approach golf course. The resident proprietors have created a wonderfully warm and friendly atmosphere, which is peaceful and relaxing. Care and attention to detail are the hallmarks of this delightful house, with service of the highest order under the personal supervision of the owners. Downrew House is very comfortable; the elegant drawing room with its log fire overlooks the garden, and adjoins the sitting room. The dining room's magnificent 18ft bow window looks over the lawns and the surrounding countryside, towards Dartmoor in the far distance. I enjoyed an excellent dinner, carefully cooked and well presented, with many of the fruits and vegetables being homegrown. A well stocked bar and specially chosen wines complement the delicious food. The hotel is open all year round. Dinner, room and breakfast from £45.00 per day including VAT. No service charge. **Special breaks** from £70 per person dinner, bed and breakfast. Two day golfing breaks from £85 with a day's free golf. Christmas from £225 for three days.

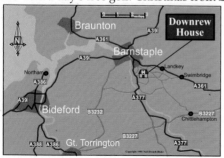

Barnstaple 3, Bideford 8, London 222

R& R licence; 12 en suite bedrooms (3 ground floor), all with telephone, colour TV and full central heating; last orders 9. 00 p.m.; bar snacks; diets; children welcome; dogs allowed; conferences up to 24; billiards; outdoor heated swimming pool; solarium; golf; tennis; fishing one mile; sauna, squash, badminton and leisure centre three miles; riding five miles; shooting, sea bathing, sailing and boating eight miles; Visa and Mastercard welcome.

THE EDGEMOOR HOTEL
Haytor Road, Bovey Tracey, Devon TQ13 9LE

Telephone 01626 832466   Fax 01626 834760

This is one of Devon's most charming small country house hotels. Standing in two acres of grounds on the edge of the Dartmoor National Park, it has the grandeur of a Victorian building and all the modern comforts of a first class hotel. The bedrooms are a delight, beautifully decorated and furnished with lovely fabrics; all have en suite bathrooms and some have four-poster and half-tester beds. The public rooms overlook the green lawns of the spacious garden, providing a perfect setting for quiet relaxation. For refreshment bar meals are available but no serious minded guest should miss Chef Edward Elliott's restaurant, which offers extensive menus of traditional French and English cuisine, using local produce and complemented by a carefully chosen wine list to suit all tastes and pockets. The location of the Edgemoor ensures excellent walking country on its doorstep as well as a number of other activities such as golf and riding which can be organised locally. The attraction of the hotel lies in the choice it offers between the shamelessly hedonistic inactivity of good food and comfort or the energetic activity of open air pursuits. If it is a dilemma it is a good one for then you must stay at least twice in this lovely place. Single room including breakfast from £39.95. Double room with breakfast from £72.50. **Leisure Breaks**: To include dinner, bed and breakfast: 2-4 days £50.00 - £ 56.95; 5 days   £92.50 - £105.90 weekend or mid-week all year.

Exeter 14 , Plymouth 32 , Newton Abbot 6, Okehampton 18 , Tavistock 26, London 181

Full licence. 17 en suite bedrooms with radio & colour TV. Direct-dial telephone; Hairdryer, trouser press, laundry service; some non-smoker bedrooms, tea/coffee making facilities. Last order for dinner 21.00 hrs. Special diets available. Full business services and two meeting rooms with capacity for 20/50 guests. AV facilities. Golf, riding, shooting, tennis nearby. Parking for 50 cars. Open all year. Major credit cards accepted.

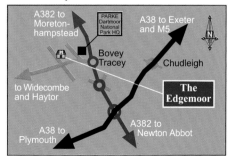

THE BERRY HEAD HOTEL
Berry Head Road, Brixham, S. Devon TQ5 9AJ

Telephone: 01803 853225   Fax: 01803 882084

The Berry Head Hotel is set in a superb water's edge position in six acres of its own gardens and woodland, in the seclusion of the Berry Head Country Park, which is noted for its bird life and rare wild flowers. The hotel is steeped in history. It was built as a military hospital in the Napoleonic Wars, and was later the home of the Reverend Francis Lyte, who wrote the famous hymn *Abide with Me* at the hotel, no doubt inspired by the glorious sunsets. The historic fishing port of Brixham, where William of Orange first landed on English soil, is only a short walk away. The hotel offers relaxing accommodation and all the en suite bedrooms have colour television, radio and tea and coffee making facilities . The comfortable lounge and the restaurant, which overlook the terrace, enjoy spectacular views of Torbay and the Devon coast. The emphasis here is upon good food, wine and company in a very special setting. Room and breakfast from £35.00, and dinner, room and breakfast from £40.00 including VAT. The hotel is always open.

Bargain breaks: Set in national parkland at the water's edge, with miles of coastal walks, fishing, birdwatching and sailing, yet close to the major resort of Torquay, this is an ideal hideaway for a short break. Two nights, dinner, bed and breakfast from £66.00

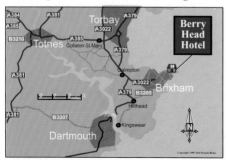

Torquay 10, Exeter 30, Bristol 100, Birmingham 200, London 180
F licence; 16 en suite bedrooms all with direct dial telephone, TV; hairdryer; tea/coffee facilities; room service; baby listening; night service; last orders for dinner 9.30p.m.; bar meals until 9.30p.m.; special diets; children welcome; dogs accepted; conferences 100 max.; boules; sea bathing 30 yds.; outdoor seawater pool 200 yds.; indoor swimming pool and squash courts $^{1}/_{2}$ mile; sailing and boating, shooting and fishing $^{1}/_{4}$ mile; tennis one mile; golf and riding two miles; Amex, Visa and Mastercard accepted.

KITTIWELL HOUSE HOTEL & RESTAURANT
Croyde, North Devon EX33 1PG

Telephone 10271 890247   Fax 01271 890469

Readers can usually picture the ideal thatched country inn but the reality often disappoints when staying or eating at such places. Kittiwell House is different. The building certainly matches the ideal but the comfort and the cuisine surpass what so often is little more than mediocre and are to the highest standards on both counts. Here the building exudes a warm and cosy atmosphere and the bedrooms, three of which are non-smoker, have all the facilities that we as guests now require including colour TV. The food, chosen from either a table d'hôte or à la carte menu is prepared from the freshest of ingredients and is perfectly cooked. There is a well thought out wine list of both local and international wines. As a centre from which to tour this lovely coast line, Exmoor or indeed the whole of North Devon Kittiwell is perfectly situated. Single room including breakfast from £42.00. Double room with breakfast from £72.00.

Leisure Breaks: October - June two nights including dinner £96.00 per person.

Bideford 20 , Barnstaple 10 , Ilfracombe 9 , London 203

Full licence. 12 en suite bedrooms with colour TV, radio, direct-dial telephone; tea/coffee making facilities; non-smoker bedrooms. Last orders for dinner 21.00 hrs. Special diets available. Fishing, golf, riding, tennis and cycle riding all by arrangement nearby. Car parking for 20 cars.

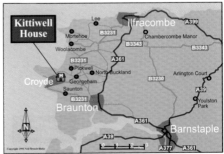

LANGSTONE CLIFF HOTEL
Dawlish, South Devon EX7 0NA

Telephone 01626 865155   Fax 01626 867166

It is hardly surprising that the Langstone Cliff is such a happy place as it is traditionally a family hotel run by a family, The Rogers, who welcomed their first guests nearly fifty years ago, have been cosseting them ever since and are justifiably proud that not many of them come only once. There are countless reasons: the hotel is set in 19 acres of grounds overlooking the sea with a footpath giving direct access to the beaches. The bedrooms are tastefully decorated with many designed as family rooms, some with balconies and most offering lovely sea or woodland views. The leisure facilities, including two swimming pools, offer everything for the energetic, whilst spacious public rooms provide more peaceful havens in comfortable lounges. The story of the catering is not just about Lincoln Restaurant, the coffee shop or the three friendly bars, but the fare that is offered there. Anyone taking advantage of the famous cabaret weekends could also enjoy a huge West Country breakfast, a traditional Sunday lunch and dinner with one of the most tempting sweet trolleys within miles. We were recommended to visit this hotel simply because it provides something for everyone. We shall return too. Single room including breakfast from £40.00. Double room with breakfast from £70.00. **Leisure Breaks**: Two days half board from £80 p.p. Special cabaret weekend prices on application.

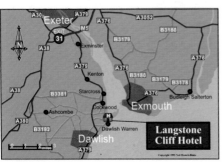

Exeter 13, Torbay 11, Honiton 26, Okehampton 30, Plymouth 40, London 179
Full licence. 68 en suite bedrooms (incl. 20 family rooms). Radio and satellite TV, direct-dial telephone, hairdryer, laundry service, trouser press, tea/coffee making facilities; 24-hr room/meal service; last dinner orders 21.00. Barber shop, beauty salon, massage; facilities for disabled; Billiards/snooker; golf nearby; indoor games room, outdoor + indoor swimming pools, tennis, table tennis. Ten meeting rooms total capacity 400 guests. AV and secretarial services available. Parking 200 cars. Airport pick-up; car rental. Most credit cards accepted.

COMBE HOUSE
Gittisham, Nr. Honiton, Devon EX14 0AD

Telephone: 01404 42756 and 43560   Fax: 01404 46004

This 14th century Elizabethan mansion lies in 2000 acres of parkland adjoining the Otter Valley, off the A30 Honiton-Exeter road to Gittisham. John and Therese Boswell own and care for the hotel, and enhance the historic country mansion atmosphere with many antiques from the Boswell ancestral Scottish home. The staff work as a cheerful, efficient and attentive team. The spacious, restful bedrooms are dignified and well appointed. Among the magnificent rooms downstairs are the Entrance Hall - a fine example of Caroline grandeur - and the large, panelled drawing room. The cosy Cocktail Bar (adjacent to the smaller drawing room) features John's interest in horse racing. He owns some wonderful horses and pictures of them adorn the walls. A wonderful candlelit dinner is served in the two lovely dining rooms. Therese and her team produce superbly cooked dishes, full of imagination. The wine list is excellent in its range and quality. Rates from 1st January 1996 which are subject to alteration without prior notice are, room and breakfast from £65.00 per person (single), £99.50 (double/twin), inclusive of VAT and service. Other terms on application, including out of season rate. Member of Pride of Britain. Open all year, but closed last week of January and all February.   **B a r g a i n breaks** available in November, December and March (except Christmas/New Year). 2-night stay - 10% discount; 3+ nights - 15%. January - stays of 2+ nights - tdh dinner included.

London 155, Birmingham 149, Bristol 61, Exeter 16, Honiton 2, Airport 14

R and R 1icence; 15 en suite bedrooms (one suite), 2 with four-poster beds, all with colour TV, direct dial telephone and hairdryer; diets available, including a vegetarian menu; children welcome, dogs welcome; small executive conferences; weekend house parties up to 20 welcome; small wedding receptions; croquet; trout fishing; riding by arragement; tennis nearby; golf by special arrangement at Woodbury Park; sea bathing seven miles; lovely walks and well kept gardens.

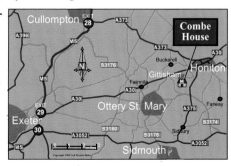

THE COTTAGE HOTEL
Hope Cove, Kingsbridge, South Devon TQ73

Telephone: 01548 561555   *Fax: 01548 561455*

The Cottage Hotel enjoys a superb position, overlooking the picturesque harbour and cove, with spectacular sea views and sunsets. The gardens descend to the beach, where you can bathe in safety. The hotel is delightful and has 35 beautifully furnished bedrooms, with 25 of them having private bathrooms / showers. I always enjoy visiting The Cottage; it has a happy and relaxing atmosphere thanks to the owners, John and Janet Ireland, who, with Patricia Bazzano personally care for this pleasant and comfortable haven. The enticing dining room, which has lovely views of the cove and coast, offers table d'hote and a la carte menus. I chose the former, which was excellent, cooked with great interest and attention, served by cheerful, efficient and courteous staff of many years' standing. The meal was supported by a selective wine list. The ground floor rooms are comfortable and nicely furnished. This hotel still remains one of the best family hotels I visit, well illustrated by the preponderance of sun-tanned, well-fed families. Dinner, room and breakfast from £45.35.

Bargain breaks are available from 1st November to 13th April inclusive. 2-night stay £27.25-£42.50. 7-night stay £26.75-£41.50 according to room. Prices are per person per night and include accommodation, 6-course dinner plus coffee, full English breakfast, service and VAT.

Totnes 18, Plymouth 25, London 236, Torquay 21, Exeter 36

F licence; 25 en suite bedrooms, all with direct dial telephone and colour TV; room service; baby listening; last orders for dinner 8.30p.m.; bar meals; children welcome; dogs accepted; conferences max. 50; games room; sea bathing; sailing/boating; riding three miles; golf four miles; indoor heated swimming pool, tennis and squash courts six miles; hotel closed from 2nd Jan. -30th Jan. inclusive; no credit cards accepted.

ILSINGTON COUNTRY HOTEL
Ilsington, Dartmoor, Devon TQ13 9RR

Telephone 01364 661452   Fax 01364 661307

This peaceful country house hotel is situated in six acres of the Dartmoor National Park and offers spectacular views over the surrounding countryside with scenery that must rate amongst the most beautiful in England. The Ilsington also provided everything we could expect of a first class hotel. The bedrooms are stylish and inviting with the full range of facilities which assured a comfortable stay. For relaxation it was pleasant to have a choice of warmly decorated public rooms from the library to the attractive lounge bar or the Victorian conservatory. Dining was a pleasure too in a room full of character with a traditional menu and intelligently chosen wine list. It is a fair sign of the versatility of the Ilsington that it has a purpose-built, fully equipped gymnasium and indoor swimming pool which was much used by the more energetic guests in preparation for enjoying the many sporting activities on the doorstep for which the area is famous. We found so much to see and do around Dartmoor and a more congenial base could hardly be imagined. Single room including breakfast from £50.00, double from £80.00.

Leisure Breaks: Two nights or more £50.00 per person per night b & b.

Exeter 16, Plymouth 31 , Torquay 7 ,London 216

Full licence. 25 en suite bedrooms with radio & satellite TV. Direct-dial telephone. Hairdryer, laundry service. Non-smoker rooms, tea/coffee making facilities. Last dinner orders 21.00. Croquet, fitness centre, indoor games room, jacuzzi, sauna, indoor heated swimming pool, tennis, bowls. Fishing, golf, water sports, riding and shooting all nearby. Open all year. All major credit cards accepted.

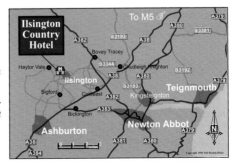

BUCKLAND-TOUT-SAINTS HOTEL
Goveton, Kingsbridge, South Devon TQ7 2DS

Telephone: 01548 853055   *Fax: 01548 856261*

John and Tove Taylor have now been at Buckland for four years and are old hands at welcoming guests, having spent 15 years running the Taychreggan Hotel in Argyllshire. Buckland-tout-Saints is a beautiful Queen Anne manor house which was built in 1690, and lies in the heart of rural South Devon. "Far from the madding crowd," you will be able to relax in comfort, in elegant surroundings. The Great Hall boasts a glorious log fire, and personal pieces of antique furniture are on display. The newly decorated and refurbished drawing room overlooks the well-kept acres of garden, and the small bar offers a warm and friendly atmosphere. The 17th-century Russian Pine panelled dining room is a fine setting for the chef's unique cooking - impeccably presented dishes from a daily-changing menu, and I highly recommend that you leave enough room for a pudding! There is an excellent choice of first class wines, suitable for the most experienced palate. Each of the 12 bedrooms is individually decorated with superb bathrooms, and good use has been made of the second floor, to create unusually shaped, smaller bedrooms, most of which overlook the grounds and surrounding countryside. Head Chef, David Newland, is responsible for the very high standard of the cuisine. The Taylors, together with their son, George, and the rest of the team, will make your stay happy and relaxed, and you will find you will want to return again and again. Room and breakfast from £50 single and £100 double, which also includes early morning tea, newspaper and VAT. Winter breaks (Oct 1st-April 1st) from £50 inc. per person for dinner, bed & breakfast.

Salcombe 6, Plymouth 20, Exeter 30, London 203 *R & R licence, 12 en suite bedrooms, all with direct-dial telephone and TV; room service; night service until 10 pm; last orders for dinner 2130; bar lunches; special diets; conferences from 12-16 people; putting green; croquet; three golf courses within ten miles; open all year; all major credit cards accepted.*

THE MAYPOOL PARK HOTEL
Maypool, Galmpton, Devon TQ5 OET

Telephone: 01803 842442   *Fax: 01803 845782*

This delightful, peaceful hotel, set 400 feet above the River Dart, has a new name and new owners: Alison and Raymond Taylor. Their enthusiasm was very evident as I was shown around - personal service and good food are their aims and these they achieve. The ten bedrooms are attractively furnished, all having their own private and beautifully equipped bathrooms. The Garden Room is available for conferences, banquets and functions, with a 30 person maximum. There is an extensive and interesting wine list featuring approx. 30 wines imported by Mr & Mrs Taylor themselves and a dozen or so if these are available in $^1/_4$ litre carafes. The food in the Taste of Taylors restaurant is based on the freshest of local ingredients - the menu reflecting the proximity of the hotel to the sea and Devon countryside. Two excellent golf courses are within easy reach of the Maypool Park, salmon and trout fishing are available on the Dart and there is still water trout fishing nearby. A trip on the Paignton and Dartmouth Steam Railway is a must for enthusiasts! I can highly recommend a stay at the Maypool Park Hotel and the Taylors will make you most welcome. Room and breakfast from £35 per person; dinner, room and breakfast from £51.00. Two or three day **breaks** available. Price on application. Special Christmas, Easter and New Year programmes available; details on request.

Kingswear/Dartmouth 5, Totnes 8, Exeter 30, London 200

Full licence, 10 en suite non-smoking bedrooms, all with direct-dial telephone and TV; room service; by arrangement; last orders for dinner 20.45; conferences max. 30; sailing, boating and fishing $^1/_2$ mile; golf two miles; sea bathing three miles; riding four miles; most credit cards accepted. ⊗

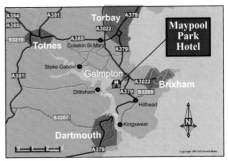

MANOR HOUSE HOTEL & COUNTRY CLUB
Moretonhampstead, Devon TQ13 8RE

Telephone: 01647 440355   Fax: 01647 440961

This imposing building with its superb grounds and golf course offers the best of everything for which the sportsman, holidaymaker or business traveller can hope for. Almost every outdoor pursuit is catered for - tennis, fishing, shooting and more. Own 18-hole golf course. Leisure Centre with indoor pool due for completion in 1996. The position of the hotel on the edge of Dartmoor, yet close to the English Riviera, makes it ideal for touring and as an out-of-the-way retreat for a conference; the Manor is big enough to accommodate all but the largest. Add to this the warmth and superb comfort of the rooms, the excellence of the cuisine and the friendliness of the staff and you have a perfect blend of all that is good in English hotel-keeping. Single £72.50; double £100. Table d'hôte dinner £18.50.
Bargain breaks advertised from time to time in the national press

Exeter 13, London 182, Ashburton 13, Crediton 11, Okehampton 13, Plymouth 29, Tavistock 21

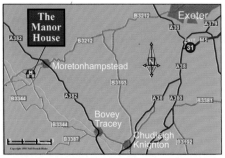

Full licence; 90 en suite bedrooms (25 double, 36 twin, 23 single), all with direct-dial telephone and colour TV, hairdyer, laundry/valet service, tea/ coffee making facilities, 24 hour room/meal service, trouser press, video films/satellite, safety deposit box.
Car parking for 90, beauty salon. Last orders for dinner 2130; Recreation: billiards and snooker, croquet, fishing, golf (own course), riding within four miles, shooting, ballooning. Business service - conference room with capacity of 120. AV equipment available.

THE BOLT HEAD HOTEL
Salcombe, South Devon TQ8 8LL

Telephone: 01548 843751   *Fax: 01548 843060*

Blessed with a climate that is said to be the mildest in Devon, and set amid imposing scenery that ends with the fantastically shaped black rocks of mighty Bolt Head, this most southerly hotel in Devon commands a marvellous view of the Salcombe Estuary and coastline, and overlooks the sheltered golden cove of South Sands Beach. There are always yachts and fishing boats to be seen in this unspoilt estuary. The hotel has been completely refurbished to a very high standard under the ownership of Mr. Colin Smith. A sun terrace leads off the main lounge. The bedrooms are also very comfortable and equipped as one would expect of this well run hotel. The hotel is renowned for its warm welcome and friendly service and the staff are courteous, attentive and cheerful. The table d'hôte menu with specialities, is interesting and provides a splendid choice carefully served, in an attractive restaurant which has panoramic views of the estuary. In spite of all that is offered at this first class establishment, it also provides peace and quiet with lovely walks in the National Trust property adjoining the grounds. Dinner, room and breakfast from £62.00 per person per night inclusive of VAT. Closed mid November to mid March, but office open. A Best Western Hotel.
Getaway Breaks available; details on request.

London 214, Kingsbridge 7, Totnes 18, Exeter 43, Plymouth 25

F licence; 29 en suite bedrooms (four ground floor), all with direct dial telephones, remote control colour TV with satellite, radio, tea/coffee making facilities; full central heating; meals to 9p.m.; diets; children welcome, baby listening; dogs at manager's discretion; games room; outdoor heated swimming pool; sailing, boating, private moorings; sea fishing; tennis ¹/₄ mile; riding seven miles; golf eight miles; major credit cards accepted.

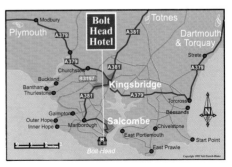

TIDES REACH HOTEL
South Sands, Salcombe, South Devon TQ8 8LJ

Telephone: 01548 843466   *Fax: 01548 843954*

The position of Tides Reach is perfect - a beautiful secluded sandy cove. The quiet luxury of the hotel strikes you as you enter the conservatory-style hall with its indoor water garden and the flower garden lounge-hall so full of sunshine and scented blooms. The décor throughout was chosen and supervised by Mrs. Edwards and the colours are wonderfully vibrant and original. The indoor heated swimming pool, around which has been built a new bar and coffee shop, is as glamorous as a Hollywood film set - there is an outdoor sun patio and sun deck leading off and below, a new hairdressing and beauty salon, multi gym, sunbed, Whirlpool Spa bath, sauna, steam baths and squash court. In addition to the new facilities the dining room has been extended and the bedrooms and public rooms have been refurnished throughout in a most comfortable and luxurious manner. The food is superb, both à la carte and table d'hôte dishes being really first class. Dinner, room and breakfast from £56.00 to £104.00 per person including VAT according to season and length of stay. Closed 22nd December-Mid-February. Resident proprietor - Roy Edwards FHCI.
Bargain Breaks available from early March-26th May 1996 (excluding Easter) and Oct,Nov Dec 1996. 2-day breaks from £120 for dinner, bed and breakfast. 4-day breaks from £224 for dinner,bed and breakfast. Extra days pro rata.

London 214, Kingsbridge 7, Totnes 19, Exeter 43, Plymouth 26

F licence; 40 en suite bedrooms with colour TV; radio, direct dial telephone; some family suites; lift; children over eight welcome ; games room; snooker room; some diets available; dogs by arrange,ment; indoor heated pool; solarium; sauna; spa bath; squash; indoor and outdoor water gardens; drying room; golf, tennis, riding nearby; sea bathing; boating; fishing, windsurfing, water sports from own boathouse.

HERON HOUSE HOTEL
Thurlestone Sands, Nr. Salcombe, South Devon TQ7 3JY
Telephone: 01548 561308/561600   *Fax: 01548 560180*

Standing only fifty yards from the beach, the Heron House enjoys a prime location in South Devon, with magnificent views across to Plymouth Sound, Burgh Island, and on a fine day, Cornwall. Situated on the coastal path - incidentally Britain's longest footpath-, guests can either swim from Thurlestone's lovely sandy beach, the adjoining beaches, or in the hotel's large and exceptionally warm outdoor swimming pool. Thurlestone has the Premier Good Beach Award for 1994, which includes superior water quality. The Rowland family take great pride in running this hotel, and personally supervise the excellent meals that are freshly prepared in their well equipped kitchen. Dinner is five courses, and the menus feature vegetarian specialities and fish which is supplied locally. All of the eighteen comfortable bedrooms enjoy first class views, and have the facilities now expected by today's guest. Keen sailors can hire craft from nearby Salcombe, Newton Ferrers and Dartmouth, golfers are offered temporary membership of the Thurlestone and Bigbury Clubs, and there is riding and sea fishing available. Room and breakfast from £35.00, dinner, room and breakfast from £45.00 including VAT. **Special Winter/Spring Short Breaks** are available from November to April (exc. Xmas & Easter) from £32 pppn d,b&b 1-6 nights; from £29 d, b&b for seven nights plus.

Kingsbridge 4, Salcombe 4, Plymouth 20, Torquay 20, London 207
F licence; 18 en suite bedrooms, all with direct dial telephone and TV; room service; baby listening; night service; 1ast orders for dinner 8.30p.m; bar meals; special diets; children welcome; dogs by arrangement; conferences max. 40; games room; pool table; outdoor heated swimming pool; solarium; sea bathing; special activities in autumn and spring; leisure centre three miles; sailing, boating, tennis, riding, shooting and fishing all nearby; golf by arrangement with Thurlestone Golf Club; open all year; Mastercard, Eurocard and Visa accepted.

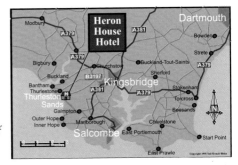

THE SAUNTON SANDS HOTEL
Saunton Sands, Nr. Braunton, Devon EX31 1LQ

Telephone: 01271 890212   *Fax: 01271 890145*

Lots of sun, miles of golden sands and tiered silvery waves advancing eagerly up the beach is what you look down on from the warm and luxurious rooms of The Saunton Sands, a member of the Brend Group of Exclusive Hotels. The hotel is light and sunny as most of the rooms face the south, the sea and the sands, and there are panoramic views from most. All the staff are efficient and attentive, creating an air of warmth and friendliness. The furnishings are elegant and comfortable, and the bedrooms have all the modern facilities that you could want. Food is of a very high standard and the wine list is well chosen. Room and breakfast from £60.00 single, £60.00 per person double, all inclusive of VAT. Other seafront hotels in the Brend Group include Carlyon Bay near St. Austell and The Victoria Hotel in Sidmouth (see pages 11 and 34). This splendid hotel provides a truly outstanding holiday for all the family, all year round. **Bargain Breaks:** A Luxury Breaks tariff is available in addition to the hotel's main tariff, with reduced rates for stays of two nights or more. Spring, June and Autumn Breaks represent excellent value with prices from £55 per person per night for dinner, room and breakfast. Child reductions are also available. Telephone the hotel and ask for the Luxury Breaks Tariff.

London 203, Bamstaple 8, llfracombe 9, Bideford 17, Exeter 48

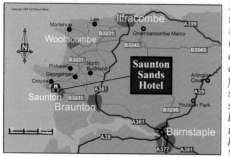

F licence; 92 en suite bedrooms, all with telephone, satellite TV, tea/coffee making facilities; lift; 24 hr room service; last orders 9.30 p.m; bar meals (lunch); afternoon teas; vegetarian and vegan diets; children welcome; baby listening; no dogs; conferences max. 200; games room; dancing frequently; full size snooker table; children's paddling pool; supervised nursery; heated indoor and outdoor swimming pools; sauna/solarium, hairdressing salon; mini cinema; miles of beach below hotel; sailing; tennis; squash; riding; shooting; fishing; helipad; golf nearby; Mastercard, Amex, Diners, Visa credit cards accepted.

THE ROYAL GLEN HOTEL
Sidmouth, Devon EX10 8RW

Telephone: 01395 513221 / 513456   *Fax: 01395 514922*

Originally built in 1700 as a farmhouse, the Royal Glen Hotel has been managed by a member of the Crane family for over 100 years. This historic and lovely hotel stands in its own grounds, 200 yards from the sea-front at Sidmouth. The cricket club is nearby as well as the golf course and shopping centre. Mr. Orson Crane proudly showed me around his lovely hotel, with its wonderful antique furniture and memorabilia from the time of Queen Victoria, whose family, the Kents, used it as a holiday cottage until the untimely death of the Duke. During the course of the young Victoria's stay, she came close to death when an apprentice boy who was shooting at birds in the garden, hit a window in the nursery, narrowly missing the future Queen. The hotel has a great deal of old world charm; the upstairs drawing room is oval with period furniture, and the dining room of the same shape houses an intriguing collection of period chairs. The food is excellent, including a superlative pudding trolley and an extensive wine list. It is possible for visitors to the hotel to stay in a Royal bedroom or Princess Victoria's nursery. The hotel also has a wonderfully up-to-date swimming pool. Prices start from £30.00 per night for bed and breakfast, and from £35.00 dinner, bed and breakfast in the winter. Open all year. **Bargain breaks** available November until the end of April, excluding Christmas and Easter. Details on application.

London 161, Torquay 35, Birmingham 159

R & R licence; 34 bedrooms, 32 with bathroom/ shower, three on ground floor; all have colour TV, radio, tea-making facilities, telephone and full central heating; last orders 8.30 p.m; children from 8 years; dogs allowed; indoor heated swimming pool; sea bathing; golf nearby; tennis one mile; Mastercard and Visa cards accepted.

THE VICTORIA HOTEL
Sidmouth, Devon EX10 8RY

Telephone: 01395 512651   *Fax: 01395 579154*

Sidmouth was discovered as a resort by the affluent in Queen Victoria's day - hence the name of this imposing hotel which dominates the west end of the promenade, and has an uninterrupted view of the wide sweeping bay. The Victoria is owned by the Brend family who own other-luxurious hotels, including the Royal Duchy at Falmouth (see page 6),Carlyon Bay at St. Austell (see page 11) and The Saunton Sands Hotel at Saunton Sands (see page 32) . Mr. John Brend, Managing Director, is very much in evidence looking after the needs of the guests, with the help of his efficient and friendly staff. The ground floor creates an impression of space and good taste; everything is planned for your comfort and well-being. The restaurant has a first class reputation for its cuisine, the table d'hôte and à la carte menus reaching high levels in quality, presentation and service. The wine list is comprehensive and well chosen. Upstairs, the well appointed bedrooms are comfortable and pleasantly furnished. Set in 5 acres of landscaped gardens, with many outside attractions, I can recommend The Victoria to all ages. Room and breakfast from £66.00 single, £61.00 double per person (including VAT). Bargain Breaks available at various times of year. Winter, Spring and Autumn breaks are particularly good value with single rooms from £54 and doubles from £49 per person, dinner , b & b, min. two nights.

London 161, Birmingham 159, Bristol 70, Exeter 15, Honiton 9, Torquay 35

F licence; 61 en suite bedrooms, all with telephone and TV; lift; night service-meals to 9 p.m.; diets and vegeterian menus; children welcome; dogs accepted at discretion of management; conferences max. 100; hairdressing salon; games room; entertainment; billiards; indoor and outdoor heated swimming pools and lido; sauna; solarium; spa bath; 18 hole putting course; sea bathing; sailing; fishing by arrangement; squash, badminton and riding all nearby; major credit cards accepted.

GABRIEL COURT HOTEL
Stoke Gabriel, Nr. Totnes, South Devon TQ9 6SF

Telephone: 01803 782206   *Fax: 01803 782333*

Situated in the picturesque village of Stoke Gabriel on the River Dart, the Gabriel Court Hotel, a 15th century manor house, is a haven of peace and tranquillity. Early maturing gardens reflecting the climatic conditions of the area, are stocked with unusual plants, magnificent magnolias, box hedges and yew archways . The garden supplies the restaurant with fresh vegetables and herbs, whilst energetic guests will enjoy the heated outdoor swimming pool. Bedrooms are well furnished, with lovely peaceful views and all have full facilities. There are several good size family suites. Michael and Eryl Beacom, assisted by their son Ross, are wonderful hosts, nothing is too much trouble for them or their excellent staff. A delightful dining room has views of the gardens enhanced by a large magnolia. Gabriel Court has always had an excellent reputation for its food, and fresh fish from Brixham and Exmoor venison are specialities. This is a thoroughly comfortable and peaceful hotel, I can highly recommend it. Dinner, room and full English breakfast from £59.50 per person, inclusive of VAT.

London 198, Paignton Station 4, Totnes 4, Kingswear 7, Torquay 6

R & R licence; 19 en suite bedrooms (two ground floor), all with telephone, colour TV,radio,hairdryer and tea/coffee making facilities; baby listening; TV lounge; diets, children welcome; dogs accepted; guests ' laundry facilities; outdoor heated swimming pool; croquet; sea bathing; fishing; riding nearby; golf (Churston three miles); open all year.

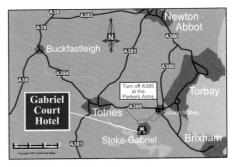

WATERSMEET HOTEL
Mortehoe, Woolacombe, Devon EX34 7EB

Telephone: 01271870333   *Fax: 01271870890*

Watersmeet, with its south facing terraced gardens and private steps leading to the beach below, commands a unique position with extensive sea views from Hartland Point to Lundy Island. This lovely hotel is owned and personally looked after by Brian and Pat Wheeldon, both very experienced, who have taken great care preserving the comfort and style of a country house. All the public rooms and bedrooms are delightfully furnished with soft colour schemes complemented by lovely fabrics. There are two bars, one an exclusive cocktail bar with comfortable lounges leading off. Candles light the octagonal Pavilion Restaurant which is designed so that every table enjoys a spectacular view of the sea. The award winning cuisine, always imaginative, has gone from strength to strength, and is simply superb. The menus are changed daily, and guests may choose from an English or an International menu. The selection of wines is well chosen. I can thoroughly recommend this well run family hotel, where the service is efficient and conveys a happy atmosphere. Dinner, room and breakfast from £49.00. Other terms, including special breaks on application. Bridge and painting holidays arranged. Closed December to February but office open for enquiries. Do write for their most attractive and informative brochure. Spring and Autumn Breaks, 2-4 days. All prices on application.

Taunton 62, Bristol 79, Barnstaple 14, Exeter 56

F licence; 26 bedrooms (one ground floor suite) all with private bathroom, remote control colour TV; direct dial telephones; children welcome; meals till 8.30p.m; light lunches; diets; pool table; games room; outdoor heated swimming pool; grass tennis court; bathing, sandy beach - private steps to sea-shore; surfing and sailing, boating, sea and river fishing, riding and three golf courses all nearby; lovely walks - National Trust; all major credit cards accepted.

WOOLACOMBE BAY HOTEL
Woolacombe, Devon EX34 7BN
Telephone: 01271 870388   Fax: 01271 870613

Rugged moors, rocky tors, endless National Trust walks on beach and headland; picturesque villages of "old worlde" charm are the feel and freedom of Devon. Set amidst six acres of quiet gardens running to three miles of golden sand is the luxurious Woolacombe Bay Hotel, built in the halcyon days of the mid 1800's. It exudes a relaxed air of friendliness, good living, comfort and traditional service. The hotel has been extensively but sensitively modernised, combining discreet old fashioned ambience with modern charm. Dining is simply a delight, the best of English and Continental cooking, using the freshest local produce. Vegetarian dishes and special diets are always available. To complement the menus, is an interesting wine list, and you can also enjoy a drink in one of the relaxed bars. Guests have unlimited use of the extensive leisure and sporting amenities (see facilities below), and the hotel's MV Frolica boat is available for charter. A magnificent ballroom and spacious lounges, combined with the outstanding facilities at the Woolacombe Bay Hotel, enables everyone to have the holiday of their choice. Energetic or relaxed - the decision is yours. Room and breakfast from £50.00 per person, dinner, room and breakfast from £65.00 per person. Prices include VAT. Special seasonal offers available. Please enquire for details.

Taunton 62, Bristol 79, Exeter 56, Barnstaple 14

F licence, 64 en suite bedrooms, all with telephone and TV, room/night service; baby listening, lift; last orders for dinner 9.30p.m; bar meals in bistro; special diets; children welcome; conferences max. 200; games room; snooker/billiards; short mat bowls; tennis coaching; indoor and outdoor heated swimming pools; new in 1995 the 'Hot House' fitness centre with aerobics studio, fitness room, beautician, masseur, trimtrail; 2 squash courts; 9 hole approach golf course; 2 floodlit all-weather tennis courts; sea bathing (blue flag beach); sailing/boating; own motor yacht; riding, shooting and fishing nearby; hotel closed Jan.-mid Feb.; all credit cards accepted.

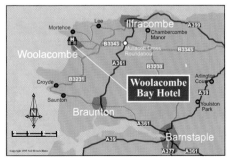

EASTON COURT HOTEL

Easton Cross,
Chagford, Devon
TQ13 8JL

Tel and Fax: 01647 433469
AA ★★ ◉
ETB ⌒⌒⌒ Commended

*Seven en suite double bedrooms.
Bed and breakfast from £42-45.
Dinner available from 1930-2030
from £16 per head. Short break
terms available.
Telephone and TV in rooms, tea/
coffee making facilities, parking.*

Easton Court is everyone's dream of a thatched cottage hotel. Beams and antiques abound; log fires glow and superb food that has created an enviable reputation in the district and beyond. Dartmoor is on the doorstep and both the North and South coasts of Devon are only a short drive away. A "must" for anyone visiting Devon for a few days. But beware - you will want to stay longer to soak up the atmosphere and the good life that Easton Court purveys.

SKINNERS ASH FARM

Fenny Bridges Honiton, Devon
EX14 OBH

Tel: 01404 850231

ETB Commended

*Two double bedrooms, both en suite;
separate flat. Bd and breakfast from
£15.50. Dinner available 1800-2000
from £7 per head. Colour TV, tea/
coffee making, parking. Farm walks
and pony rides; no dogs.*

This is a fine place to stay (also known as 'Berties's Barn') especially if you have children. Basically a 16th century farmhouse, still run as a farm, it provides traditional comfort and fare for the holiday maker. There are rare breeds to look at and you can help on the farm. The countryside round about is delightful and the South Devon coast is easily accessible by car. What could be better than to start the day with a proper farmhouse breakfast, spend the day sightseeing and then return to either a cream tea or a dinner usually prepared with ingredients straight from the farm.

BALCOMBE HOUSE HOTEL
Stevenstone Road, Exmouth, Devon EX8 2EP
Telephone 01395 266349

Balcombe House is ideally situated in half an acre of lawns and gardens which brings the feel of the English countryside to this idyllic setting, although it is near to the sea front with its 2 miles of golden sand and not far from the town centre. All rooms, both public and bedrooms, are comfortably furnished and decorated, whilst books in the lounge, a well-stocked bar and garden views add to the homely ambiance. The dining room offers an interesting and varied menu accompanied by an extensive and reasonably priced wine list. Free use can be made of the nearby Cranford sports club where almost all types of activities are available. The resident proprietors are proud of the peace and quiet of the Balcombe House and of their philosophy that guests come first. It shows. Single room with breakfast from £31.00. Double room including breakfast from £56.00.

Leisure Breaks: Special off season bargain breaks include up to half price accommodation.

Exeter 11, Honiton 17, Lyme Regis 27, Axminster 26 , London 170

Full licence. 12 en suite bedrooms with radio, video, colour TV; hairdryer, tea/ coffee making facilities. Partial facilities for disabled. Last orders for dinner 20.45. Special diets available. Sea fishing. Three local golf courses, watersports, riding, squash, swimming pool, tennis - all nearby. No bookings for children under 10. Car parking for 12 cars. Open all year. All major credit cards accepted.

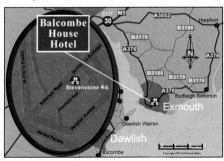

LEUSDON LODGE HOTEL
Leusdon, Poundsgate, Ashburton, Newton Abbot, Devon TQ13 7PE

Tel: 01364 631304; Fax: 01364 631599

Seven double bedrooms, all en suite. Bed and breakfast from £30-£60. Dinner available from 1930-2045 from £21 per head. AA ★★ TV/ Video films, telephone, tea/coffee making, ample parking

A traditional stone Victorian lodge in the Dartmoor National Park. Worth a detour from the A38 for its splendid cuisine and enviable views. Recently refurbished to a high standard of comfort. Situated in a tranquil spot within easy reach of eight local golf courses. Special terms for some courses through the hotel. Salmon trout and game in season with home grown vegetables. Nearby attractions: walking, riding, fishing, National Trust houses and gardens.

Three single, 30 double bedrooms, all en suite. Bed and breakfast from £20-£25. Lunch available 1230-1330 from £3.50 per head. Dinner available from 1830-2000 from £7.50 per head. Tea/coffee making facilities; colour TV; parking.

THE APSLEY HOTEL
Torwood Gardens Road, Torquay, Devon TQ11 1EG

Tel: 01803 292058

ETB ⌒⌒⌒ RAC ★★

This small family run hotel is situated in a quiet corner of Torquay and yet it is only a few minutes' walk to the harbour, the marina and the shops. A varied menu offers good food; there is a reasonably priced wine list and well stocked bar. Live entertainment is provided during the season and all rooms are comfortably furnished. Good value for money for those visiting the *English Riviera*. Coastal cruises and coach tours to historical and other places of interest can be organised from the hotel.

THE TORBAY HOLIDAY MOTEL
Totnes Road, Paignton, Devon TQ4 7PP

Telephone 01803 558226   Fax 01803 663375

This hotel probably offers as good value for money as you will get anywhere in the area and it is especially good for families because of its wealth of facilities. Here you have an indoor and outdoor swimming pool, a mini-gym an adventure playground, a 35-acre picnic area, Sky television, a launderette and a shop. The rooms are varied as well and range from the conventional motel style to studio apartments and nicely appointed luxury suites. In a popular resort hotel the Spinnaker Restaurant is aptly named: it serves English and continental breakfasts and there is a full choice of table d'hôte or à la carte menus in the evening whilst the Rally Bar nearby provides for every type of refreshments including light snacks. The outstanding views towards Torbay and Dartmoor remind you of the excellent location of the motel situated as it is between the beautiful South Hams district and the "English Riviera" with its historic towns and villages such as Dartmouth and Brixham. The harbour of Paignton itself and the Torbay Leisure Centre are only a short drive away. There is so much to see and do so whatever the weather you can be sure that there will never be a dull moment during your stay in this active place. Single room including breakfast from £29.00. Double room with breakfast from £46.00.
Leisure Breaks: Enquire about off season special offers for stays of three nights or more. Also senior citizen discounts.

Torquay 3 , Totnes 6 , Plymouth 29 , Dartmouth 8 (ferry), Exeter 26 , London 191

Full licence. 18 en suite bedrooms with radio, satellite TV, direct-dial telephone; hairdryer, laundry service; tea/ coffee making facilities. Last orders for dinner 21.00 hrs. Special diets available. Fitness centre, indoor games room, sauna; Indoor and outdoor swimming pools. News-stand/shop. Car parking for 120 cars. Open all year (limited service 24/12-31/1). Access, Visa, Amex accepted.

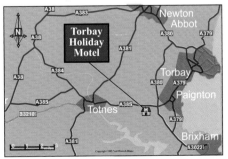

THE ANCHOR INN
Beer, Nr. Seaton, Devon EX12 3ET
Telephone 01297 20386

When I crossed the threshold of The Anchor, the hallmarks of a good seaside inn were all there: the friendliness, sense of tradition and inviting aroma of food. Beer is an unspoilt fishing town set amongst fine coastal scenery and The Anchor is unspoilt too, with its position on the waters edge overlooking the boats and the beach from the Inn, and sea views from most of the bedrooms. This free house serves Real Ale in its popular cliff-top beer garden, whilst in winter you relax in front of an open fire amid the warm decor of one of the cosy bars. These public areas are much patronised by locals, so the atmosphere is one of participating in the life of the neighbourhood. The bedrooms are welcoming, attractively decorated and en suite. Leaving the best until last: it is the cuisine which tempts you back to The Anchor with its well deserved reputation for serving fresh local seafood and an enormous choice of other dishes. The small, friendly seaside inn is a marvellous place to stay because you get close to the area and its people, which gives added value to exploring such beautiful regions as East Devon. The Anchor Inn is a classic example of this enduring genre. Double room with breakfast from £24.50 pp.

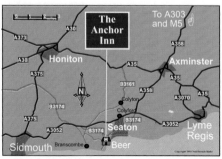

Leisure Breaks: 1st November - 31st March 25% reduction for 2 nights or more except public holidays.

Sidmouth 7, Exeter 22 , Hiniton 11 , Axminster 8 , London 153

Full licence. Eight en suite bedrooms, most en suite with colour TV; tea/coffee making facilities. Hairdryer, trouser press on request. Last orders for dinner 21.30 hrs. Special diets available. Sea fishing. Golf - six local courses. Riding by arrangement. Open all year. Visa, Access, Switch accepted.

MOUNT EDGCOMBE HOTEL
23 Avenue Road, Torquay, Devon TQ2 5LB
Tel: (01803) 292310

Nine double bedrooms, eight en suite. Bed and breakfast from £13-£23; dinner available from £7.50 per head; colour TV, tea/coffee making facilities; ample parking.

The Mount Edgcombe Hotel is situated centrally for all the attractions of Torquay and is close to both the rail and bus stations. It is family run and the owners put great emphasis on the cuisine. There is an Olde Worlde Bar. In a town where accommodation is often at a premium, this hotel gives remarkable value. Well located for Torre Abbey and the English Riviera Conference and Leisure Centre; a level walk to the sea front and Abbey Gardens. Sun patio.

SHIRLEY HOTEL
Braddons Hill Road East
Torquay TQ1 1HF
Tel: 01803 293016

ETB ━━━ Commended   RAC Acclaimed

Two single bedrooms, eleven double - 10 en suite. Bed and breakfast from £17 to £22 per head. Dinner available from £8 per head. Children over five welcomed; sauna & jacuzzi; outdoor pool;TV + satellite; tea/coffee making facilities; no dogs.

Close to the heart of this attractive Riviera town, a family run detached and comfortable hotel where guests consistently return to enjoy a varied menu and commendable standards of accommodation. 500 yards from the harbour and shops of Torquay, the Shirley Hotel makes a convenient base for touring the 22 miles of unspoiled coastline, 18 beaches , secluded coves and spectacular Dartmoor National Park nearby.

QUEEN'S HOTEL
Meyrick Rd, East Cliff, Bournemouth, Dorset BHl 3DL

Telephone: 01202 554415　　　　　*Fax: 01202 294810*

The Queen's Hotel, set in a prime position on Bournemouth's East Cliff, enjoys a southerly aspect, benefitting from wonderful views across Poole Bay. It is part of the Arthur Young Hotel Group, with The Cumberland, The Trouville and The Cliffeside, all being "sister" hotels, within the central Bournemouth area. A truly warm welcome awaits guests. All the bedrooms are stylishly decorated, and have excellent en suite facilities. Many of the rooms have their own balconies (some with seaviews) and a number of luxury four-poster bedrooms and family suites are available. The restaurant has established an enviable reputation for its excellent cuisine. Menus are well chosen with wide and varied combinations offered daily. A well selected wine list complements the culinary flair, and wines to suit every palate can be savoured. The Garden Room, leading out onto a sunny patio, is the ideal venue for either a coffee, or perhaps cocktails with friends. The new Queensbury Leisure Club is the most superb addition. Facilities including the indoor pool are of the highest standards, providing a truly luxurious fitness centre. Conferences are well catered for, with purpose built seminar and syndicate rooms available, providing for all your business needs. All in all, the Queen's Hotel is an excellent venue, whether your stay in Bournemouth is for business or pleasure. A fitting motto used by the group is *"Stay Young, Stay Happy"*, and I personally could not agree more! Room and breakfast from £39.50. An AA Rosette has been awarded for the cuisine. **Bargain breaks:** October-April two night stay £94.50

pppn, d, b&b. Mini breaks, Christmas, New Year and Easter programmes.
London 100, New Forest 10, Southampton 35
R &R licence; 114 en suite bedrooms, with radio, TV, direct dial telephone, tea and coffee making facilities; lift; night service; dinner to 9. 00 p.m; diets; children welcome; baby listening; dogs accepted; wide range of conference facilities -new syndicate rooms; beauty salon; leisure club with indoor swimming pool, sauna, steam rm, spa pool, trymnasium/ solarium; games room; dancing; sea and sailing; open all year; all major credit cards.

THE MANOR HOTEL
West Bexington, Dorchester,Dorset DT2 9DF

Telephone: 01308 897616   Fax: 01308 897035

The Manor Hotel, located amidst some of the most dramatic scenery on the South Dorset coast, is somewhere very special just waiting to be discovered. This ancient manor house steeped in history is well mellowed with age, offering a wonderful combination of flagstone floors, panelled walls, beamed ceilings, cellar rooms, yet has been provided with en suite bedrooms including every modern comfort and facility that guests could require. The décor of the en suite rooms certainly brings the vibrance of Dorset flowers and countryside through every window. Views are breathtaking. The natural gardens of the hotel are colourful and well established. Beyond is the sweeping geographical landmark of Chesil Bank with the clear seas of Lyme Bay lapping and ebbing over miles of pebbles. A more dramatic and scenic, yet quiet and relaxing situation for an hotel, one could not wish to better. The Cellar Bar provides a varied choice of bar meals through the day and in the evening, the elegant restaurant enjoys a fine reputation for well chosen culinary specialities, with fresh local produce, vegetables and especially seafood being used by the chef to present an excellent menu. A fine wine list satisfies all tastes. Historic Dorset, Weymouth, Lyme Regis and Abbotsbury are within easy reach of the Manor Hotel. With the owners, Richard and Jane Childs stating that, for their guests "nothing is too much trouble", please discover and pamper yourself with a visit to the Manor Hotel - a real treat! Room and breakfast from £37; weekly charge from £330.

Bargain breaks: Two-day stay - dinner, bed & breakfast £112 per person; five-day stay - dinner, bed & breakfast £260 per person.

Bridport 7, Dorchester 10, Weymouth 11, Lyme Regis 14, Bournemouth 50, Exeter 50, London 135
F licence; 13 en suite bedrooms, all with TV, direct dial telephone, room service; baby listening; last orders 9.30 pm; bar meals; special diets; children welcome; conferences max 60; sea bathing; golf 5 miles; riding 2 miles; open all year; credit cards accepted.

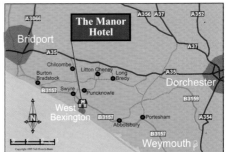

DEVON HOTEL
Lyme Road, Uplyme, Lyme Regis, Dorset DT7 3TQ

Telephone 01297 443231   Fax 01297 445836

If you are looking for a quiet retreat to explore a beautiful local area, then the Devon Hotel is the place. Set in eight acres of grounds, it is a fine period country house overlooking the Lyme Valley, one of the loveliest parts of Dorset, and not far from rural Devon; Lyme Regis with its quaint harbour and the famous Undercliff Gardens is but a mile away. The Devon is family-run and character mingles with traditional style to produce an atmosphere which is relaxed, welcoming and most comfortable. All the bedrooms are en suite with modern facilities and the many which enjoy rural views have a matching décor reflecting the light and freshness of the countryside. There is an elegant lounge, a welcoming bar area and a dining-room which is a feature in itself with carved panelling, ornate relief on the ceiling and an imposing fireplace which dominates the splendid room. We enjoyed the menu, in particular the fresh local produce and a well-chosen wine list. Refreshments are also served by the swimming pool and on the terrace. The needs of the active are met by a gymnasium, a putting green and a games room. This is the sort of hotel which is a pleasure to visit at any time of the year. Single room including breakfast from £31.00. Double room rate including breakfast from £62.00.

Leisure Breaks: 2 day breaks or longer from £31.00 p.p. per night b & b; £41.00 p.p. including dinner. Golfing Breaks offer green fee reduction of £4.00 per player at Lyme Regis golf course.

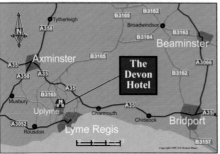

Lyme Regis 1 mile, Axminster 5 , Dorchester 26, Exeter 28, Crewkerne 15, London 147
Full licence, 21 en suite bedrooms with radio & colour TV; direct dial telephone. Coffee/tea making facilities. Last orders dinner 21.00 hrs. Billiards (pool); putting green, outdoor swimming pool. Fishing, golf, water sports, riding, tennis, all nearby. One meeting room for 30. Secretarial services. Facilities for disabled. Parking 21 cars. Open all year. All major credit cards accepted.

THE HAVEN HOTEL
Banks Road, Sandbanks, Poole, Dorset BH13 7QL

Telephone: 01202 707333   Fax: 01202 708796

The Haven Hotel at Sandbanks must occupy one of the finest positions of any hotel on the south coast of England. It is situated on the deep water entrance to Poole Harbour where marine activity abounds. All 96 bedrooms are well-appointed, and decor reaches new heights of excellence. The public rooms, bars, sun lounge and Sea View Restaurant are tastefully presented, creating an aura of sophistication throughout, with friendly attentive service by a professional team of staff. The luxury of relaxing on leather sofas prevails in the Marconi Lounge from where Guglielmo Marconi sent his first wireless messages; the "message" transmitted today is of a first class hotel. The Sea View Restaurant's cuisine is supervised by an award winning chef, Carl Heinz-Nagler, who provides a buffet and carvery luncheon, and in the evenings, discerning diners can savour culinary delights from the table d'hôte and gourmet selected menus. La Roche Restaurant also serves excellent food from à la carte menus, and overlooks the sea. The purpose built Business Centre has individual suites and seminar rooms to cater for all requirements, and the numerous facilities of the Leisure Centre are again superb. The ultimate luxury must be to charter the hotel's own yacht for a cruise around the bay. All in all, this is a first class hotel. Room and breakfast from £69.00 to £89.00 per night; dinner, bed & breakfast £75.00-£97.50. **Bargain breaks** - on application.

London 105, Southampton 28, Dorchester 23

F licence; 96 en suite bedrooms, all with telephone and TV; room/night service; baby listening, lift, last orders 9. 30 p.m., bar meals, special diets on request; children welcome, no dogs; conferences max. 200; indoor/outdoor heated swimming pools; American hot tub; sauna; spa pool; solarium; jacuzzi; gym; all weather floodlit tennis court, squash court, aromatherapist/masseuse, sea bathing, sailing/boating; golf and riding 3 miles; shooting/fishing by arrangement; open all year; major credit cards accepted.

THE EASTBURY
Long Street, Sherborne, Dorset DT9 3BY

Telephone 01935 813131   Fax 01935 817296

Built in 1740 this Georgian town house hotel situated in a quiet street has retained much of its former grandeur. The atmosphere at the Eastbury is one of style and sophistication with the public rooms setting the tone from the elegant entrance hall to the warm décor of the lounge, not forgetting the library and a cosy cocktail bar. Bedrooms are named after English garden flowers and the bright colour schemes and polished furniture reflect the floral theme, particularly in those rooms with views onto the colourful and well cultivated walled garden. Excellent food is served in the restaurant which extends into a light and tented conservatory feature also with the benefit of garden views. I enjoyed the traditional cooking using local Dorset produce. It was well presented and the service was particularly attentive. Whether a visit here is for business or pleasure,Thomas Hardy's Dorset is on the doorstep to be discovered and the Eastbury Hotel, just a short distance from Sherborne's 8th Century Abbey, is an ideal and most relaxing base from which to do it. Double room with breakfast from £65.00.

Shaftesbury 16 , Crewkerne 14 , Dorchester 18 , Blandford Forum 20 , Taunton 31 , Salisbury 36, Bournemouth 39, London 120

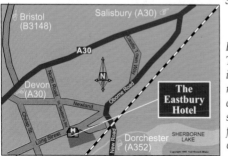

Full licence. 15 en suite bedrooms with satellite TV; direct-dial telephone, hairdryer, laundry service; tea/coffee making facilities. Last order for dinner 21.30. Theatre style conference room with capacity for 65 guests. Fishing, golf, riding, indoor swimming pool all nearby. Car rental. Car parking for 20 cars. Open all year. Major credit cards accepted.

MANOR HOUSE HOTEL
Studland Bay, Nr. Swanage, Dorset BH19 3AU

Telephone: 01929 450288

The site of the Manor House Hotel is mentioned in the Domesday Book and parts of the present rambling Gothic House date back to 1750. Set within 16 acres of elevated grounds, the hotel commands beautiful views overlooking the beaches and waters of Studland Bay. History and character are in abundance; the hotel's medieval carvings are said to have come from the residential quarters of Corfe Castle, home of the famous Mary Banks, who defended it so bravely against Cromwell's troops . The bedrooms are all en suite, and are individually decorated with great charm and style. Four rooms have four-poster beds, and most have spectacular views over the bay and out to Old Harry Rocks. Wall carvings in the Westminster Bedroom are of particular interest, reputed to have been from the old Palace of Westminster, circa 1636. All the reception rooms enjoy lovely views and those with old panelling glow on winters evenings when the fires are lit. A delightful conservatory has extended the dining area, where décor is sophisticated, and the atmosphere and service is most warming. The menu has an excellent choice of fresh local produce and the delicious Studland Lobster is a must ! The hotel has recently been awarded an AA Rosette for Good Food. The Manor House Hotel is the ideal base from which to explore the beauty of Studland, its conservation area, beaches, nature trails and in general, the many attractions of Dorset. Dinner, room and breakfast from £46.00. Hotel closed Christmas and January.

London 113, Swanage 3, Bournemouth 8, Dorchester 26, Corfe Castle 6

R & R licence; 18 en suite bedrooms, all with colour TV, radio, tea/coffee making facilities, telephone, hairdryer and full central heating; last orders for dinner 8.30 p.m; bar lunches; vegetarian diets; children over five welcome; dogs allowed; sea bathing three miles, with sandy beach, sailing and boating; two tennis courts (hard); riding; golf within two miles; Mastercard and Visa cards accepted.

KNOLL HOUSE HOTEL
Studland Bay, Dorset BH19 2AH

Telephone: 01929 450450 Fax: 01929 450423

This delightful hotel is situated on the finest stretch of Dorset heritage coastline surrounded by some of the prettiest countryside in the West and it is well worth a visit. It is within a National Trust Reserve and overlooks three miles of golden beach with first class swimming, fishing, boating and wind-surfing. Knoll House is an independent country house hotel under the personal management of its family owners and is set in pine trees with the most attractive gardens where you can relax away from the cares of everyday life. The sporting facilities are numerous - tennis courts, a nine-hole par 3 golf course and outdoor heated swimming pool. For relaxation there is a sauna, steam-room, Jacuzzi, plunge-pool, solarium and gym set in a marvellous health hydro complex with fruit juice and coffee bar. Many of the bedrooms are arranged as suites, ideal for families. Log fires and an attractive cocktail bar add to the unique atmosphere of this extremely efficiently run hotel. The quality, choice and presentation of the menus is excellent. At lunchtime a superb hors d'oeuvres selection and buffet table laden with cold meats, pies and salads is a speciality, fol-

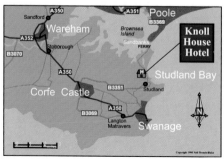

lowed by delicious puddings and a good English cheeseboard. Young children are catered for in their own dining room and there are many and varied facilities to keep them amused all day. Sandbanks and Bournemouth are easily reached by the nearby car ferry with Dorchester, Corfe Castle and the picturesque villages of Dorset only a short drive away. The hotel is open from April to October. Half board from £53.00 daily, or full board (weekly) £380.00 (April) - £550.00 (August). Generous full board terms for five nights out of season.

Old Harry Rocks and Studland Bay.

Special breaks: 'Family Five' (two adults, one or two children under 13) - five nights full board in low season £745. Purbeck Five (single or twin rooms without private bathroom) five nights full board in low season £254 .00 per person. September 22nd-October 17th, two nights full board £115-£133 per person. Prices include VAT. There is no service charge.

London 113, Swanage 3, Bournemouth 8, Studland 1, Corfe Castle 6

C licence; 79 bedrooms (many ground floor), comprising 30 family suites, 29 single, 20 twin bedded rooms; 57 private bathrooms; five lounges; children 's dining room; self-service laundry; three games rooms; solarium; children 's disco in season; colour TV room; 9 acre golf course; two hard tennis courts, playground, outdoor swimming and paddling pools; full leisure centre; giftshop; adjoins clean sandy beach, safe bathing; Isle of Purbeck Golf Club two miles, two courses; no credit cards.

PLUMBER MANOR
Sturminster Newton, Dorset DT10 2AF
Telephone 01258 472507   Fax 01258 473370

This imposing Jacobean manor house hotel is set in idyllic countryside in the heart of beautiful Dorset. Most certainly "far from the madding crowd", tranquillity prevails throughout. The Divelish stream weaves its way through delightful grounds, extensive lawns and fine old trees making a rich and peaceful setting. Dating from the 17th Century the manor has been and remains the home of the Prideaux-Brune family. Since 1973 the careful management by Richard, Alison and Brian has indeed led to the creation of a first class hotel and restaurant. Situated half-way between London and Cornwall, the location is perfect for travelling or simply exploring the picturesque and unspoilt Dorset countryside. There are six elegant en suite bedrooms within the main house and a further ten en suite rooms are located in the courtyard and converted barn overlooking the stream and gardens. Rooms are individually furnished with style, flair and the colour schemes of the country warmly reflected. The highly acclaimed restaurant, subdivided into three rooms, provides imaginative and traditional cuisine using the finest of fresh local ingredients where possible. The extensive wine list is excellent. Plumber Manor is welcoming, comfortable and has the most charming atmosphere in which to relax and savour first class hospitality, cuisine and service. A fine hotel. Single room rate including breakfast from £65. Double room rate with breakfast from £42 per person.

Leisure Breaks: 10% disc. on two nights (or more), 15% on 3 nights or more October - April. **London 123, Bournemouth 30, Bristol 49, Salisbury 28, Taunton 41**

Full licence. 16 en suite bedrooms with radio & colour TV. Direct-dial telephone. Tea/coffee making facilities, hairdryer, trouser press. Last orders for dinner 21.30. Croquet, tennis, fishing, golf, riding, shooting and massage facility all nearby by arrangement. Meeting room for 12 guests. Photocopying fax, o/h pro-jector available. Car rental, car parking. Open March-January. All major credit cards accepted.

SPRINGFIELD COUNTRY HOTEL & LEISURE CLUB
Grange Road, Wareham, Dorset BH20 5AL

Telephone: 01929 552177   Fax: 01929 551862

The Springfield Country Hotel is set in six acres of beautifully landscaped gardens at the foot of the Purbeck Hills. It is ideal for visiting local attractions such as Lulworth Cove, Corfe Castle, Dorchester and the nearby resorts of Poole and Swanage. For golf enthusiasts, there are three 18 hole golf courses within the locality, one of whom can arrange a discount. Each of the 48 bedrooms has delightful views across the grounds, which feature an ornamental lake and waterwheel. All types of rooms are available, including family suites and ground floor rooms, and there is a lift to take you to the first floor. Both the à la carte and table d'hôte menus offer a wide choice of delicious dishes, cooked to perfection and complemented by good value, quality wines from around the world. The oak beamed lounge bar leads out onto an attractive patio area, providing the perfect setting for bar meals, afternoon teas or evening aperitifs. The new large function suite can accommodate conferences or wedding receptions. Syndicate rooms and audio visual aids are also available. Springfield's new leisure club includes a large gymnasium with the latest computerised equipment. This 4 Crown Commended hotel is a first class family run establishment with outstanding facilities, where a warm Dorset welcome is always guaranteed. Room and breakfast from £63 single, £100 double, new luxury rooms from £130 inc. VAT. **Bargain breaks:** 2 nights £118-£148 inc. dinner, b & b; 3 nights £177-£222 pp. **Poole 10, Bournemouth 15, Southampton 35, London 120.**

F licence; 48 en suite bedrooms with showers and direct dial telephone, TV, radio,tea/coffee making facilities; lift; room service; night porter, last orders for dinner Sun.-Fri. 9.00p.m/Sat.9.30p.m; bar meals; special diets; children welcome; dogs by arrangement; games room; snooker/billiards; tennis court; outdoor heated swimming pool; new sports and leisure club with indoor heated swimming pool, spa, saunas, steam rooms, solarium, gymnasium & squash courts; open all year; most credit cards accepted.

MOONFLEET MANOR HOTEL
Moonfleet Nr. Weymouth Dorset DT3 4ED

Telephone 01305 786948   Fax 01305 774395

Moonfleet Manor is a mix of the ancient and modern. It is situated by Chesil Bank, a unique natural wonder of geographical interest and beauty on the Dorset coast whilst the hotel itself has origins going back to 1564, since when many stories of smuggling and adventure have left their mark on history. Today's excitement is amongst the quality comforts and exceptional sporting facilities of the hotel, created by Bruce and Jan Hemingway, the resident proprietors. The rooms are appointed to a good standard with glorious sea or open countryside views. The lounges are spacious and include a residents' bar and conservatory for light lunches. There is a main restaurant as well for more substantial meals and also the cosy Blue Moon bistro cellar bar which puts on a discreet disco. The Country Club - called The Ball Park is a natural for family activity offering everything from tennis to skittles , snooker and an indoor Adventure Playroom. In addition there is The Blue Lagoon with pools for all ages as well as keep fit classes and weight training. Moonfleet Manor is ideal for families but also caters expertly for conferences and if you are simply looking for a friendly place from which to explore the beauties of Dorset then this would be a perfect base. Single room with breakfast from £37.50. Double room with breakfast from £30.00.

Leisure Breaks: £42.00 per person per night dinner, room and breakfast.

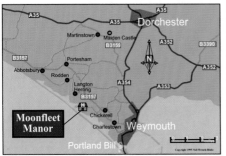

London 130 , Bournemouth 35 , Axminster 30, Lyme Regis 28, Wareham 17, Bristol 68, Exeter 59 *Full licence. 40 en suite bedrooms with colour TV, radio, direct-dial telephone; hairdryer, trouser press, laundry service, tea/coffee making facilities. Last orders for dinner 21.00 hrs. Special diets available. Facilities for disabled. Billiards, snooker, fitness centre, indoor games room; jogging track, indoor swimming pool, indoor bowls. Squash, tennis, golf, watersports, riding - 3-5 miles. Business services and meeting room - capacity 50 guests. AV equipment available. Safety deposit box. Car rental. Car parking for 200 cars. Open all year. All credit cards accepted.*

BRITMEAD HOUSE
West Bay Road, Bridport, West Dorset DT6 4EG
Tel: 01308 422941

4 doubles, 3 twin rooms, all en suite; single rate £24; double £46. Dinner (1800 hrs) £12. Colour TV, hairdryer, minibar, car parking. Fishing, golf and riding can be arranged nearby.

With a reputation for friendliness, hospitality and high standards, Britmead House is situated between the historic town of Bridport and the Dorset coast at West Bay. The seven bedrooms all have en suite facilities, fresh, light décor and include "many little extras".

Meals at Britmead are of a consistently high standard. Dinner menus change daily and are well chosen to include local produce and seafood. Breakfasts are excellent; there is a carefully chosen wine list and bar service. Both the lounge and dining room have a lovely southwesterly aspect across open fields to the hills, cliffs and coastal pathways. Mr & Mrs Walker, the resident proprietors will ensure that your stay at Britmead will be memorable.

THE OLD BAKEHOUSE
Lower Church Street, Colyton, Devon EX13 6ND
Tel: 01297 552518
AA★★RAC

6 doubles, all en suite; bed and breakfast from £21.50. Lunch available from noon-1400 from £1.95 per head; dinner 1900-2130 from £6.95 per head. Colour TV, tea/coffee making facilities, car parking, children welcome. Four-day breaks (3 nights) b&b £55.50; dinner,b&b £82.50.

This lovely little hotel in the centre of Colyton has been cleverly and tastefully converted from a 17th-century building without in any way detracting from the original ambience. The owners have gained a reputation far and wide for the excellence of their food and to dine in the cosy, candle-lit dining-room is a delight. Colyton is ionly three miles from the sea, thus making the Old Bakehouse an ideal venue from which to tour the south coasts of Devon and Dorset and the lovely areas inland around Ottery St Mary, Chard and Axminster.

THE WALNUT TREE HOTEL
North Petherton, Bridgwater, Somerset TA6 6QA

Telephone: 01278 662255   Fax: 01278 663946

The Walnut Tree Inn is a former 18th Century coaching inn, set in the heart of the pretty Somerset village of North Petherton, on the A38. Traditional values have been maintained here over the years. All the rooms are quietly located at the rear of the Inn, and every possible comfort is provided for guests. Each of the thirty three bedrooms offer superb amenities. The décor is tasteful and warming, and the four-poster bed suite is a popular choice for those seeking a special or romantic weekend break. Three spacious meeting rooms are available, seating up to seventy people. These have all the usual support facilities, along with visual aids. Any business meeting here is bound to be successful! The Walnut Tree also specialises in receptions and parties - or whatever the celebration may be. The public rooms of the hotel have an abundance of charm and character. The popular bar with Cottage Room Restaurant, can tempt you with real ales, light bar snacks and succulent steaks. However, first class international cuisine can be savoured in the beautiful Sedgemoor Restaurant. Presentation service and excellent wines complement this more formal setting in which to enjoy a memorable repast. The Walnut Tree Hotel is a hostelry of high standards with friendly staff attending to your

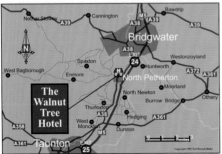

every need. Well located for touring the South West. Do sample the charm of this hotel, and you are bound to return. Room and breakfast from £33, dinner, room and breakfast from £44 inc. VAT. Special weekend packages available.
Bridgwater 1½, M5 (exit 24) 1, Taunton 8, Wells 12, Bristol 35, Exeter 40, London 150.
F licence; 33 en suite bedrooms (inc. suites) (3 for the disabled) all with direct dial telephone and TV; room service; baby listening; night service; last orders for dinner 10 p.m., bar meals, special diets, children welcome; conferences max. 70; solarium; extensive parking facilities; open all year; all major credit cards accepted.

ALFOXTON PARK
Holford, Bridgwater, Somerset TA5 1SG

Telephone: 01278 741211

After a mile's drive through the lovely woodland, off the main A39 road, you arrive at Alfoxton Park. The hotel is a fine Queen Anne period house, set in fifty acres of undulating parkland and woods. From the position of Alfoxton, on the slopes of the Quantock Hills, the location commands the most spectacular and breathtaking views across the Bristol Channel and on to the distant Welsh coast. A thousand years of history can be directly traced to dwellings on the site, and dating from 1710, Alfoxton Park has many original features giving it a wonderful character and atmosphere. All the bedrooms are en suite and provide the facilities that ensure the comfort of guests. The décor is light and attractive, and complements the warm, historic, relaxing atmosphere that can be found throughout the hotel. The bar is set in a fine panelled room, and the dining room, of more classical style, commands beautiful views across the grounds. A wonderful walled kitchen and herb garden provide oganically grown produce which is constantly used in the varied menus, based upon the best of British cooking. The well selected wine list, and friendly, attentive service are most welcoming. Alfoxton Park is a lovely hotel at which to stay, and for walking, swimming, or simply travelling through Somerset, I can thoroughly recommend it as a homely base.

Room and breakfast from £38.00 and dinner, room and breakfast from £50.00. Prices are per person and include VAT. **Bargain breaks:** Any two nights or more £45 pppn, d, b & b. **Bridgwater 11, Taunton 13, Minehead 15, London 167** *R & R licence; 18 en suite bedrooms (one for the disabled), all with TV, room service; last orders for dinner 8.45 p.m; bar meals available for residents; special diets on request; children welcome; outdoor heated swimming pool; riding approx. two miles; 18 hole golf course approx. seven miles; hotel closed during the winter; major credit cards accepted.*

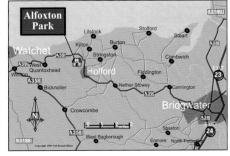

COMBE HOUSE HOTEL
Holford, Nr. Bridgwater, Somerset TA5 1RZ

Telephone: 01278 741382

This 17th century house is situated off the A39 at Holford amid romantic and beautiful surroundings in the heart of the Quantock Hills, famous for their wildlife, red deer and ponies. Combe House Hotel, which was acquired in 1976 by the resident proprietors, Mr. and Mrs . Bjergfelt, stands in its own grounds of five acres half a mile from the main road, with lovely gardens and a wonderful 100 year-old monkey puzzle tree. For the actively inclined there is a hard tennis court, croquet lawn and indoor heated swimming pool. The hotel is furnished to a high standard with genuine period furniture and attractive décor throughout and there is a fine collection of Royal Danish Christmas plates. Of the well appointed and comfortable bedrooms, seventeen have private bathrooms en suite. Great care is taken over the preparation and presentation of the meals, where fresh fruit and vegetables feature prominently on the menu. Good riding stables nearby provide suitable mounts for all ages to ride over the moors and forests of the surrounding hills. Golf is available at Minehead and Enmore and a championship course at Burnham-on-Sea. Room and breakfast from £35.00 (single) and £68.00 (twin) . Open March to November. Write for colour brochure to R. S. Bjergfelt.
Bargain breaks available from September to May from £75 for two nights, dinner, bed & breakfast.

London 153, Birmingham 132, Bridgwater 12, Bristol 45, Minehead 15, Dunster Castle 12

R & R licence, 19 bedrooms all with direct dial telephone and tea/coffee facilities; colour TV; 17 with private bathrooms, four poster bed; central heating; children welcome; meals to 8.30p.m.; dogs welcome but not in public rooms; tennis; croquet; indoor swimming pool; solarium; Visa, Mastercard, Amex accepted.

THE MANOR ARMS
North Perrott, Crewkerne, Somerset TA18 7SG

Telephone: 01460 72901   *Fax: 01460 72901*

If you seek fellowship on holiday there can be few better places than this charming "inn" situated in the lovely unspoilt village of North Perrott. The whole place was once owned by the same family and the feeling of kinship lingers on, so as you stroll on the Green opposite the Arms and chat with the locals, you are temporarily part of the everyday life of the village. So you are in this 16th Century grade II listed building which is at the heart of the community and with its log fires, oak beams and flagstone floors is the epitome of an English inn which despite the provision of good modern comfort has lost nothing of its old world character. You may also marvel, as I did, at the food in the restaurant which is so in keeping with the whole place, being quite simply beautifully cooked home-made English fare. The accommodation set in the quiet gardens behind the inn is homely. If you can tear yourself away from that mix of peace and conviviality which is village life, North Perrott is ideally situated for touring the beautiful country side and the nearby coastal resorts on your doorstep. Single room including breakfast from £29.00. Double room with breakfast from £42.00.

Leisure Breaks: available most of the year: two for the price of one rate of £32.00 per night per couple including English breakfast - min. two nights, must include dinner on one night.

Exeter 38 , Southampton 81 , Taunton 20 , London 145

Full licence. Five en suite bedrooms - all non-smoking - with colour TV; tea/coffee making facilities. Last orders for dinner 21.30 hrs. Vegetarian diets available. Fishing, golf, riding nearby. One meeting room with capacity for 16-24. Car parking for 36 cars. Open all year. Visa, Access, Mastercard accepted.

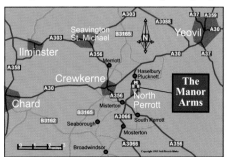

THE CASTLE INN
Castle Combe, Wiltshire, SN14 7HN

Telephone 01249 783030   Fax 01249 782315

The Castle Inn with origins dating back to the 12th Century nestles in the heart of what has been described as one of the prettiest villages in England. The inn has been sympathetically restored with comfort and character being the hallmarks. The en suite bedrooms are literally a dream with their individual furnishings complementing the natural features of the ancient inn but providing every modern day convenience and luxury including a choice of two rooms with whirlpool baths and an elegant Victorian slipper bath. All public areas of the Inn are warm and welcoming with the bar room still retaining the unique atmosphere of an old English inn where ales and traditional English fare can be savoured to the full. For sophisticated dining Oliver's Restaurant is a perfect example of imaginative menus being created with the freshest of produce and beautifully presented. For more informal occasions, or private parties, the conservatory and patio areas offer a lighter and more relaxed atmosphere. With Bath and the Cotswolds' historic and natural interests close to hand the Castle Inn is an ideal place to stay, relax and enjoy the picturesque charm, style and truly "old-fashioned" ambience combined with superlative service. Highly recommended. Single room including breakfast from £55.00. Double room with breakfast from £70.00.

Leisure Breaks: Two night scenechanger break from £95.00 per couple per night, includes English breakfast, daily newspaper, residents' dinner.

Cirencester 22 , Chippenham 6 , Bristol 18, Frome 22 , Tetbury 12 , London 97.

Full licence. Seven en suite bedrooms with radio, TV and video films. Direct-dial telephone, hairdryer, trouser press, tea/coffee making facilities. Last orders for dinner 21.30. Special diets available. Golf, fishing nearby. Squash, tennis six miles. Business services include meeting room with capacity for 30 guests. AV on request. Open all year. All major credit cards accepted.

CRUDWELL COURT HOTEL AND RESTAURANT
Crudwell, Nr. Malmesbury, Wiltshire SN16 9EP

Telephone: 01666 577194   Fax: 01666 577853

What a lovely surprise to find this enchanting little hotel on my travels near to Cirencester and Malmesbury. It is a 17th century former vicarage, set alongside a Saxon church in three acres of beautiful walled gardens. It is really like staying in a private home - I had the most warm welcome and I certainly look forward to a return visit. The house has recently been completely refurbished and all fifteen bedrooms are individually decorated. The gracious panelled dining room and the beautiful conservatory overlook the church. The excellent cuisine is freshly prepared to order, all complemented by an extensive wine list. Crudwell Court is run by its resident owners, who give that extra personal touch to the warm, country house atmosphere. Room and breakfast from £50.00 single/£90.00 double. Weekly terms on application. Hotel is open all year.
Bargain breaks available - tariff on application.

London 97, Cirencester 6, Swindon 12, Malmesbury 3

R & R licence; 15 en suite bedrooms, all with telephone, remote control colour TV, radio, tea/coffee making facilities, full central heating; night service until 12 midnight; last orders 9.30 p.m., bar meals, diets, children welcome, baby listening; dogs accepted; conferences max. 25; heated outdoor swimming pool; croquet; leisure centre, sailing, golf, tennis, squash, badminton, riding, shooting, fishing all nearby; Mastercard, Visa, Amex, Diners credit cards accepted.

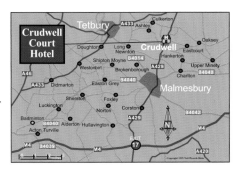

WHATLEY MANOR
Nr. Easton Grey, Malmesbury, Wiltshire SN16 ORB

Telephone: 01666 822888   Fax: 01666 826120

Whatley Manor, located on the borders of Wiltshire and Gloucestershire and on the edge of the Cotswolds, is noted for the luxury and spaciousness of both the bedrooms and public rooms. It has a real feeling of comfort and opulence, backed by unobtrusive service and excellent cuisine. The dining room has lovely views over the gardens, beyond which paddocks run down to a peaceful stretch of the river Avon . The pine panelled lounge and oak panelled drawing room, both with log fires, are elegant and provide relaxing surroundings . The Library Bar offers drinks and volumes of Punch dating back to the 19th century. The Manor bedrooms are furnished to a very high standard indeed. The Court House, 70 yards from the Manor, has ten more bedrooms overlooking the tennis court and grounds. The hotel is within easy reach of Badminton, Westonbirt Arboretum, Stonehenge and Longleat, to name but a few places, and the towns of Bath, Bristol, Cirencester and Swindon. Convenient for M4 and M5 Bed and full English breakfast from £85.00 single, double £112.00, inclusive of VAT.
Two-night breaks including English breakfast and dinner from £121 per person. Special stay-on rates for longer breaks are available.

London 98, Chippenham 10, Swindon 16, Bristol 30

R and R licence, 29 en suite bedrooms (12 ground floor), all with telephone, TV, tea/coffee making facilities, radio; full central heating; night service; diets; children welcome, baby-listening; dogs welcome; conferences; sauna; solarium, jacuzzi, croquet, billiards, heated outdoor swimming pool, tennis; golf five miles, squash two miles, riding one mile; Amex, Mastercard, Diners, Visa cards accepted.

THE PEAR TREE AT PURTON
Church End, Purton, Nr. Swindon, Wiltshire SN5 9ED

Telephone 01793 772100   Fax 01793 772369

The former Purton vicarage of traditional Cotswold Stone has been transformed into a most sophisticated hotel by Francis and Anne Young. Set in 7 $1/2$ acres of grounds, it is an elegant haven in the Wiltshire country side, a fine place, graciously well managed and the deserved recipient of many awards of excellence. The Conservatory Restaurant, decorated in soft tones of pink and white, overlooks the beautiful gardens. There is a creative menu of good English food with the freshest of local produce and home grown herbs whilst the wine list offers a fine choice from "wines of the world". The 18 rooms and suites are named after characters associated with the village of Purton. They are decorated to high standards and guests are welcomed by fresh fruit, mineral water and a decanter of Sherry. Public rooms are spacious with warming decor reflecting the charm and character of this beautiful building. Nestling in the Vale of the White Horse, the hotel is well located for exploring the surrounding English heritage and countryside and if on business in the area, the centre of Swindon is only five miles away. The Pear Tree at Purton is a lovely hotel in a fine setting, highly recommended for a stay whether on business or for pleasure. Single room with breakfast from £75.00. Double room including breakfast £75.00.

Swindon 5 , Oxford 34, Tetbury 17 , Bristol 40, Bath 35, Reading 45, London 82

Full licence. 18 en suite bedrooms with radio and satellite TV, direct-dial telephone, hairdryer, trouser press, laundry service. Last orders for dinner 21.15. Special diets available. Fishing, golf, watersports, riding, squash, tennis all nearby. Full business services. Four meeting rooms - capacity up to 50 guests. Car parking for 70 cars. Open all year. All major credit cards accepted.

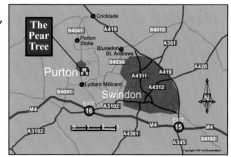

BLUNSDON HOUSE HOTEL & LEISURE CLUB
Blunsdon, Nr. Swindon, Wiltshire SN2 4AD

Telephone: 01793 721701   Fax: 01793 721056

Blunsdon House stands in 30 acres of grounds off the A419, just north of Swindon. During the last thirty years, the Clifford family have worked hard making this hotel the fine, modern, four-star establishment it is today. In spite of the size of the hotel, the emphasis is still on personal service, starting with the courteous hall porter who escorts you to your room and explains the location and operation of the many facilities. All the accommodation is spacious and comfortable, and there is no extra charge for children sharing their parents' room. The Ridge Restaurant offers a high standard of food, English and continental dishes, from daily fixed price or à la carte menus. I found the dinner and service excellent. For a more informal meal, try *Carrie's Carverie*, where there is a good choice from a fixed price menu. Three bars provide a choice of venue for your pre-lunch or dinner drink. The hotel is seven miles from junction 15 on M4 and on the link road to the M5. On the edge of the Cotswolds, it is an ideal centre for Bath, Longleat, Stonehenge, Salisbury and many other interesting places. Room only from £77.50, twin/double £92.50 inclusive of VAT and service. Open all year.
Getaway Weekend Breaks from £62.00 per person per night. Seven-day break from £375.00 per person.

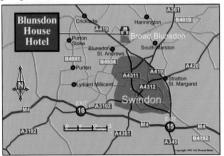

London 91, Oxford 29, Reading 40, Bristol 41, Southampton 64, Birmingham 80

F licence; 88 en suite rooms (29 ground floor), all with telephone, radio, TV; lift; night service; late meals to 10.30 p.m.; diets; children welcome, baby listening; no dogs; conferences; dancing by arrangement; sauna, solarium, spa bath, gym, beauty salon; snooker room; games room; children's adventure playground; heated indoor swimming pool; squash; tennis; pétanque; 1 mile woodland walk/jog; 9 hole, par 3 golf course; major credit cards accepted.

■ **Historic Houses, Gardens & Parks**

LONDON
Carlyle's House, Chelsea
Fenton House, Hampstead
Kensington Palace, Kensington Gardens, W8
Osterley Park, Isleworth
Tower of London, Tower Hill, EC3
Westminster Abbey Chapter House, SWI

BEDFORDSHIRE
Luton Hoo, Luton
The Swiss Garden, Old Warden
Woburn Abbey, Woburn
Wrest Park House & Gardens, Silsoe

BERKSHIRE
Beale Wildlife Gardens, Lower Basildon
Cliveden, Nr. Maidenhead
Dorney Court, Nr. Windsor
Forbury Gardens, Reading
Highclere Castle, Nr. Newbury
Mapledurham House and Watermill, Nr. Reading
Stonor House Henley-on-Thames
Stratfield Saye House, Nr. Reading

BUCKINGHAMSHIRE
Claydon House, Nr. Winslow
Hughenden Manor, High Wycombe
Stowe Landscape Gardens, Nr. Buckingham
Waddesdon Manor, Nr. Aylesbury
West Wycombe Park, Nr. High Wycombe

HAMPSHIRE
Breamore House & Museums, Nr. Fordingbridge
Broadlands, Romsey
Exbury Gardens, Nr. Southampton
Furzey Gardens Minstead, Nr. Lyndhurst
Highclere Castle
Lymington Vineyard
Lymore Valley Herb Garden, Nr. Milford-on-Sea
Sir Harold Hillier Gardens & Arboretum,
   Ampfield, Nr. Romsey
Stratfield Saye House & Wellington Country Park

HERTFORDSHIRE
Ashridge Estate, Nr, Berkhamsted
Cedars Park, Waltham Cross
The Gardens of the Rose, Chiswell Green, St. Albans
Hatfield House
Knebworth House
Ihe National Trust Wimpole Hall, Arrington, Nr. Royston
Priory Gardens, Royston
Verulamium Park, St Albams

KENT
Bedgebury National Pinetum, Nr. Goudhurst
Chilham Castle Gardens, Nr Canterbury
Doddington Place Gardens, Nr Sittingboume
Godington House & Gardens, Godington Park, Ashford
Goodnestone Park, Wingham, Nr. Canterbury
Iden Croft Herbs, Staplehurst
Kent Garden Vineyard, Headcorn
Penshurst Place & Gardens, Nr. Tonbndge
Sissinghurst Garden

OXFORDSHIRE
Basildon Park, Nr. Pangboume
Blenheim Palace, Woodstock
Peoples Park, Banbury
Rousham House & Gardens, Steeple Aston

Waterperry Gardens, Wheatley

SURREY
Clandon Park, West Clandon
Claremont Landscape Garden, Esher
Ham House, Richmond
Hampton Court Palace, East Molesey
Hatchlands Park, East Clandon
Kew Gardens (Royal Botanic Gardens), Richmond
Polesden Lacey, Great Bookham, Nr. Dorking
The RHS Garden, Wisley, Nr. Woking
The Savill Garden, Nr. Egham
Winkworth Arboretum, Hascombe, Nr. Godalming

EAST SUSSEX
Alfriston Clergy House, Alfriston
Battle Abbey, Battle
Brickwall House & Gardens, Northiam, Nr. Rye
Carr Taylor Vineyards, Hastings
Great Dixter House & Gardens, Northiam, Nr. Rye
Michelham Priory, Upper Dicker, Nr. Hailsham
Merriments Gardens, Hurst Green
Pashley Manor Gardens Ticehurst
Preston Manor, Preston Park, Brighton
Sheffield Park Garden, Danehill, Nr. Uckfield

WEST SUSSEX
Denmans Garden, Fontwell, Nr. Arundel
Goodwood House, Goodwood
Leonardslee Gardens, Lower Beeding, Nr. Horsham
Parham House & Gardens, Parham Park, Nr. Pulborough
Petworth House & Park
St. Mary's House, Bramber, Nr. Steyning
Standen, East Grinstead
Wakehurst Place Gardens, Ardingly, Nr. Haywards Heath

■ **Walks & Nature Trails**

BEDFORDSHIRE
Greensand Ridge Walk, from Leighton Buzzard to
   Gamlingay
Upper Lea Valley Walk, from Leagrave Common to E. Hyde

BERKSHIRE
Riverside & Country Walk to Speen Moors
Heritage Walk, Reading
Look Out Countryside & Heritage Centre Nr.   Bracknell
Reading Town Trails

HAMPSHIRE
Avon Valley Path, Salisbury to Christchurch
Itchin Way, Southampton to Hinton Ampner
Solent Way, Milford on-Sea to Emsworth
Three Castles Path, Windsor to Winchester

HERTFORDSHIRE
The Lea Valley Walk, from Ware to Stanborough Lakes
Tring Reservoirs

WEST SUSSEX
Burton Pond Nature Trail
Worth Way Walk, from Worth Way to East Grinstead

KENT
Bewl Water Walks and Rides, Nr. Lamberhurst
Cobtree Manor Park Nature Trail
The Ecological Park, Elms Vale
Hastings Country Park, Hastings
Haysden Country Park Nature Trail
The Western Heights, Dover
White Cliffs Country Trail (various walks), around Kent

OXFORDSHIRE
Guided Walking Tours of Oxford
Oxford Ecology Trail

■ Historic Sites & Museuns

LONDON
Bntish Museum Great Russell Street, WC1
Guinness World of Records, The Trocadero Centre
The London Dungeon, 28 -34 Tooley Street, SE1
Mall Galleries The Mall, SWl
National Portrait Gallery, St. Martin's Place, WC2
Natural History Museurn, Cromwell Road, SW7
The Oueen's Gallery, Buckingham Palace, SWl
Royal Mews Buckingham Palace Road, SWI
Science Museums, Exhibihon Road, SW7
The Tate Gallery, Millbank, SWl
Tower Bridge SEl
Victoria & Albert Museum, Cromwell Road, SW7

BEDFORDSHIRE
Bunyan Museum, Bedford
Elstow Moot Hall, Church End
Stockwood Craft Museum & Gardens
Shuttleworth Collection, Biggleswade

BERKSHIRE
Blake's Lock Museum, Reading
Foxhill Collection of Historic Carriages, Nr. Reading
Newbury Museum
Reading Abbey
St. George's Chapel, Windsor Castle
Windsor Castle

BUCKINGHAMSHIRE
Buckinghamshire County Museum, Aylesbury
Chiltern Brewery, Terrick, Aylesbury

HAMPSHIRE
D Day Museum, Portsmouth
Hurst Castle, Keyhaven
New Forest Museum & Visitor Centre, Ashurst,
Portchester Castle
The Sammy Miller Museum, New Milton

HERTFORDSHIRE
Berkhamstead Castle
Hertford Castle
Roman Baths, Welwyn Garden City
Roman Theatre St. Albans
Verulamium Museum, St. Albans

EAST SUSSEX
Anne of Cleves House Museum, Lewes
Bodiam Castle, Bodiam
Brighton Museum & Art Gallery
Filching Manor Motor Museum, Polegate
Hastings Castle and 1066 Story, West Hill, Hastings
Hove Museum & Art Gallery
Quarry Farm Rural Experience, Robertsbridge

WEST SUSSEX
Arundel Castle, Arundel

KENT
Canterbury Cathedral
The Canterbury Tales, Canterbury
The Dickens Centre, Rochester
Dover Castle & Hellfire Comer
Eurotunnel Exhibihon Centre, Folkestone
Guildhall Museum, Rochester
Leeds Castle, Nr. Maidstone

Lympne Castle, Nr. Hythe
Rochester Castle

OXFORDSHIRE
Banbury Museum & Art Gallery
Broughton Castle, Banbury
Cogges Manor Farm Museum, Witney
Didcot Railway Museum
The Oxford Story, Oxford

SURREY
Brooklands Museum, Weybndge

■ Entertaimnent Venues

LONDON
Madame Tussaud's & The London Planetarium, NWl
London Zoo, Regent's Park, NWl

BEDFORDSHIRE
Stagsden Bird Gardens
Whipsnade Wild Anmmal Park, Dunstable
Woburn Safari Park, Woburn

BERKSHIRE
Bucklebury Farm Park Nr. Reading
Crown Jewels of the World Exhibition, Windsor
Holme Grange Craft Centre/Art Gallery, Wokingham
Trilakes Country Park & Fishery, Sandhurst
Wyld Court Rainforest, Nr. Newbury

BUCKINGHAMSHIRE
Flamingo Gardens & Zoological Park, Olney
Glass Craft, Holtspur, Nr. Beaconsfield
West Wycombe Caves

HAMPSHIRE
Lepe Country Park, Exbury
Marwell Zoological Park, Winchester
New Forest Butterfly Farm, Ashurst
Paultons Park, Nr. Lyndhurst
Portsmouth Sea Life Centre

HERTFORDSHIRE
Maltings Centre, St. Albans
Paradise Wildlife Park, Broxboume
Water Hall Farm & Craft Centre, Nr. Hitchin

EAST SUSSEX
The Bluebell Railway - Living Museum, Shenfield Park
Hastings Sea Life Centre

WEST SUSSEX
Butlins Southcoast World, Bognor Regis
Coombes Farm Tours, Lancing
Pulborough Brooks RSPB Nature Reserve

KENT
The Buttefly Centre, Swingfield Dover
Kent & East Sussex Steam Railway, Tenterden
Port Lympne Wild Anmmal Park, Mansion & Gardens
Toy & Model Museum, Lamberhurst

OXFORDSHIRE
Cotswold WildDife Park, Burford
CuriOXiTy (Science Gallery) Oxford
The Oxford Story, Oxford
Waterfowl Sanctuary, Nr. Hook Norton

SURREY
Birdworld, Nr. Farnham
Gatwick Zoo, Charlwood
Thorpe Park, Chertsey

January 5-14	42nd LONDON INTERNATIONAL BOAT SHOW Earls Court, London SW5.
February 11	HORSE RACING, TOTE GOLD TROPHY Newbury Racecourse, Berkshire.
February 27- March 3	FINE ART AND ANTIQUES FAIR Olympia, London W14
March 14-23	CHELSEA ANTIQUES FAIR Chelsea Old Town Hall, London SW3
March 14 to April 6	IDEAL HOME EXHIBITION Earls Court, London SW5.
April 1	OXFORD v. CAMBRIDGE BOAT RACE Putney to Mortlake, River Thames, London.
April 21	FLORA LONDON MARATHON Blackheath/Greenwich to the Mall.
April 27	RUGBY LEAGUE CHALLENGE CUP FINAL Wembley Stadium, Wembley, London
April 29	HORSE RACING, THE WHITBREAD GOLD CUP Sandown Park Racecourse, Esher, Surrey.
May 3-26	BRIGHTON INTERNATIONAL FESTIVAL Various venues, Brighton, East Sussex
May 3-6	EASTBOURNE INTERNATIONAL FOLK FESTIVAL Various venues, Eastbourne, East Sussex.
May 6	RUGBY: PILKINGTON CUP FINAL Twickenham, Middlesex
May 8-12	ROYAL WINDSOR HORSE SHOW Home Park, Windsor, Berkshire.
May 11	FA CHALLENGE CUP FINAL Wembley Stadium, Wembley, London.
May 19 to June 2	RAMSGATE SPRING FESTIVAL Various venues, Ramsgate, Kent.
May 21-24	CHELSEA FLOWER SHOW Royal Hospital, London SW3.
May 25-27	PORTSMOUTH NAVY DAYS '96 HM Naval Base, Portsmouth
May 27	SURREY COUNTY SHOW Stoke Park, Guildford, Surrey.
May 30-June 2	DICKENS FESTIVAL Various Venues, Rochester, Kent
June 7-9	DERBY DAY, CORONATION CUP & OAKS DAY Epsom Racecourse, Surrey.
June 5-6	BEATING THE RETREAT - MASSED BANDS OF THE HOUSE- HOLD DIVISION, Horse Guards Parade, London SW1.
June 6-8	SOUTH OF ENGLAND AGRICULTURAL SHOW Showground, Ardingly, West Sussex.
June 9-August 18*	ROYAL ACADEMY SUMMER EXHIBITION Royal Academy of Arts, Piccadilly, London W1
June 13-22	GROSVENOR HOUSE ANTIQUES FAIR Grosvenor House Hotel, London W1
June 15	TROOPING THE COLOUR Horse Guards Parade, London SW1.
June 10-16	STELLA ARTOIS TENNIS CHAMPIONSHIPS Queen's Club, London W14.
June 15-22	BROADSTAIRS DICKENS FESTIVAL Various venues, Broadstairs, Kent.
June 15-22	EASTBOURNE INTERNATIONAL LADIES TENNIS CHAMPIONSHIP Int'l Lawn Tennis Centre, Eastbourne, East Sussex.

June 18-21	HORSE RACING, ROYAL WEEK
	Royal Ascot Racecourse, Berkshire.
June 28-30	OPEN AIR CONCERTS IN PETWORTH PARK
	Petworth, West Sussex.
June 29-30	MIDDLESEX SHOW
	Uxbridge Showground, Middlesex
June 24 to	WIMBLEDON LAWN TENNIS CHAMPIONSHIPS
July 7	All England Lawn Tennis Club, London SW19.
July 3-7	HENLEY ROYAL REGATTA
	Henley-on-Thames, Oxfordshire.
July 11-13	KENT COUNTY SHOW
	Showground, Detling, Kent.
July 9-20	ROYAL TOURNAMENT
	Earls Court, London SW5.
July 19 to	BBC HENRY WOOD PROMENADE CONCERTS
September 14	Royal Albert Hall, London SW7.
July 30-Aug 1	NEW FOREST & HAMPSHIRE COUNTY SHOW '96
	New Park Farm, Brockenhurst, Hampshire.
July 30-Aug 3	HORSE RACING, GLORIOUS GOODWOOD
	Goodwood Racecourse, Goodwood, West Sussex.
August 3-10	SKANDIALIFE COWES WEEK 96
	High Seas, Cowes, Isle of Wight
August 9-15	BROADSTAIRS FOLK WEEK
	Various venues, Broadstairs, Kent.
August 23 to	ARUNDEL FESTIVAL
September 1	Various venues, Arundel, West Sussex.
September 2-8	FARNBOROUGH INT'L AIR SHOW
	Farnborough Airfield, Hants
September 2-3	ENGLISH WINE FESTIVAL & REGIONAL FOOD FAIR
	English Wine Centre, Alfriston, East Sussex.
September 14-22	SOUTHAMPTON INT'L BOAT SHOW 96
	Western Esplanade, Southampton, Hants
October 2-6	HORSE OF THE YEAR SHOW
	Wembley Arena, Wembley, London.
October 19-29	LONDON MOTOR SHOW
	Earls Court, London SW5.
November 3	LONDON TO BRIGHTON RAC VETERAN CAR RUN
November 10	LORD MAYOR'S SHOW, CITY OF LONDON
November 12	REMEMBRANCE SUNDAY CEREMONY
	Cenotaph, London SW1.
November 25	HORSE RACING, HENNESSY GOLD CUP
	Newbury Racecourse, Berkshire.
December 26	HORSE RACING, KING GEORGE VI CHASE
	Kempton Racecourse, Sunbury-on-Thames, Middlesex.

*Denotes provisional date   *For further details contact:*

The Southern Tourist Board
40 Chamberlayne Road
Eastleigh
Hampshire S05 5JH.
Tel: 01703 620006

The South East England Tourist Board
The Old Brew House
Warwick Park, Tunbridge Wells
Kent TN2 5TU.
Tel: 01892 540766

London Tourist Board & Convention Bureau
26, Grosvenor Gardens Victoria
London SW1W ODU.
Tel: 0171 730 3450

THE ABBEY COURT
20 Pembridge Gardens, London W2 4DU
Telephone 0171 221 7518   Fax 0171 792 0858

This handsome five-storey Victorian building is the epitome of a traditional town house hotel. You enter into a welcoming reception area with deep sofas and armchairs, which is one of the two public rooms - the other being the very pleasant conservatory downstairs where breakfast is served and there is also a well-stocked honesty bar. The bedrooms are the most superb feature. Each of them has been individually designed and decorated incorporating carefully chosen antiques, desks and tables and smart button-back chairs. There is a variety of beds ranging from brass to four-posters whilst the Italian marble bathrooms are equipped with whirlpool baths and offer the additional luxuries of toiletries and bathrobes. The personal touch to make you feel at home is a supply of books and magazines and even a tin of home made shortbread. The Abbey Court is situated in peaceful Pembridge Gardens in the "village of Kensington" with its shops, quality restaurants and antique markets all nearby and the West End just ten minutes away by public transport. It is something of a work of art to be able to create a place of such flair whilst retaining the restful ambience of a hospitable home. The Abbey Court is a special place of the highest quality and whether you are there on business or pleasure you could not ask for better all round value. Single room with breakfast from £80.00. Double room including breakfast from £120.00.

22 en suite bedrooms with radio, colour TV, direct-dial telephone; hairdryer, trouser press, laundry service; 24 hour room service; whirlpool bath in rooms; honesty bar, safety deposit box. Open all year. Main credit cards accepted.

THE BEAUFORT

33 Beaufort Gardens, Knightsbridge, London SW3 1PP

Telephone 0171 584 5252   Fax 0171 589 2834

The Beaufort deserves to retain its award as one of the best hotels in the world, for the owner's philosophy of putting the guest first is apparent in every facet of the hotel. The Beaufort is situated in a quiet tree-lined square only 150 yards from Harrods, and you are made to feel at home immediately on your arrival when you are given the front door key to your "house" and shown to your room. Later you will linger awhile with a drink chosen from an array of bottles, in the airy drawing room with its floral curtains, deep squashy chairs and books and magazines. The bedrooms are beautifully decorated in warm pastel colours with every personal luxury for guests - even umbrellas are provided- and flowers are everywhere: on which subject the hotel displays on its walls one of the largest collections of original English floral water colours. Our day at the Beaufort starts with a wonderful breakfast in your room where everything is fresh or home made from the croissants to the delicious jams, whilst local knowledge of the restaurants guarantees you will not go hungry for the remainder of the day. Unashamed pampering of guests by each and every member of the friendly staff in the superbly comfortable surroundings is the speciality of this special hotel, and it makes a great experience for all who stay there. Single room excluding breakfast from £110.00. Double room excl. breakfast from £150.00.

28 en suite bedroom with airconditioning; radio, satellite TV; direct-dial telephone, hairdryer, laundry service; non-smoker bedrooms; tea/coffee making facilities; safety deposit box. 18 hour room service. Light snacks available. Riding, squash, tennis 1-2 miles. Free membership of leisure club. Full business services and meeting room for 6-12 guests. AV equipment available. Airport pick-up. Car rental. Open all year. All credit cards accepted.

THE CRANLEY HOTEL
10-12 Bina Gardens, South Kensington, London SW5 OLA

Telephone 0171 373 0123   *Fax 0171 373 9497*

Recapturing the age of grandeur, The Cranley is set in the heart of the Royal Borough of Kensington and Chelsea, one of London's smartest residential districts. The antiques, stylish décor and delicate period details of The Cranley will captivate the most discerning guest. It's exclusive. Loving restoration has been carried out to provide 36 rooms, including executive-type suites and one-bedroom apartments, giving the impression of a private residence rather than a hotel. Antique furnishings and exquisite decoration make each room individual yet luxurious. A fully equipped and concealed kitchenette offers all the comforts of home and each room is fully equipped with every conceivable modern comfort and luxury. Whether relaxing in the deep tub bath or freshening up under a powerful shower, it is the extra touches such as the soft white towels and bathrobes that go to make a stay at The Cranley an experience of luxury. The Cranley is ideally situated for direct links to Gatwick and Heathrow Airports and London's underground rail system. The famous museums and shopping areas of Knightsbridge and the King's Road are within easy walking distance, as are the exhibition areas of Earls Court and Olympia. Single room incl. VAT from £120.00. Double room incl. VAT from £140.00. Continental breakfast £8.50. English breakfast £12.00.

38 en suite rooms with satellite TV, radio, direct-dial telephone; hairdryer, trouser press, laundry service, tea/coffee making facilities. Room service from 0700 hrs. Open all year. Credit cards accepted.

THE EXECUTIVE HOTEL
57, Pont Street, Knightsbridge, London SW1X 0BD

Telephone 0171 581 2424   Fax 0171 589 9456

The blue plaque tells you that this distinguished and listed Victorian town house was once the private address of actor/manager Sir George Alexander. Nowadays you enter through its imposing arch flanked by brass plates announcing The Executive Hotel. The hallway is theatrical for, although it is simply furnished incorporating a lounge area, the remainder is dominated by a magnificent curved staircase leading to the bedrooms, and the walls are decorated with brass lamps and oval friezes in unusual style like Wedgwood China. The twenty-nine bedrooms come in all shapes and sizes - there is one where a large four-poster takes up most of the space and another which is eccentrically located at the corner of the building. They are all extremely comfortable and provide the full range of luxuries for guests. I enjoyed visiting the breakfast room via a panelled foyer in the basement. It is light and airy with colourful striped wall paper, chintz curtains and pink chairs. It seemed a very good way to start the day. The Executive is set in London's exclusive residential district and claims Harrods as its "corner shop". It is a fine bed and breakfast hotel, offering comfort with character at exceptionally good rates. Single room rate including breakfast from £75.00. Double room rate with breakfast from £90.00.

27 en suite bedrooms with colour TV, direct-dial telephone; hairdryer, trouser press, laundry serv-ice, tea/coffee making facilities; safety deposit box. Golf by arrangement seven miles. Riding in Hyde Park. Open all year. Major credit cards accepted.

HARRINGTON HALL HOTEL
5-25 Harrington Gardens, London SW7 4JW
Telephone 0171 396 9696   Fax 0171 396 9090

Harrington Hall, a hotel of elegance located in the heart of London is one of the few remaining privately owned hotels. This luxury 200 bedroom, fully air conditioned property is situated in the exclusive Royal Borough of Kensington and Chelsea, within easy reach of Knightsbridge. Behind the splendour of the original period facade, Harrington Hall is a new hotel providing every modern convenience in a beautifully designed, classical setting. In the open plan lounge, which combines warmth and elegance with comfortable traditional furnishings and a beautiful marble fireplace, snacks and refreshments are offered. Wetherby's, the spacious and refreshingly airy restaurant, has a tempting selection of dishes available from the choice of buffet or à la carte menu. Harrington Hall's bedrooms are large and all contain an extensive array of facilities which include satellite TV, mini-bar, a state of the art message system and of course air conditioning. A number of rooms have been allocated for non-smoking guests. Harrington Hall's 10 conference and banqueting suites provide a sophisticated venue for conferences, or corporate hospitality and are ideal for luncheons, or receptions. Harrington Hall also has a Business Centre for the exclusive use of guests, which provides a range of secretarial services including word processing and facsimile. Guests can tone up in the private Fitness Centre which boasts a multi-gym as well as saunas and showers. Room rates from £120.00 incl. VAT and service. Continental breakfast £7.50 and English breakfast £11.00. *Full licence. 200 en suite air conditioned bedrooms with radio, satellite TV, direct dial telephone; hairdryer, trouser press, laundry service; tea/coffee making facilities, mini-bar, safety deposit box; 24-hour room service; non-smoker bedrooms. Last orders for dinner 22.30 hrs. Special diets available. Fitness centre/gym, sauna. Full business services; ten meeting rooms with a maximum capacity for 250 guests for lunch/dinner. Car parking off site. Car rental. Open all year. Credit cards accepted.*

HOLLAND PARK HOTEL
6, Ladbroke Terrace, Holland Park, London W11 3PG

Telephone 0171 792 0216   *Fax 0171 727 8166*

It is very difficult to find good bed and breakfast places in London and I was pleasantly surprised to be introduced to this modest town house hotel, which provides accommodation to suit all needs at reasonable prices. The Holland Park is a classic example of a place which is unpretentious in terms of style but full of character, and it lives well up to its reputation of a small friendly hotel that feels like home. The Victorian house is situated in a quiet tree-lined avenue near to the shops and restaurants of Kensington and close to transport services offering easy access to the West End. There is a welcoming atmosphere from the moment you enter the reception area which gives on to the warm and elegant sitting room with its period furniture, interesting pictures and deep sofas. You can relax in this room and look out over the spacious garden which is available for guests and visitors. There are twenty three individually decorated bedrooms, ranging from a cosy single to a spacious family room. They are all a fair size, very comfortable and some are idiosyncratic with nooks and crannies and ceiling beams; with an on-going programme of refurbishment most of them have full en suite facilities. The Holland Park has its own special charm and only one cause for modesty which is in the tariff. Anyone looking for a home from home which offers value for money should stay here again and again. Single room including breakfast from £49.00. Double room with breakfast from £66.00.

23 bedrooms; 17 en suite with Colour TV; direct-dial telephone, tea/coffee making facilities; fax transmission service. Closed for Christmas holiday. Main credit cards accepted.

THE HOWARD HOTEL
Temple Place, Strand, London WC2R 2PR

Telephone: 0171 836 3555   *Fax: 0171 379 4547*

Ideally located for business or leisure, this unique, luxury hotel is imposingly situated on the Thames where the City meets the West End. Many of the elegantly designed bedrooms which feature French marquetry furniture and tasteful marble bathrooms, enjoy the stunning panoramic view of the river as it winds between St . Paul' s and Westminster. All rooms are fully air conditioned and have every possible modern convenience, including 24 hour room service. The Surrey and Westminster suites cater for small parties, while larger meetings, to a maximum of 200, may be held in the Arundel and Fitzalan suites. One can relax over an aperitif in the Temple Bar overlooking an attractively landscaped terrace, planted with flowers and shrubs. I enjoyed an excellent luncheon, beautifully presented and served, in the justifiably famous Quai d'Or Restaurant, where the Renaissance décor, domed ceiling and thoughtfully chosen paintings, complemented the French haute cuisine and wines. Attentive staff anticipate your every need, some having been at the hotel for many years. This rather special hotel is under the direction of Mr. Michael P. Day, Resident Director and Mr. Nicolino Martini, General Manager. Single £210.00, twin/double £236.00 and suites from £255.00. Rates inclusive of $17^1/_2\%$ VAT.

Heathrow 16, Gatwick 28, London City Airport 6

F licence; 135 en suite bedrooms, all with direct dial telephones, TV; 24 hour room service; 3 lifts; last orders 10.30 p.m.; special diets; children welcome; conferences 200 max; major credit cards accepted.

LANGORF HOTEL
20 Frognal, Hampstead, London NW3 6AG

Telephone 0171 794 4483   Fax 0171 435 9055

This delightful Edwardian residence is so discreetly located in a quiet residential street that you almost pass it without realising it is an elegant town house hotel. The picturesque black and white tiled path leads into the public areas remarkable for their freshness in an ambience of rich comfort. The bright lounge is a happy blend of floral curtains and dark blue Chesterfield furniture; it gives onto an airy breakfast room and bar and you can have light snacks here as well, overlooking the peaceful garden area. The bedrooms are gracious and uniform in soft colours, décor and furnishings, although they vary in other ways for many are suitable for families and there are some serviced apartments as well which are ideal for businessmen or longer staying guests. The bathrooms throughout are sparkling and well appointed with one unique element being the most impressive high pressure showers. It is unique in another way, namely its location for there are no other places of this genre that enjoy such proximity to fashionable Hampstead with its exquisite shops and fine restaurants as well as the Heath and Kenwood House of fine art and open-air concerts fame. Nor is it far from central London by the nearby tube or bus routes. My lasting impression of this intimate little hotel is of the attentive and friendly staff who treat guests as members of a family and for whom nothing is too much trouble. Single room with continental breakfast from £55.00. Double room including continental breakfast from £80.00.
Leisure Breaks: On application according to season.
F licence. 31 en suite bedrooms with satellite TV, radio, direct-dial telephone, hairdryer, laundry service, tea/coffee making facilities. 24 hour service of bar and light snacks. Safety deposit box. Local leisure centre is 15 mins. walk. Horse riding in Regents Park. Open all year. All major credit cards accepted.

NUMBER 11 CADOGAN GARDENS
11 Cadogan Gardens, London SW3 2RJ

Telephone 0171 730 3426   Fax 0171 730 5217

Eleven Cadogan Gardens occupies a block of stately red Victorian houses not far from Knightsbridge in a quiet tree-lined square between Sloane Street and the Kings Road. It has no name, just the number outside, no reception, no restaurant nor bar. The atmosphere is that of a home and guests who never tire of the number 11 experience return again and again as friends. It is easy to see why, because this exclusive place was the first of the town house genre in London and remains very much in the top league. With the best traditions of antique furniture, fine oil paintings, the book-lined lounge and a grand winding staircase, Number Eleven is still wholly modern in the provision of services for today's guests. There is a lift and 24-hour room service and a chauffeur-driven Rolls Royce available. There is a private room for business meetings as well and the most recent innovation has been the introduction of a fully equipped gymnasium in the basement. The bedrooms are quite lovely, thoughtfully furnished with antiques and pictures and decorated in understated fashion with touches of luxury. Each of them is different in content and character, but have beautifully fitted marbled bathrooms in common. For a total indulgence you can book the self-contained two-bedroom Garden Suite with its own 26 foot drawing-room overlooking the rear garden. Number Eleven is supreme, and its combination of elegance with high standards of hospitality has few equals in London. Single room from £108.00. Double room from £158.00.
F licence. 6 suites and 55 en suite bedrooms with airconditioning (some); radio, satellite TV; direct-dial telephone; hairdryer, laundry and valet service, tea/coffee making facilities; safety deposit box. 24-hour room/meal service. Last order for dinner 23.00 hrs. Special diets available. Fitness centre, jogging track, tennis, riding, squash nearby. Full business services, including meeting room for 14. AV equipment available. Beauty salon. Airport pickup. Car rental. Open all year. Credit cards accepted.

PARKES HOTEL
41 Beaufort Gardens, Knightsbridge, London SW3 1PW

Telephone 0171 581 9944   *Fax 0171 581 1999*

Stepping from a quiet tree-lined square in Knightsbridge into this elegant Victorian hotel you are welcomed by the pleasant foyer whose warm colours, fresh flowers and prints sets the tone for the rest of the place. The ambience is one of intimacy and restfulness; one is apparent in the quiet sitting room with its white marble fireplace where you can relax with a cup of coffee and read the daily newspapers. The breakfast room in the basement where a full buffet is available is also cosy and brightly decorated. Although there are six double rooms, Parkes' accommodation consists mainly of suites and these provide the tranquil element, being individually decorated in restful colours, they are also large with a fully equipped kitchenette, minibar and bedroom, in some cases split level. The suites are supremely comfortable and they can be put to work during the day, being ideal for business meetings and social gatherings. Parkes does not provide a meal service, but it encourages guests to make themselves at home with their kitchenette - Harrod's food hall is close - and also supplies a list of restaurants, which includes those in nearby Beauchamp Place to satisfy any appetite. Parkes' spacious accommodation combined with the discreet and friendly character of the hotel makes it an ideal place for long or short term guests seeking to enjoy peace and privacy. Suites including breakfast from £170.00. Double room with breakfast from £115.00.

6 double rooms. 27 suites all en suite with radio, satellite TV, direct-dial telephone, hairdryer, trouser press, laundry service, tea/coffee making facilities. Safety deposit box. Business services including availability of AV equipment. Airport pick-up. Open all year. All major credit cards accepted.

THE RITZ
Piccadilly, London SW1V 9DG

Telephone 0171 493 8181   Fax 0171 493 2687

The Ritz is not only a famous London landmark but, since it was opened by César Ritz in 1906, it has remained consistently in the top league for hospitality. The standards of comfort are outstandingly high and a reflection of the stylish elegance of a bygone age. The pink and gold beauty of the ground floor remains faithful to the original splendour and the spacious bedrooms with their marble bathrooms have been lovingly restored, many with original fireplaces and gold leaf decoration in the style of Louis XVI. The terrace and gardens have been opened for dining al fresco and the elegant restaurant overlooking Green Park is one of the most beautiful dining-rooms in Europe, where the menu is complemented by an extensive selection of wines including the Ritz's own family of Champagnes. Afternoon tea at the Ritz is a part of London folklore and the Palm Court is a supremely gracious place to partake of the finely presented scene and cucumber sandwiches. Amidst such grandeur it is always gratifying to find friendly staff providing a personal and caring service in the best traditions of one of the finest hotels in the country. Tariff on application.

Full licence; 130 en suite bedrooms, all with telephone, TV, satellite TV and personal bar; two lifts; 24-hour room service; valet service; last orders for dinner Louis XVI restaurant 11.30 p.m. (Sundays 10.30 pm); special diets; children welcome; baby listening; no dogs; conferences, dinner dances Fri./Sat. in restaurant; all major credit cards accepted.

THE GREAT HOUSE AT SONNING
Thames Street, Sonning-on-Thames, Nr. Reading RG4 6UT

Telephone: 01734 692277   *Fax: 01734 441296*

The Great House Estate is situated in an English village with a Thameside setting, four acres of grounds and beautiful gardens, and the hotel must be one of the few with private river mooring for guests. The original 16th Century White Hart, renamed the Great House, is the centrepiece of this spacious paradise. The Bedrooms are here, in the 16th Century Palace Yard Buildings, the 17th Century Coach House and a 19th Century House. Many have four-poster beds, two are suites and all rooms are stylishly decorated, providing the highest standards of comfort for guests. The Moorings Restaurant is a perfect compliment to the ambience. Overlooking terrace and lawns to the water it is a romance in itself. There is a choice of table d'hôte or à la carte accompanied by an excellent selection of wines. There is a choice of restaurants too where more informal needs are catered for in the Ferryman's Bar and the Hideaway Restaurant. The Great House at Sonning has character, atmosphere and a sense of history. It is quite lovely and the stay there was a memorable experience. Single room exc. breakfast from £69.50. Double room excluding breakfast from £89.50. **Bargain breaks**: weekends - Friday, Saturday, Sunday evenings b & b from £39.50 one-night stay to d, b & b from £129.00 three-night stay.(Excludes Royal Ascot week, Henley, Christmas/ New Year and Sonning's Mill theatre weekend at £20 supplement.)

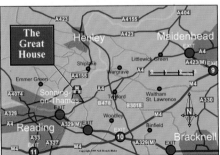

Reading 4, Henley 8 , Windsor 17 , Heathrow Airport 14 , London 48

Full licence, 36 en suite bedrooms with TV and radio; direct dial telephone, coffee/tea making facilities; laundry service; 24-hour room service; hairdryer, trouser press. Last orders for dinner 22.30. Golf - three miles; fishing, tennis; 9 meeting rooms providing for between 5 to 90 guests. AV equipment, typing, photocopying available. Parking 100 cars. Open all year. All major credit cards accepted.

THE SWAN DIPLOMAT
Streatley-on-Thames, Berkshire RG8 9HR
Telephone: 01491873737   Telex: 848259   Fax: 01491872554

Set on the banks of the River Thames in 23 acres of grounds, this well established hotel offers a welcoming and caring service to its guests. The spacious bedrooms, some with balconies, are individually designed and furnished and many look on to the river or have views to the Streatley hills. The comfortable lounge overlooks the river and the hotel's own island. The Riverside Restaurant enjoys an enviable reputation for its classical French cuisine, wine list and high standard of service. In addition, the hotel operates the Duck Room Brasserie, in which guests may enjoy a variety of light, seasonal dishes. Other facilities include the Reflexions Leisure Club (free membership for hotel guests during stay) and the rebuilt 19th-century Magdalen College barge - a wonderful venue for meetings or cocktail parties. There are many short walks around the hotel, a number of National Trust properties and stately homes within easy reach and arrangements can be made for golf at local courses or the hire of a river cruiser. To sum up, this is a luxurious hotel in a marvellous setting which offers plenty to do and see - or you can even just relax by the river! Bed and full English breakfast Monday to Thursday from £96.00; Friday-Sunday from £59. Service charge at guests' discretion. Open all year. **Breaks:** Please apply for your copy of CYGNET for information on a variety of breaks and activities. 1st October 1995-30th September 1996 weekend breaks from £69.50 pppn. **London 50, Reading 9, Oxford 20, Newbury 13, Windsor 30, Henley 20**

F licence; 46 en suite bedrooms, all with telephone, colour TV + satellite channels, minibar, hairdryer; 24 hour room service; last orders 9.30p.m; light lunches; diets; children welcome, baby listening; dogs by arrangement; conferences up to 90; indoor, heated fit-pool; spa bath; multi-gym; sauna; solarium, row boat and bicycle hire, beauty treatments; golf, tennis and fishing ¹/₂ mile; shooting and riding five miles; Amex, Diners, Barclaycard and Mastercard accepted.

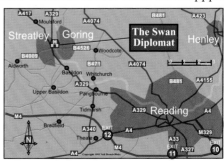

SIR CHRISTOPHER WREN'S HOUSE
Thames Street, Windsor, Berks SL4 1PX
Telephone: 01753 861354   Fax: 01753 860172

Set on the riverside, adjacent to Eton Bridge and beneath the ramparts of the castle, nestles Sir Christopher Wren's house as he designed it in 1676. Furthermore the interior of this town house style hotel has all the attributes of the architect's home with some tasteful additions through the years. It is furnished with fine antiques in keeping with the architecture; the public rooms and particularly the drawing room and entrance are supreme, helping to provide so friendly and peaceful an atmosphere that it is hard to imagine you are at the heart of busy Windsor. The bedrooms are all en suite, spacious and well-designed, and most provide lovely views of the river, terraced gardens or the castle. There are four poster beds too, but the unique feature is the Sir Christopher Wren's spectacular suite bedroom which is ideal for meetings but also attractive as family accommodation. The Orangerie Restaurant is pure elegance. It overlooks the Thames and Eton and, on the summer day when we visited, it had been extended outside on to the terrace gardens where guests were dining and absorbing the atmosphere of one very traditional corner of England. The cuisine is excellent as is the wine list with a fixed price menu and à la carte catering for all tastes and pockets. Perhaps "once a home, always a home" is a fair description for that's the way it felt. Single room exc. breakfast from £99.50. Double room excluding breakfast from £119.50. **Bargain week-end breaks:** Friday, Saturday, Sunday evenings b & b from £39.50 for one night stay to d, b & b from £129.00 for 3-night stay.

Visit to Theatre Royal Windsor is available for supplement of £10 per person. (Tariffs exclude Royal Ascot week, Henley, Xmas and New Year.)

Reading 19, Heathrow Airport 5, London 28
Full licence, 40 en suite bedrooms with TV and radio, direct dial telephone. Hairdryer, trouser press, laundry service. Tea/coffee-making facilities, 24 hr room service. Last orders dinner 22.30. Fishing, riding, squash and tennis facilities available nearby. 6 meeting rooms total capacity 100 guests. AV facilities, typing, photocopying, fax. Parking for 20 cars. Open all year. All major credit cards accepted.

DANESFIELD HOUSE
Marlow, Nr. Henley-on-Thames, Buckinghamshire SL7 2EY

Telephone 01628 891010   Fax 01628 890408

This majestic hotel could be classified as a monument for it is the third house since 1664 to occupy the site and its Victorian splendour pays tribute to the architecture of its predecessors. Every thing about Danesfield is grand: starting with the fine view from its stone terrace overlooking the Thames and Chilterns, then its 64 acres of formal and water gardens and parkland which contains the hotels extensive leisure facilities including swimming pool and walking trails. The public rooms are equal to the spectacular views particularly the Grand Hall with its beamed roof and gallery. You can relax here, in an atrium or in the sophisticated cocktail bar. The main restaurant is the fine panelled Oak Room where the international cuisine is superb. The de luxe quality of the Danesfield extends to its bedrooms which are spacious, beautifully furnished - some have four posters and all have two telephone lines. Within the ambience of chandeliers, mirrored doors, ornate fireplaces and rich floral displays the hotel has provided every possible top class facility - even running a chauffeur driven Rolls Royce. If you want the ultimate in style and service Danesfield is close to perfection. Single room with Breakfast from £125.00. Double room with breakfast from £145.00.

Leisure Breaks: "Weekend in England's Oldest Parish - Welcomed by Champagne and Flowers Weekend" includes 2 nights d,b&b from £185pp sharing.

Henley-on-Thames 5, High Wycombe 4¹/₂, Oxford 27, Reading 13, Windsor 15, London 31. *Full licence. 88 en suite bedrooms with radio; satellite TV, direct-dial telephone; hairdryer, trouser press, laundry service; mini bar; 24 hour room service; safety deposit box. Last orders for dinner 22.00 hrs. Special diets available. Billiards, snooker, croquet, outdoor swimming pool. Tennis, golf, riding, watersports within 4/5 miles. Full business services with 5 meeting rooms with capacity for 2-80 guests. Airport pick-up. Car rental. Car parking for 100 cars. Open all year. Major credit cards accepted.*

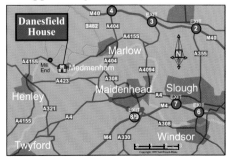

COCKLE WARREN COTTAGE HOTEL
36 Seafront, Hayling Island, Hampshire PO11 9HL

Telephone 01705 464961   *Fax 01705 464838*

As the inviting name suggests, the resident proprietors David and Diane Skelton have created a true gem on the seafront of Hayling Island. The highly acclaimed hotel is a genuine tile-hung cottage full of character. The large garden has white picket fencing to the front and a heated swimming pool and attractive patio area to the rear of the hotel. Each of the six ensuite bedrooms are quite lovely and much thought has gone into creating an individual style in each, with colour schemes that are crisp and bright with floral freshness and warm pine, creating an aura of comfort. The little extras such as magazines, chocolates, sophisticated toiletries and a decanter of Madeira emphasise the high standards to be found throughout Cockle Warren Cottage. The lounge with its antiques and memorabilia is welcoming for pre-dinner drinks and is especially cosy in the winter with a log fire burning and candles glowing to the sound of the Solent surf breaking outside. Café Le Jardin is an intimate conservatory restaurant offering award winning French and English country cooking. Fresh local produce from land and sea is used and a speciality is the mouth-watering home made bread. The historic and natural sights of Chichester, Portsmouth and the Isle of Wight are within easy reach, making Cockle Warren Cottage the ideal place to escape to and be wonderfully pampered at any time of year. A truly charming hotel. Single room with breakfast from £45.00. Double room including breakfast from £68.00.

Leisure Breaks: available except Bank Holidays; please enquire for further details.

Portsmouth 6, Chichester 10, Southampton 28, Brighton 45, London 74

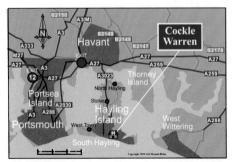

Full licence. 6 en suite bedrooms with radio and colour TV; direct-dial telephone; hairdryer, trouser press; laundry/valet service; non-smoker bedrooms; outdoor heated swimming pool. Fishing, golf, water-sports, riding, squash, tennis nearby; car rental. Car parking for 7. Open all year. Amex, Access & Visa accepted.

PASSFORD HOUSE HOTEL
Nr. Lymington, Hampshire SO41 8LS

Telephone: 01590 682398　　　*Fax: 01590 683494*

This lovely country house hotel is set in nine acres of grounds on the edge of the New Forest and was originally the home of Lord Arthur Cecil. It has been carefully adapted to an elegant hotel run under the personal supervision of the owners, Mr and Mrs Patrick Heritage. Passford House is ideally suited for the pursuit of many interests and forest walks and drives begin at the hotel entrance. In addition to the many outdoor activities which include a new hard tennis court swimming pool, croquet and putting green, a very comprehensive purpose-built leisure centre has been added, providing an indoor swimming pool, spa pool, sauna, solarium, multi-gym, including cycling, rowing and treadmill equipment, pool table and table tennis. In the hotel the spacious lounges are elegantly furnished and comfortable with wood fires in autumn and winter. The restaurant prides itself on its high standard of cuisine which is complemented by an extensive and varied wine list. 18 of the bedrooms have been recently redesigned (one with a four-poster) and all have bathrooms en suite with shower and are maintained to a very high standard. Room and breakfast from £81 single, £112 double. Open all year.

Special seasonal breaks available (min 2 nights)
London 93, Lymington 2, Brockenhurst 3¹/₂, Bournemouth 17

F licence; 55 bedrooms (13 ground floor), 2 suites, all with private baths, trouser press, hairdryer, telephone, radio, colour TV; children welcome; dogs by arrangement; diets on application; indoor leisure complex with swimming pool; tennis court; croquet lawn; putting green; outdoor swimming pool - heated in season; sea bathing, sailing, golf, riding all nearby; major credit cards accepted.

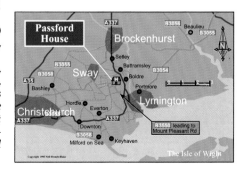

SOUTH LAWN HOTEL
Milford-on-Sea, Lymington, Hampshire SO41 0RF

Telephone: 01590 643911   Fax: 01590 644820

It was a letter of recommendation from a local resident that led me to South Lawn Hotel which is situated about a mile from the sea at Milford. Ernst Barten and his wife have owned the hotel since 1971 and are constantly effecting improvements. Mr. Barten can be justifiably proud of the standard of cuisine that is available. The quality is particularly emphasised and French, German and English dishes predominate. Mr. Barten supervises all the cooking himself and the kitchen is absolutely spotless. The spacious bedrooms are comfortably furnished and all have private bathrooms. Here, then, is a most attractive venue from which to explore the New Forest, or take advantage of the many sporting activities that are available in the vicinity. If you approach the hotel from the direction of Christchurch and Bournemouth, please note that you have to travel through the village of Milford-on-Sea, but then South Lawn is easily found on the left hand side of the road about half a mile beyond. The Bartens are always very helpful and courteous; they extend a warm welcome to every guest. Room and English breakfast from £47.50 single, £60.00 double, including VAT. Two day **Winter Breaks** (twin/double) Nov-Dec £97.50; Jan-May £99.00 except Easter and Bank Holidays. Closed Christmas & New Year.

London 96, Lymington 4, Brockenhurst 5, Barton-on-Sea 3

R and R licence; 22 bedrooms and 2 deluxe all with en suite bathrooms, ground floor bedrooms available, colour TV, radio, telephone, trouser press, hairdryers; £18 table d'hôte dinner til 2030; children over 7 years welcome, no dogs; diets; full central heating; sea bathing, sailing, boating, golf, tennis, squash, riding, shooting and fishing all nearby. Visa & Access accepted.

CHEWTON GLEN HOTEL
New Milton, Hampshire BH25 6QS

Telephone: 01425 275341   *Fax: 01425 272310*

Undoubtedly Chewton Glen is one of the finest hotels that Great Britain has to offer - the only privately owned, 5 Red Star hotel in the U.K. It is somewhat off the beaten track, but is within easy reach of such places as Salisbury and Winchester with their famous cathedrals, Wilton House, Broadlands, Stonehenge, Exbury Gardens, the Mary Rose and Kingston Lacy. The bedrooms are beautifully furnished and spacious, and the decor and fittings in the public rooms are of an exceptionally high standard. The guest will particularly appreciate the friendly and attentive service, which is not to be found everywhere nowadays. The luxury health club incorporates two indoor tennis courts, indoor heated swimming pool, six treatment rooms, gymnasium, saunas, steam room, spa and hairdressing salon. These are some of the finest facilities of their kind in the U.K. To locate this lovely old house, the traveller should find Chewton Farm Road in Walkford, off the Ringwood Road, which itself lies between the A35 and the A337. The hotel is at the end of a long drive, thus ensuring quiet and privacy. A member of The Leading Hotels of the World and Relais & Chateaux. Room and breakfast for two persons from £214, inclusive of VAT.

London 97, Bournemouth 10, Lymington 7, Lyndhurst 12

F licence; 53 bedrooms with private bath and colour TV; satellite television; meals until 9.30 p.m.; no children under seven; no dogs; croquet and putting on the lawn; chauffeur service; indoor and outdoor heated swimming pools; en-tout-cas tennis court + two indoor tennis courts; health club; 9-hole golf course in grounds; boating, fishing, shooting, riding, sea bathing nearby.

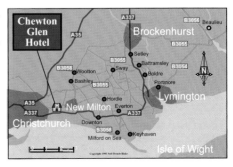

STOCKS HOTEL, GOLF & COUNTRY CLUB
Stocks Road, Aldbury, Nr. Tring, Hertfordshire HP723 5RX

Telephone: 01442 851341　　　　　*Fax: 01442 851253*

Stocks, an historically elegant country house hotel, dates back to 1176 and was the former home of entrepreneur Victor Lownes who turned the house into a training school for his "Bunny Girls". The house is situated in 182 acres of parkland surrounded by 10,000 acres of National Trust forests and land. This peaceful setting provides the perfect atmosphere for relaxing, unwinding and enjoying the delightful range of sporting and leisure facilities. The golf course has been designed and built to the highest specification and provides a challenging test of length and accuracy at over 7000 yards from the blue tees. There are extensive practice facilities and a team of teaching professionals, offering modern training services and a well stocked golf shop. One can take advantage of the riding stables which offer many beautiful and picturesque hacks in and around Ashridge Forest, including picnic riding and jumping is offered in the menage. The energetic can have a thorough work out in the gym, followed by relaxation in the sauna, steam room or jacuzzi (one of the country's largest). The Tapestry Restaurant features a daily table d'hôte menu, using fresh local produce with a varied wine list. The Orangery offers views of the golf course and serves light snacks in a less formal setting. A visit to Stocks is thoroughly recommended whether on business or pleasure. You will find the atmosphere relaxing and the service friendly and efficient. Room and breakfast from £75.

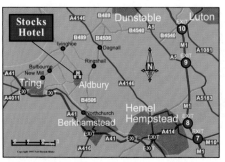

Weekend packages available from £110 inc. per person, dinner, bed & breakfast.
Heathrow 29, Luton Airport 19, Ml & M25 9, Tring station 2 (mainline Euston-London)
F licence; 18 bedrooms (15 en suite), all with telephone and TV; room service; night porter service; last orders for dinner 9.30 p.m.; bar meals; children welcome; conferences 65 max; 18 hole par72 championship standard golf course; putting green; PGA Game Improvement Centre; golf shop; snooker; outdoor heated swimming pool; sauna; solarium; jacuzzi; steam room; gymnasium; 4 tennis courts; croquet; riding & livery stables; menage; open all year; credit cards accepted.

REDCOATS FARMHOUSE HOTEL
Redcoats Green, Nr. Hitchin, Hertfordshire SG4 7JR

Telephone: 01438 729500   *Fax: 01438 723322*

Near Little Wymondley village, set amidst the rolling Hertfordshire countryside, yet only a few minutes away from the A1, lies the 15th century Redcoats Farmhouse. It has been in the Butterfield family for generations and in 1971 Peter and his sister Jackie Gainsford converted the building into an hotel. Today, the hotel still retains its relaxed and easy-going country atmosphere. The bedrooms, where pictures abound, are in the main house or in the adjacent converted stables, and some have exposed beams. One room is particularly suitable for a long stay as it opens onto the very pretty country garden where marquees can be erected for weddings. There are three intimate dining rooms serving outstanding cuisine, and the new conservatory which offers a less formal type of menu, is very successful. The menus, which are changed every two weeks, include a good choice of delicious dishes such as Danish herring with dill sauce and new potatoes, half a Gressingham Duckling with peach and ginger sauce or a Fillet Steak Carpetbagger. Redcoats is ideal for visiting Knebworth and Woburn Parks, Hatfield House or the Shuttleworth Aircraft Collection. To find the hotel from Junction 8 of the A1(M), take the road to Little Wymondley - not the A602 to Hitchin. Redcoats is closed from December 24th to January 5th except for Christmas lunch and New Year's Eve dinner. Room and breakfast from £60.00, other terms on application. **Bargain weekend breaks** from £95 per person for two nights. You could leave after Sunday lunch in the conservatory at £16 per head. **London 35, Cambridge 25, Hitchin 3, Hatfield 10, Woburn 15, A1(M) 1**

F licence, 12 en suite bedrooms, 2 with shared bathroom (9 ground floor), all with telephone, colour TV; last orders 9.30 p.m. for Club Suppers; children welcome; baby listening; conferences max. 20; garden suitable for marquees; tennis one mile; Mastercard, Amex, Visa and Switch credit cards accepted.

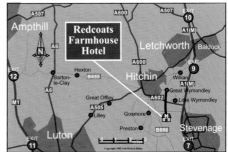

ST. MICHAEL'S MANOR
St. Albans,
Hertfordshire
AL3 4RY

Telephone: 01727 864444
Fax: 01727 848909

It was a delightful surprise to discover this manor house, which has celebrated over 400 years of history, in 5 acres of beautiful grounds at the heart of Roman Verulamium, offering guests complete tranquillity. The comforts, character and quality of the house combine the best of old and new in a way which has won praise from leading commentators on British Tourism, including an award from a 'Grounds for Delight' competition. They noted as we did, the influence of the Newling Ward family, who have owned the hotel for over 30 years. They are assisted by a very professional team, and all the staff are very proud of their hotel, and take great pains to ensure their guests have a happy stay. The restaurant, with its Victorian style conservatory, enjoys lovely views over the gardens. The Head Chef provides delicious menu . On Sunday evenings, there is also a very popular buffet supper. I noticed too, that everything was cooked traditionally, using fresh herbs from the garden. The bedrooms are interesting, as they are all so different, with picturesque views, and all have been recently refurbished . Single £76; executive single £86; double / twin £86; executive double £106. Special weekend rates available. Please ask for details.

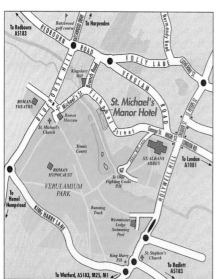

London 20, Luton 8, Heathrow 35, Gatwick 60.

F licence; 24 en suite rooms, all with telephone, radio, TV; night service; late meals to 9.00 p.m.; dogs by arrangement; conferences welcome; golf nearby; tennis one mile; Visa, Diners, Amex and Master Card accepted.

APPLES HOTEL
133 London Road, St. Albans, Hertfordshire AL1 1TA

ETB ⌢⌢⌢ Commended

Telephone: 01727 844111; Fax: 01727 861100

Apples offers luxury at sensible prices, is close to the city centre and railway station, minutes from local motorways yet standing in a beautiful half acre of garden with heated pool during summer.

One single, eight double bedrooms, all en suite. Bed and breakfast from £25.00 to £29.50. Lunch available from 12.30 pm to 14.30 from £12.50 per head. Dinner available from 1900-2115 from £14.50 per head. Colour TV, tea/coffee making facilities, direct dial telephone, ample parking, wheelchair access, swimming pool, licensed bar.

THE WATERMILL HOTEL
(formerly Hemel Hempstead Moat House)
London Road, Bourne End, Hemel Hempstead, Hertfordshire AL1 1TA

Telephone: 01442 349955; Fax: 01442 866130

High standard of service and décor with motel-style accommodation. A converted watermill, the river still runs under the lounge, giving superb views. Bargain weekend breaks available - £42 per person per night, dinner, bed and breakfast. Also Watercolour Weekends, - £95 per person including tuition, Backgammon Weekends and Writers Weekends - prices on application.

40 single, eight twin, 13 triple bedrooms, all en suite. Bed and breakfast from £48.25 (single) to £57.00 (double). Lunch available from 12.30 pm to 14.00 from £5.00 per head. Dinner available from 19.00-22.00 from £14.95 per head. Last orders 22.00. Colour TV + satellite, tea/coffee making facilities, direct dial telephone, hairdryer, trouser press, car parking for 100. 24-hour room service; non-smoker bedrooms available. Billiards/pool, fishing (200 yards away), golf 1¹/₂ miles, riding & squash one mile, tennis two miles. Visa, Diners, Access and Amex cards accepted.

COUNTRY GARDEN HOTEL
Church Hill, Totland Bay, Isle of Wight PO39 0ET

Telephone: 01983 754521   *Fax: 01983 754521*

This aptly named hotel is not far from the picturesque village of Totland and is indeed a true picture of a traditional English country garden. The landscaping, the quiet pools and the rich colour of the flowers are a joy. Bedrooms are en suite and are comfortably furnished with light colours. Some rooms have a view out towards Totland Bay, whilst others overlook peaceful countryside. The public rooms are welcoming too with the style and atmosphere of a friendly and relaxing country home nicely contrasting with the striking dark green and white decor of the elegant restaurant. The hotel has a reputation for fine food and I found the menus interesting with local seafood and shellfish an absolute must and flambé dishes being a speciality. The Country Garden Hotel is ideally located for walks in the beautiful Totland area and also as a base from which to explore this island which has so many attractions and a character of its own. A good hotel with excellent food, a friendly and informal atmosphere and attentive service. Well worth a stay. Single room including breakfast from £38.00. Double room with breakfast from £76.00.

Leisure Breaks: Up to June and from October: 2 nights or more at special rates. Gourmet dinners Saturday & Wednesday at no extra charge. £44.00 per day half board. Reduced rate ferries.

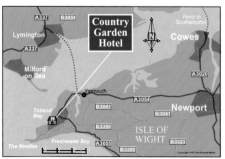

F Licence. 15 en suite bedrooms with satellite TV and direct-dial telephone. Hairdryer, laundry service, tea/coffee making facilities. Facilities for the disabled. Last order for dinner 21.30 hrs. Special diets available. Car rental. Car parking for 40 cars. Open February to December (incl.). Access/Visa accepted.

ROWHILL GRANGE COUNTRY HOUSE HOTEL
Hextable, Nr. Wilmington, Dartford, Kent DA2 7QH

Telephone 01322 615136   *Fax 01322 615137*

Anyone seeking relief from the M25 would do well to discover Kent's best kept secret. Completely renovated by its new proprietors, the Rowhill Grange is one of the most exquisite country house hotels I have visited. Nestling in nine acres of woodlands and mature gardens which descend to a picturesque lake, its seclusion and tranquillity are its greatest assets. You are welcomed as guests to a country house and shown to one of the eighteen lovely en suite bedrooms, each named after flowers in the Grange's gardens, and individually decorated to the highest standards. The garden restaurant is in character with the hotel and extends into a conservatory; you can dine on the terrace too, sharing a glorious view with the swans and peacocks. The cuisine is great - based on fresh produce and ranging from the traditional to the exotic. It is an attractive place for weddings and conferences and the Clockhouse Suite is an enchanting venue; formerly the stables, it has been restored to the same standard as the hotel and is a self-contained suite with its lounge, bar and dancing area. Rowhill Grange has found a magic formula combining the luxury of a hotel with the friendliness and informality of a country house atmosphere. It won't stay secret for long. Single room rate with breakfast from £75.00. Double room rate including breakfast from £95.00.

Leisure Breaks: Dinner, bed and breakfast from £65.00 pp in double room.
London 12 , Dartford 3 , Maidstone 21 , Dover 62, Canterbury 48 , M25 Junction 3 one mile.
Full licence. 18 en suite bedrooms with radio & colour TV. Direct-dial telephone. Hairdryer, laundry service. Non-smoker bedrooms. Last order for dinner 21.00 hrs. Special diets available. From April 1996 beauty parlour, jacuzzi, swimming pool, sauna, massage. Golf nearby. Full business services and three meeting rooms with capacity from 8 to 100 guests. Car parking for 100 cars. Open all year. Major credit cards accepted.

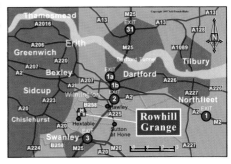

THANINGTON HOTEL
140 Wincheap, Canterbury, Kent CT1 3RY

Telephone: 01227 453227;
Fax: 01227 453225

Imposing Georgian bed and breakfast hotel with lounge, snooker
room, bar and courtyard parking.
Convenient access to Channel ter-
minals; ten minutes' walk from city centre and B.R. East station; 15 minutes' walk to the
cathedral. Attractive modern en suite accommodation with indoor swimming pool. Bargain breaks Jan-March two nights £116-120/April-Dec £120-124 for two persons sharing a
double or twin room, inc breakfast and VAT.

*Five single, five double, all en suite. Bed and breakfast from £42.00 (single) to £60.00 (double). No
restaurant. Colour TV, tea/coffee making facilities, direct dial telephone, hairdryer, trouser press,
car parking for 10; non-smoker bedrooms available; safety deposit box; billiards/snooker; indoor
swimming pool. Visa, Diners, Access, JCB and Amex cards accepted.*

THE OLD GATE INN
162 New Dover Road, Canterbury, Kent CT1 3EL

Telephone: 01227 452154
Fax: 01227 456561

ETB ━━━ Commended

Conveniently situated on its own 1 1/2 acre prime site, the Old Gate Inn and Restaurant is
one of the most accessible hotels in Canterbury, convenient for the city centre and for the
Channel terminals. A coaching inn dating from the early 1800s, it was built on the site of an
original toll gate on Watling Street. The Kentish Pub type bar offers snacks and the restaurant can accommodate up to 60 persons in light, airy comfort.

*11 single/double, all en suite. Bed and breakfast from £45 (single) to £55 (double) in Executive
Rooms. £10 less in Tourist rooms. Family rooms (four persons) £75. Lunch available from 12 noon
to 2 pm from £4 per head; dinner available from 7 to 10 pm from £12 per head. Colour TV, tea/coffee
making facilities, direct dial telephone, hairdryer, trouser press, ample car parking (60 cars); major
credit cards accepted.*

THE BAY TREE HOTEL
Sheep Street, Burford, Oxfordshire OX18 4LW
Telephone: 01993 822791   Fax 01993 823008

You enter a bygone age in this charming Cotswold hotel tucked away down a pretty side street. Built in 1584 the Bay Tree was the home of one Sir Lawrence Tanfield and the character of the house remains with original flagstones, oak beams, enormous fireplaces, a raftered hall and galleried staircase. The bedrooms, all named after indigenous trees, are particularly characterful and individually decorated, furnished with antiques and very spacious, as are the bathrooms which were formerly dressing-rooms and where the guests' luxuries leave nothing to chance. The Woolsack bar with its polished wood floor, vast log fireplace and beamed ceiling is the place for a delicious light lunch, whilst the flagstoned restaurant, which opens onto a terraced garden, is for savouring the Bay Tree's chef's concise menus of freshly prepared, seasonal local produce. The conservatory lounge overlooking the grounds offers relaxation after your meal. This historic hotel thrives on informality and a willing service to the guests' every need. There is a wealth of places to visit within 20 miles including Oxford, Blenheim Palace and Chedworth's Roman Villa, whilst Burford itself is one of the Cotswold's most attractive villages. Single room with breakfast from £60.00. Double room including breakfast from £110.00 **Leisure Breaks**: Sunday-Thursday double room at £135.00 min. stay 2 nights. Weekend Breaks: min. stay 2 nights Fri/Sat only double room at £145.00. Both rates are per room per day based on two people sharing and includes full English breakfast and dinner. **Oxford 15, Cheltenham 20, Stratford-upon-Avon 30, Banbury 25, Birmingham, London 76** *Full licence. 23 en suite bedrooms with colour TV. Direct-dial telephone, hairdryer, laundry service, tea/coffee making facilities. Last dinner orders 21.00. Croquet, golf, riding, shooting - five miles. Business services and AV equipment available. Car parking 25 cars. Open all year. All major credit cards accepted.*

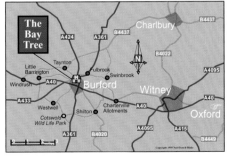

THE PLOUGH AT CLANFIELD
Clanfield, Oxon OX18 2RB

Telephone 01367 810222　　Fax 01367 810596

The Plough is no ordinary inn for this fine Cotswolds manor house in the Oxfordshire village of Clanfield was built in 1560 and has been painstakingly restored and attractively furnished to provide guests with every modern comfort in an Elizabethan setting. The combined lounge and bar area is invitingly cosy with its magnificent fireplace, oak beams and homely armchairs in which to relax. However, you will wish to sample the delights of the award-winning Tapestry Room Restaurant which is famous throughout the Cotswolds. Here in elegant surroundings you will enjoy excellent French and English cooking and a wide choice of wines from throughout the world. There is also the charming Portrait Room which provides for a more private occasion. All the bedrooms are traditionally furnished and stocked with complimentary toiletries, baskets of fruit, home-made biscuits and mineral water and, as if these luxuries were insufficient, there are rooms with jacuzzis and a mini-suite with a four-poster bed. Clanfield is not far from Burford sometimes called The Gateway to the Cotswolds. There are many historic houses and gardens in the area and Oxford is only a few miles down the road. Anyone seeking to be pampered in sleepy English village tranquillity needs look no further than the Plough. Single room inc. breakfast from £68. Double room with breakfast from £88.

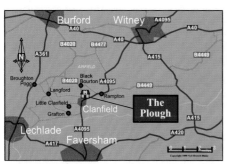

Leisure Breaks: Two night scenechanger break from £120 per couple per night, includes English breakfast, daily newspaper, residents' dinner.

Oxford 20 , Swindon 17, Lechlade 5 , London 76

Full licence. Six en suite bedrooms with radio,TV with video films, direct-dial telephone, hairdryer, trouser press, laundry service, tea/coffee making facilities. Last orders for dinner 21.30. Special diets available. Fishing, golf, watersports, riding, shooting, squash, tennis - all by arrangement in the area. Business services and conference room with capacity for 10; AV equipment on request. Car parking for 30 cars. Open all year. All major credit cards accepted.

STUDLEY PRIORY HOTEL
Horton-Cum-Studley, Oxford OX33 1AZ

Telephone 01865 351203   Fax 01865 351613

Set in 13 acres of garden and woodland Studley Priory formerly housed a Benedictine nunnery founded in the 12th Century, and the sense of history was preserved by the Parke family who converted it into a standard bearer among hotels hundreds of years later. Passing through the magnificent wood-panelled hall I was immediately aware of the enchantment of the place. It is beautifully furnished with antiques, whilst many 16th and 17th Century features also remain, blending perfectly with all the comforts of the 20th Century, and warmed by log fires in the public rooms. Then there is the excellent award winning restaurant which combines the best of modern French and British cooking at a fixed price or à la carte, complemented by a wide-ranging wine list. The bedrooms are lovely, whether in the main building or in the Jacobean wing reached through a maze of corridors, and the jewel in the crown is the Elizabethan Suite with its oak panelling and early 18th Century half-tester bed. Most rooms have views towards the Cotswolds, the Chilterns or the Vale of Aylesbury - and indeed this is an ideal base from which to explore the beautiful countryside and many historic sights around Oxford. The ambience of this lovely old country house hotel guarantees a most enjoyable stay. Single room including breakfast from £95. Double room with breakfast from £105.

Leisure Breaks: Two night scenechanger break from £145 per couple per night includes English breakfast, daily newspaper, residents' dinner. **Oxford 7, Aylesbury 23, London 57**
Full licence. 19 en suite bedrooms with radio, satellite TV, direct-dial telephone, hairdryer, trouser press, laundry service; non-smoker bedrooms, coffee/tea making facilities; 24 hour room service. Last orders for dinner 21.15 hrs. Special diets available. Croquet, tennis, golf, riding nearby; squash, watersports 7 miles. Business service available and four meeting rooms with capacity of 40 guests. AV on request. Car parking for 100 cars. Open all year. All major credit cards accepted.

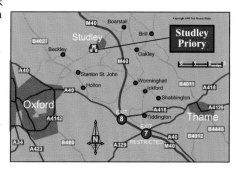

CHASE LODGE
10 Park Road, Hampton Wick, Kingston-upon-Thames, Surrey KT1 4AS

Telephone: 0181 943 1862   *Fax: 0181 943 9363*

Nigel and Denise Stafford Haworth own and personally run this extremely popular little gem of an hotel, situated just 20 minutes from the heart of London. Chase Lodge has been cleverly amalgamated from two old cottages dating back to 1870, and Nigel himself has done most of the work. Whether you are in the pretty lounge and bar area, or in one of the gorgeous bedrooms, Denise has designed the style and décor of all the rooms with such flair and charm that you will immediately feel relaxed and at ease. Nigel also runs the kitchen with equal aplomb. The menu is imaginative, and the food is cooked and presented to perfection. Avocado with crab, langoustine and pernod, followed by roast barbary duck with a kumquat or black cherry sauce are just an example of the delicious dishes available, which can be complemented by a bottle from the very fine wine list. Meals are served in the conservatory, which is surrounded by the prettiest little floodlit courtyard garden, and light bar snacks can also be enjoyed in the adjoining sitting room. I can thoroughly recommend this hotel to anyone who is looking for comfort, relaxation and good food. They will understand Chase Lodge's popularity. Room and breakfast from £26 (single); £55 (double). Dinner, room and breakfast from £42.50, inc. VAT.

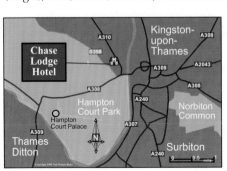

Bargain breaks: Discounts available for stays of 3 nights or more. Also Xmas/New Year programmes. **Hampton Court 1½, Kew Gardens 4, London 7, Wimbledon 7, Heathrow 8**

R & R licence; 10 en suite bedrooms, all with direct dial telephone and TV; tea/coffee making facilities; room service; baby listening; night service; last orders for dinner 9.30 p.m; bar meals; special diets; children welcome; dogs accepted; conferences max. 50; gymnasium 500 yds; tennis ½ mile; indoor heated swimming pool, leisure centre, squash, golf and riding 1 ½ miles; open all year; ample parking; all major credit cards accepted.

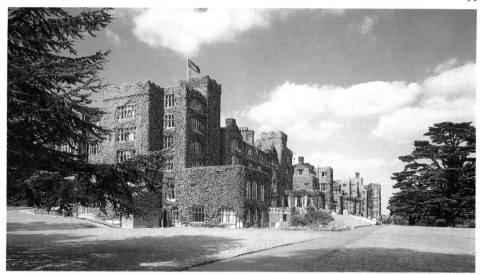

SELSDON PARK HOTEL
Sanderstead, Nr. Croydon, Surrey CR2 8YA

Telephone 0181 657 8811   Fax 0181 651 6171

"The Home of Hospitality", this luxurious and highly commended hotel is outstanding for its amenities, personal service and efficiency. The historic building, originally one of England's finest country houses going back to 891 AD, is situated in 200 parkland acres of the Surrey hills, with its own J H Taylor-designed 18-hole championship golf course. There is a country house feeling and friendly atmosphere at Selsdon Park. The public rooms are most comfortable and the bedrooms are decorated and furnished with care. Cuisine under the direction of Maître Chef de Cuisine, Jean-Marie Zimmermann is imaginative and perfectly cooked and there is a carefully chosen selection of excellent wines presented by Barrie Larvin, Master Sommelier. There are admirable facilities for large or small conferences, including an exclusive Leisure Complex. Chauffeur-driven cars and helicopter are available by prior arrangement. Room only, from £85 single, £120 double, including VAT. Always open. **Leisure Breaks:** The hotel offers an impressive variety of short breaks from dinner bed & breakfast including full use of the leisure club from £70 pppn to *Fly Away* Weekends which include a helicopter tour for two from £188. There are Shopping Weekends, Summer Packages between mid-July and early September, Children's Breaks in half-term and August from £35 per child per night d,b&b. Golf Weekends: d,b&b and one round of golf from £85 pppn. Health & Beauty Weekends and Tennis and Fitness Weekends from £112 pppn. **London 13 , Croydon 3, Epsom 9, Reigate 10, Kingston 11, Heathrow 1 hour, Gatwick** $^{1}/_{2}$ **hour, Victoria 17 mins Hotel car service.**
Full licence. 170 en suite bedrooms with AC, radio, satellite TV, direct dial telephone; hairdryer, trouser press, safety deposit box, laundry service, minibar, non-smoker bedrooms, 24 hour room service. Last orders for dinner 21.30. Special diets available. Dinner dance Friday & Saturday evenings. Billiards/snooker, croquet, golf, jogging track; fitness centre, jacuzzi, massage, sauna; beauty salon; indoor and outdoor swimming, tennis, squash. Full business services include 25 meeting rooms with capacity for up to 220. News stand. Car rental. Parking for 350 cars. Open all year. All major credit cards accepted.

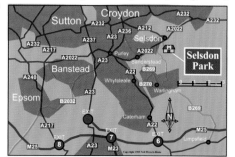

GRANVILLE HOTEL
124, Kings Road, Brighton BN1 2FA
Telephone 01273 326302   Fax 01273 728294

The Granville Hotel promises something "excitingly different" in store for you and how right that is! Situated on Brighton's Regency sea front, just 300 yards from the Brighton Conference Centre and opposite the majestic ruin of the West Pier with the Lanes, the Royal Pavilion and the best of Brighton on your doorstep, the location of the Granville is ideal. No description can really do justice to the flair, atmosphere and decor throughout. To whet your appetite - the Brighton Rock room is a sweet fantasy in pink and white. Decadence drifts through the Noël Coward room with its superb art deco bathroom, the Marina Room is complete with water bed and the Black Rock room a stunning symphony in black. The remaining en suite bedrooms all have individual style themes. Considerable thought and flair has also gone into the imaginative cuisine served in Trogs Restaurant. Organic and the freshest of produce only is used with presentation, service and the setting being quite brilliant. You will discover "roulade" you have never experienced before. For light snacks and drinks the more informal Café Bar has a genuine continental influence. Traditional English and vegetarian breakfasts are also outstanding. The Granville is worth a visit time and time again - a refreshingly different fun place and certainly one of the most exciting hotels we have encountered. Single room including breakfast from £45.00. Double room with breakfast from £55.00.

Leisure Breaks: Midweek breaks Sunday - Thursday from £29.95 p.p. per night minimum 3 nights subject to availability.

Haywards Heath 14, Arundel 20 , Lewes 8, Gatwick Airport 23, London 53

Full licence. 23 en suite bedrooms with colour TV; direct-dial telephone; laundry/ valet service; tea/ coffee making facilities. Hairdryer and trouser press availability. Last orders for dinner 21.30. Meeting room for 10 guests; Av equipment. Open all year. All major credit cards accepted.

LANSDOWNE HOTEL
King Edward's Parade, Eastbourne, East Sussex BN21 4EE

Telephone 01323 725174   Fax 01323 739721

The Lansdowne Hotel commands a fine view over Eastbourne's beach to the sea beyond. Owned by the same family since 1912, this hotel has the true hallmark of hospitality and comfort. Bedrooms are gracefully furnished with many rooms overlooking the sea-front. There is a choice of elegant lounges all of which benefit from a view across the Western Lawns as well as several refreshment places from the popular meeting place of the Regency Bar to the stylish Devonshire Restaurant serving fixed price menus of traditional English cuisine. The elegant Lawns Restaurant, is open from Spring to October. Conferences and seminars are well provided for in a selection of rooms. Two snooker rooms, table tennis, darts and a pool table provide every opportunity of relaxation. Eastbourne is an active resort offering a world famous tennis centre, a first class yachting marina, 200 acres of parks and gardens and the Lansdowne hotel is the ideal base from which to explore all that is offered here. Single room rate including breakfast from £49.00. Double room with breakfast from £73.00. Weekend and Weekday **Bargain Breaks** from 14th January - 12th May (exc. Easter) & 27th October -22nd December. Prices from £28.00 pppn d,b&b. Bridge Weekends once a month excepting June, July, September & October prices pp from £66 (2 nights) or £91 (3 nights). Golf Breaks all year from £110 per golfer for 2 days.

Tunbridge Wells 29, Winchester 80 , Hastings 20, Newhaven 12 ,Brighton 25, Dover 61, London 63. *Full licence. 122 en suite bedrooms with satellite TV, direct-dial telephone, hairdryer, laundry service, minibar, tea/coffee making facilities. 24-hour room service. Trouser press. Last orders for dinner 20.30. Billiards, indoor games room. Special arrangements for golf with seven local clubs. Five fully equipped conference rooms with total capacity of 330. Complete business service available, e.g. secretarial. Car parking: 23 lock-ups. Hotel closed 1-13 January. All major credit cards accepted.*

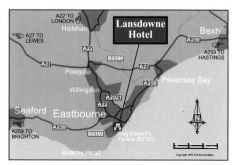

FLACKLEY ASH HOTEL
Peasmarsh, Near Rye, East Sussex TN31 6YH

Telephone: 01797 230651   *Fax: 01797 230510*

This is one of Sussex's charming, small country house hotels . It is set in five acres in a quiet rural setting. Rye is only a few miles away with its many historic buildings including the 15th century church, the Ypres Tower, the famous Landgate and Henry James' Georgian residence, Lamb House. Local activities are many and varied, with antique shops, potteries, local crafts and boutiques. There is a market on Thursdays. Camber Sands with its beautiful beaches and safe bathing is only a few miles further on; and of course there are castles, abbeys, a cathedral and many gardens to be visited, by those who are interested in places of beauty. The hotel has an indoor swimming pool and leisure complex, with whirlpool spa, mini gymnasium, steam room, sun bed, aromatherapy and beautician, new hairdressing salon, sun terrace and croquet lawn. There are endless sporting facilities in the vicinity of Flackley Ash including tennis, golf, riding, sea bathing etc, and it is easily accessible by road from London or by train via Ashford to Rye. This Georgian house offers its visitors a warm and friendly atmosphere and comfortable en suite bedrooms . The dining room has an AA Rosette for its food. Dishes are interesting and well presented by friendly and willing staff. Most vegetables are locally grown and emphasis is put on fresh local fish and seafood. Good conference and reception facilities for up to 100 are available. Room and breakfast from £49.00 per person, per night weekly rate. **Getaway Breaks** from £49.50 - £65 pppn - min. 2 nights. Winter price buster £100 pp for 3 nights. Summer price buster £180 pp for 3 nights or £280 pp 5 nights; weekly £299-£399. **Rye 3, Dover 36, Folkestone 29, London 60, Hastings 11.**

F licence; 32 en suite bedrooms, all with direct dial telephone and TV; last orders 9.30 p.m.; bar meals; children welcome; dogs accepted; conferences 80 max; indoor heated swimming pool; leisure centre; sauna; solarium; spa pool; steam room; gymnasium; opera all year; all major credit cards accepted.

JEAKE'S HOUSE
Mermaid Street,
Rye, East Sussex
TN31 7ET

Telephone: 01797 222828

Fax: 01797 222623

To stay here is to take a step back into history. The creeper clad elegant facade of Jeake's House stands on an incline in one of the prettiest old cobbled streets of Rye. Origins dating back to 1689 ,when the building was a wool store, add to its sheer charm. It was later a Baptist school and in the early 1900's the residence of an American poet and author. The history and atmosphere throughout makes Jeake's House quite unique. Jenny and Francis Hadfield own and manage the House in a traditional manner offering attentive service and high standards of comfort in the most tranquil and timeless of settings. Bedrooms have been individually restored, each highlighting characteristic features of this fine building, coupled with decorative elegance and the luxuries of modern facilities for guests' comfort. The dining room is situated in the imposing galleried chapel. Superb traditional English breakfasts are served here with a choice also of a vegetarian breakfast selection. Relaxing in the oak beamed parlour, guests can study the fascinating collection of pictures or have a drink in the comfortable book- lined bar area. Standards throughout Jeake's House are excellent and attention to detail paramount in every respect. Stepping out across the cobbles, Rye is a bustling market town with fine examples of medieval architecture. The style and ambience of Jeake's House certainly leaves a lasting impression. Single room with breakfast from £22.50. Double room including breakfast from £41.00 to £59.00.

Leisure Breaks: Reduction for stays of four or more nights.

Hastings 11 , Folkstone 25 , Dover 32, Brighton 49, Maidstone 33,London 63 .

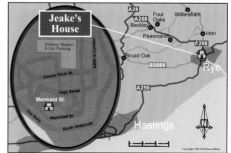

Full licence; 10 en suite bedrooms with colour TV; direct-dial telephone; hairdryer; tea/coffee making facilities. Open all year. All major credit cards accepted.

DALE HILL HOTEL AND GOLF CLUB

Ticehurst,
Wadhurst, East
Sussex TN5 7DQ

Telephone: 01580 200112;
Fax: 01580 201249

Unique comfort, style and location, together with superb facilities, can be found at the Dale Hill Hotel and Golf Club. This modern hotel is set in 300 spectacular acres, on an established, highly acclaimed parkland golf course. From the covered portico entrance, through to the open plan, two storey classic reception area, the warmth and charm of this hotel is already established. The Fairway Restaurant, from its unusual elevated situation, commands wonderful views and serves outstanding cuisine, together with a fine selection of wines. The highest standards of decor are apparent throughout the hotel, creating a stylish, sophisticated atmosphere. Each of the attractive 32 bedrooms is appointed with every facility required by the discerning guest, and most of the rooms enjoy breathtaking views. The golf course itself has been upgraded over the past few years, and you can enjoy unlimited golf during your stay at Dale Hill. A second championship standard course, designed by Ian Woosnam, will be opened in 1997. Professionally coached golfing sessions can be arranged. The amenities in the luxurious health complex are all appointed to very high standards, including, massage and selected beauty treatments. Full conference facilities and technical equipment are ready for use, and the support and advice provided, ensures the success of any meeting. This truly first class hotel is within easy reach of Tunbridge Wells and the stunning Sussex countryside where you will find historic medieval forts and castles. A stay at Dale Hill is highly recommended, whether on business or pleasure. Room and breakfast from £35.00. **Bargain breaks** are available from £75 per person, per night, to include dinner, bed and breakfast and all-day golf.

London 50, Tunbridge Wells 10, Eastbourne 30, Hastings 11, Gatwick 40, Heathrow 45

F licence; 32 en suite bedrooms, all with telephone and TV; baby listening; Lift; last orders 21.30; bar meals; special diets; children welcome; dogs accepted; conferences max. 50; pool table; indoor heated swimming pool; leisure centre; sauna; solarium; gymnasium; golf; tennis; riding, shooting and fishing available nearby; open all year; Visa, Mastercard, Switch and Amex accepted.

THE BEACH HOTEL

Marine Parade, Worthing, West Sussex BN11 3QJ

Telephone 01903 234001

Fax 01903 234567

A family run hotel, the Beach Hotel commands one of the finest sea front locations in Worthing. It is within walking distance of the shops, two first class golf courses less than two and a half miles away and with beautiful countryside for walking within easy reach. Chichester and Arundel are close by with entertainment in Brighton or racing at Goodwood about half an hour from the hotel. The double-glazed bedrooms are en suite and the decor light and bright with comfortable furnishings and all modern facilities. The front bedrooms on the first floor have private balconies with spectacular views out to sea. The open foyer and lounge are spacious and beautifully decorated with fresh floral displays. The cocktail bar provides a pleasant setting for a pre dinner drink and the restaurant serves an excellent table d'hôte menu with an à la carte choice available and a comprehensive wine list. With an open terrace running the length of the ground floor adjacent to the restaurant, lounge areas and terrace bar guests can relax enjoying the glorious views out to sea. The Beach Hotel is one of the finest in Worthing, well run with friendly and attentive staff. Single room with breakfast from £51.00. Double room including breakfast from £81.50.

Leisure Breaks: Weekends - Friday, Saturday - minimum stay 2 nights from £45.00 per person. Midweek breaks Monday-Thursday minimum stay 3 nights and take advantage of special weekend rate. Special offer: stay for 7 nights, pay for 6 **Brighton 11, Hastings, Southampton 50, Chichester 20 , Gatwick Airport 35, London 56** *Full licence. 80 en suite bedrooms with radio, satellite TV, direct-dial telephone; hairdryer, laundry/ valet service, tea/ coffee making facilities. Last orders for dinner 20.45. Special diets available. Indoor games room; safety deposit box. Car parking for 50 cars. Open all year. Credit cards accepted.*

■ Historic Houses, Gardens & Parks

CAMBRIDGESHIRE
Anglesey Abbey Nr. Cambndge
Chilford Hundred Vineyard, Linton
Docwra's Manor Garden, Shepreth
Elton Hall, Elton, Peterborough
Hincbingbrooke House, Huntingdon
Kimbolton Castle
Peckover House, Wisbech
University of Cambridge Botanic Garden

DERBYSHIRE
Calke Abbey, Park & Gardens, Ticknall
Chatsworth House & Garden, Bakewell
Eyam Hall, Eyam
Haddon Hall, Bakewell
Kedleston Hall, Derby
Lea Gardens, Matlock
Melbourne Hall Gardens & Craft Centre
Sudbury Hall & Museum of Childhood, Sudbury

ESSEX
Audley End House & Park, Saffron Walden
BBC Essex Garden, Abridge
Bridge End Gardens, Saffron Walden
Felsted Vineyard
New Hall Vineyards, Purleigh
Ingatestone Hall
Layer Marney Tower
Priory Vineyards, Little Dunmow
RHS Garden, Rettendon, Chelmsford

LEICESTERSHIRE
Belgrave Hall, Belgrave
Stanford Hall, Lutterworth
Whatton Gardens, Loughborough

LINCOLNSHIRE
Belvoir Castle, Nr. Grantham
Belton House, Grantham
Burghley House, Stamford
Doddington Hall, Lincoln
Fulbeck Hall, Grantham
Grimsthorpe Castle, Bourne
Harlaxton Manor Gardens, Grantham
Springfields, Spalding

NORFOLK
Beeston Hall, Beeston St Lawrence
Bickling Hall
Fairhaven Garden Trust, South Walsham
Felbrigg Hall
Fritton Lake Countryworld
Holkham Hall, Wells-next-the-Sea
Sandringham
Hoveton Hall Gardens, Wroxham
Mannington Gardens, Norwich
Norfolk Lavender Ltd, Heacham
Rainham Hall and Gardens, Tasburgh

NORTHAMPTONSHIRE
Castle Ashby Gardens, Castle Ashby
Canons Ashby House, Daventry
Cottesbrooke Hall, Cottesbrooke
Elton Hall, Peterborough
Deene Park, Nr. Corby
Holdenby House Gardens, Northampton
Hill Farm Herbs, Brigstock
Lamport Hall, Lamport
Rockingham Castle, Market Harborough

NOTTINGHAMSHIRE
Naturescape Wildflower Farm, Langar
Newstead Abbey Linby
Wollaton Hall Natural History Museum

SUFFOLK
Blakenham Woodland Garden, Nr Ipswich
Bruisyard Vineyard and Herb Centte
Euston Hall, Thetford
Haughley Park
Helmingham Hall Gardens
Kentwell Hall, Long Melford
Melford Hall, Long Melford
Somerleyton Hall & Gardens

■ Walks & Nature Trails

CAMBRIDGESHIRE
Bishops Way, north of Ely
Devil's Dyke, from north of Feach to south of Stechworth
Grafham Water Circular

DERBYSHIRE
Carsington Water, Ashbourne
Gulliver's Kingdom, Matlock Bath
Longshaw Estate, Hathersage

LEICESTERSHIRE
Beacon Hill Country Park, Woodhouse Eaves
Bradgate Park, Newtown Linford
Burbage Common Visitors' Centre
Melton Country Park, Melton Mowbray
Watermead Country Park, Syston
Rutland Water, Oakham

LINCOLNSHIRE
Chambers Farm Wood Forest Nature Resrve, Aply, Lincoln
Hartwholme Country Park, Lincoln
Tattershall Park Country Club, Tattershall, Lincoln

NORFOLK
Peddars Way & Norfolk Coast Path with Weavers Way
Marriott's Way, between Norwich & Aylsham

NORTHAMPTONSHIRE
Barnwell Country Park, Oundle
Brigstock Country Park, Kettering
Daventry Country Park, Daventry
Pitsford Water, Brixworth
Sywell Country Park, Northampton

NOTTINGHAMSHIRE
Burnstump Country Park, Arnold
Clumber Park, Worksop
Colwick Park, Colwick
Portland Park & Visitor Centre, Kirkby-in-Ashfield
Rufford Country Park & Craft Centre
Rushcliffe Country Park, Ruddington
Sherwood Pines Forest Park, Edwinstowe

SUFFOLK
Constable Trail
Painters Way from Sudbury to Manningtree
Suffolk Coastal Path, from Bawdsey to Kessingland
Suffolk Way, from Flatford to Lavenham

■ Historical Sites & Museums

CAMBRIDGESHIRE
Ely Cathedral
Imperial War Museum, Duxford
Fitzwilliam Museum, Cambridge
Oliver Cromwell's House, Ely
Cromwell Museum, Huntingdon

DERBYSHIRE
Arkwright's Cromford Mill, Matlock
Bolsover Castle, Bolsover
Blue John Museum Ollernshaw Collection, Castleton
Hardwick Old Hall, Doe Lea
Midland Railway Centre, Ripley
National Trust Museum of Childhood, Sudbury Hall
National Tramway Museum, Crick
Peveril Castle, Castleton

ESSEX
Central Museum and Planetarium, Southend-on-Sea
Colchester Castle
Hedingham Castle, Castle Hedingham
Maritime Museum, Harwich
National Motorboat Museum, Pitsea
Working Silk Museum, Braintree

LEICESTERSHIRE
Ashby-de-la-Zouch Castle
Bradgate House, Newtown Linford
Oakham Castle
Stanford Hall, Lutterworth
Bosworth Battlefield Visitor Centre & Country Park
Donington Collection of Grand Prix Racing Cars, Castle
 Donington

LINCOLNSHIRE
Bishop's Palace, Lincoln
Bolingbroke Castle, Spilsby
Lincoln Castle
Lincoln Guildhall
Woolsthorpe Manor, Nr. Grantham
The Incredibly Fantastic Old Toy Show, Lincoln

NORFOLK
100th Bomb Group Memorial Museum, Dickleburgh
Alby Lace Museum and Study Centre
Ancient House Museum, Thetford
Bygones Collection, Holkham Hall, Wells-next-the-Sea
Bygone Heritage Villa, Burgh St Margaret
Charles Burrell Museum, Thetford
City of Norwich Aviation Museum, Horsham St Faith
Maritime Museum, Great Yarmouth
Muckleburgh Collection, Weybourne
Shrine of our Lady of Walsingham, Walsingham
Wolverton Station Museum
Tales of the Old Gaol House, King's Lynn

NORTHAMPTONSHfRE
Boughton House, Nr Kettering
The Canal Museum, Stoke Bruerne
Chichele College, Higham Ferrers
Lyveden New Bield, Oundle
Rushton Triangular Lodge, Rushton

NOTTINGHAMSHIRE
Holme Pierrepont Hall, Nottingham
Newark Castle
Newstead Abbey, Linby
Brewhouse Yard Museum of Social History, Nottingham
D H Lawrence Birthplace Museum, Eastwood, Nottingham
Nottingham Castle Museum & Art Gallery

SUFFOLK
Bridge Cottage, Flatford
Dunwich Underwater Exploration Exhibition, Orford
Framlingham Castle
Gainsborough's House, Sudbury
Guildhall of Corpus Christi, Lavenham
Moot Hall & Museum, Aldeburgh
National Horse Racing Museum, Newmarket
Sizewell Visitors Centre, Sizewell B Power Station
Sue Ryder Foundation Museum, Cavendish
Tolly Cobbold Brewery, Ipswich
Woodbndge Museum

■ Entertainment Venues

CAMBRIDGESHIRE
Grays Honey Farm, Warboys
Hamerton Wildlife Centre
Linton Zoo
Peakirk Waterfowl Gardens Trust
Sacrewell Farm & Country Centre, Thornhaugh

DERBYSHRE
American Adventure, llkeston
Cauldwell's Mill & Craft Centre, Rowsley
Bentley Fields Open Farm Longford
Denby Pottery Visitors Centre, Denby
Lathkill Dale Craft Centre, Bakewell
Royal Crown Derby Museum & Factory, Derby

ESSEX
Colchester Zoo
Dedham Rare Breed Farm
Layer Marney Tower
Mole Hall Wildlife Park, Widdington
Southend Sea Life Centre

LINCOLNSHIrRE
Brandy Wharf Cider Centre, Gainsborough
Battle of Britain Memorial Flight, RAF Coningsby, Lincoln
The Butterfly & Falconry Park, Long Sutton
Skegness Natureland Sea Sanctuary, Skegness
Cobb Hall Craft Centre, Lincoln

NORFOLK
Banham Zoo
Kingdom of the Sea, Great Yarrnouth
Norfolk Wildlife Centre & Country Park, Great
 Witchingham
Otter Trust, Earsham
Park Farm & Norfolk Farmyard Crafts Centre,
 Snettisham
Pensthorpe Waterfowl Park
Thrigby Hall Wildlife Gardens, Filby

NORTHAMPTONSHIRE
Peakirk Waterfowl Gardens Trust, Peterborough

NOTTINGHAMSHIRE
The Lace Centre, Nottingham
The Tales of Robin Hood, Nottingham
Newark Air Museum
Nottingham Industrial Museum, Nottingham
Patchings Farm Art Centre, Calverton
Sherwod Forest Visitor Centre & Country Park, Edwinstowe

SUFFOLK
East of England Birds of Prey and Conservation Centre,
 Laxfield
Suffolk Wildlife Park, Kessingland

March 28-April 1   ALDEBURGH EARLY MUSIC FESTIVAL
Snape Maltings Concert Hall, Snape, Suffolk
March 30-31   THRIPLOW DAFFODIL WEEKEND
Thriplow, Cambridgeshire
April 6-8   AMERICAN CIVIL WAR RE-ENACTMENT
Knebworth House, Knebworth, Hertfordshire
May 4-5   NOTTINGHAMSHIRE COUNTY SHOW
Newark and Notts Showground, Winthorpe, Newark, Nottinghamshire
May 4-6   SPALDING FLOWER SHOW
Streets of Spalding, Springfields Gardens and Festival Site, Spalding, Lincolnshire.
May 5-6   THE KNEBWORTH COUNTY SHOW
Knebworth House, Hertfordshire.
May 5-7   HORSE RACING, THE GUINEAS MEETING
Newmarket Racecourse, Newmarket, Suffolk.
May 9-25   BURY ST. EDMUNDS FESTIVAL
Various venues in Bury St. Edmunds, Suffolk.
May 11-12   HERTFORDSHIRE GARDEN SHOW
Knebworth House, Hertfordshire.
May 11-12   FIGHTER MEET '96
Northweald Airfield Museum, Epping, Essex
May 11-18   32nd BUXTON ANTIQUES FAIR
St John's Rd, Buxton, Derbyshire
May 16-19   NOTTINGHAM BOAT SHOW
Trent Bridge, Nottingham
May 25-26   AIR FETE '96
RAF Mildenhall, Mildenhall, Suffolk.
May 26-27   SOUTHEND AIR SHOW
Southend-on-Sea, Essex
MAY 27   LUTON CARNIVAL
Luton, Bedfordshire
May 27-29   FELLBRIGG COAST & COUNTY CRAFT FAIR Fellbrigg Hall, Fellbrigg, Norfolk.
May 29-30   SUFFOLK SHOW 1996
Suffolk Showground, Ipswich, Suffolk.
June 7-27   49TH ALDEBURGH FESTIVAL OF MUSIC AND THE ARTS
Snape Maltings (and various venues), Aldeburgh, Suffolk. World renowned festival including operas, concerts, recitals and exhibitions etc.
June 19-20   LINCOLNSHIRE SHOW
Showground, Grange-de-Lings, Lincoln.
June 26-27   ROYAL NORFOLK SHOW 1996 (agricultural)
Norfolk Showground, Norwich, Norfolk.
July 12-14   BRITISH GRAND PRIX '96
Silverstone Race Circuit, Towcester, Northamptonshire.
July 18-Aug 4   BUXTON INTERNATIONAL FESTIVAL
Buxton Opera House, Buxton, Derbyshire.
July 20-Aug 3   KINGS LYNN FESTIVAL
Kings Lynn, Norfolk
July 31   SANDRINGHAM FLOWER SHOW
Sandringharn, Norfolk. Large flower show held in the grounds of H.M. The Queen's country retreat.
August 15-18   GILBERT & SULLIVAN FESTIVAL
Various venues, Buxton, Derbyshire.
August*   ROBIN HOOD FESTIVAL
Sherwood Forest Visitor Centre & Country Park, Edwinstowe, Mansfield, Nottinghamshire.

August 1-31   SNAPE PROMS
              Snape Maltings, Aldeburgh, Suffolk
August 7-8   166TH BAKEWELL SHOW
              The Showground, Coombe Road, Bakewell, Derbyshire.
August 10-14 ENGLAND v WEST INDIES 5TH TEST MATCH
              Nottinghamshire County Cricket Club, Trent Bridge, Nottinghamshire.
August 16-18 NORTHAMPTON HOT AIR BALLOON FESTIVAL
              Northampton Racecourse, Northampton
September 5-8 BURGHLEY PEDIGREE CHUM HORSE TRIALS
              Burghley Park, Stamford, Lincolnshire
Sept. 14-15   RAF WADDINGTON AIR SHOW
              Waddington, Lincoln
Sept. 23-24   N.A.F.A.S. FESTIVAL OF FLOWERS
              The Story of Knebworth House. Knebworth, Hertfordshire.
October 13   WORLD CONKER CHAMPIONSHIP
              Village Green, Ashton, Nr. Northampton.
October 10-20 NORFOLK & NORWICH FESTIVAL '96
              Various venues, Norwich, Norfolk

*Denotes provisional date

For further information contact:
East Anglia Tourist Board   East Midlands Tourist Board
Toppesfield Road   Exchequergate
Hadleigh   Lincoln
Suffolk IP7 5DN.   LN2 1PZ
Tel: 01473 822922   Tel: 01522 531521

BUDGET SECTION - EAST MIDLANDS - SUTTON IN ASHFIELD, NOTTS

DALESTORTH GUEST HOUSE
Skegby Lane, Skeby, Sutton-in-Ashfield, Nottinghamshire NG17 3DH

Telephone: 01623 551110;
Fax: 01623 442241

Fully modernised 18th Century ancestral home in pleasant gardens. Well situated between Mansfield and Sutton-in-Ashfield, five miles from M1, Junction 28. Ideal for business and pleasure visits. Close to local golf courses, stately homes and Sherwood Forest.

Three double, seven twin and five single bedrooms. Single £16; double £30. Evening meal optional - three course dinner for £6. Colour TV, tea/coffee making facilities, large car park (100cars). Garden centre adjoins premises.

RIBER HALL
Matlock, Derbyshire DE4 5JU

Telephone: 01629 582795   Fax: 01629 580475

This lovely peaceful Elizabethan manor house, featured in all major guides and recently nominated by the A.A. as one of "The most romantic hotels in Britain", is set in the heart of the Derbyshire countryside, surrounded by woods and meadows with an old established English country walled garden full of birdlife and birdsong. Situated on the border of the Peak National Park and close to five of the finest stately houses in England, Riber Hall enjoys pure tranquillity in a picturesque setting. The bedrooms are set around the courtyard and are appointed to the highest standard. Established nearly twenty-five years ago, Riber Hall is renowned for its outstanding cuisine and extensive wine lists. There is no room to describe all the pleasures at Riber Hall, so do try it and I am sure you will return for more. Room and continental breakfast from £83.00 single and £99.50 double, including VAT. Hotel and restaurant open seven days a week for luncheon and dinner throughout the year. **Leisure Breaks:** Information on special offers including "Hideaway Breaks" is available on application.

Derby 20, Nottingham 26, Chesterfield 11, Sheffield 25, M1 Motorway (exit 28) 20 minutes, London 144.

R & R licence; 11 en suite bedrooms (7 ground floor), with radio, tea/coffee making and bar facilities, colour TV, direct dial telephone; children over 10 welcome; meals to 9.30 p.m. (last orders), service to 11.00 p.m. Breakfast from 7.00 a.m. Small conferences. All weather tennis court; indoor swimming pool and golf two miles. Sailing on Carsington water and water sports facilities nearby. Fishing and clay-pigeon shooting by arrangement. All credit cards accepted.

THE PEACOCK HOTEL
Rowsley, Nr Matlock, Derbyshire DE4 2EB

Telephone: 01629 733518   Fax: 01629 732671

I always enjoy my visits to the Peacock, part of the Jarvis Hotel Group. where the welcome is warm and the unwinding process begins immediately. This 17th Century house, set on the banks of the river Derwent, is furnished with antiques and the many original features are well-preserved. The Peacock Bar with its oak beams and rough stone walls is a fine example and an excellent place to enjoy a pre-dinner drink after a busy day visiting the sights for which Derbyshire is justly famous. The Garden Restaurant provides a perfect setting for a delicious dinner or lunch, where the menus focus on modern British cooking using a variety of local, fresh ingredients. Some of the en suite bedrooms have four-posters or half-testers and all are appointed to a high standard with the added luxury of bath robes. The many attractions in the neighbourhood include historic houses such as Chatsworth, Riber Castle Wildlife Park and the Heights of Abraham; yet understandably the hotel's speciality is fishing and, for the enthusiasts of whatever standard, I can recommend their fishing packages which come with tuition. All in all the Peacock should be a favourite with Signposters! Single room with breakfast from £55.00. Double room with breakfast from £99.00.

Leisure Breaks: Min 2-night stay to include room, breakfast & dinner from £85.00 to £123.00. **Derby 23, Nottingham 30, Chesterfield 11, Sheffield 16, M1(exit 28) 20 minutes, London 148..**

Full licence. 14 en suite bedrooms with colour TV; direct-dial telephone; hair-dryer, trouser press; laundry service; tea/coffee making facilities. Last orders for dinner 21.00. Fishing. Three meeting rooms with capacity up to 20. Car parking for 40 cars. Open all year. All major credit cards accepted.

STAPLEFORD PARK
Nr. Melton Mowbray, Leicestershire LE14 2EF

Telephone: 01572 787522   Fax: 01572 787651

Casual luxury at its very best is how Stapleford has been described and with its character and sumptuous comforts it is one of the finest country house hotels in the world. Across acres of parkland, a tree lined avenue, through the arched stable block you reach the mellow facade of this Stately Home with every architectural style since the 16th Century. The public rooms reflect the majesty of the house: high ceilings, mahogany panelling, open fires and unique features such as a trompe d'oeil and a 450 years old vaulted kitchen - meals are taken here and in the ornately carved Grinling Gibbons restaurant which serves an outstanding cuisine conveying an eclectic mix of the Mediterranean, Californian and English. The bedrooms have been individually created by famous designers and more unexpectedly by names such as Tiffany and Wedgwood, and they are unashamedly luxurious, offering simply everything including splendid marble bathrooms. A four bedroom cottage is also available nearby. All conventional leisure activities are possible here, and of course more exotic pursuits such as carriage driving and falconry. Stapleford is ideally situated for exploring England's finest heritage from York or Lincoln to Stratford. A stay here is unforgettable, combining as it does the grand style of bygone centuries with present day luxury, whilst the attentive service instils the feeling of home with none of its worries. Room rate including breakfast from £145.00.
Leisure Breaks: £99.75 pppn - casual lunch and full dinner (with allowances totalling £35.00) - King-size or double bedded standard room. **Kettering 29, Grantham 16, Leicester 15, Loughborough 15, London 104.**

Full licence. 43 en suite bedrooms with radio & colour TV; direct-dial telephone; hairdryer, trouser press, laundry service, safety deposit box. 24 hour room service. Last orders for dinner 21.30 hrs weekdays, 22.00 hrs weekends. Special diets available. Croquet, jogging track, riding, shooting, tennis, falconry. Fishing and golf nearby. All business services including 10 meeting rooms with capacity up to 260 in largest room. Newsstand/ shops; Airport pick-up. Car rental can be arranged. Facilities for the disabled. Ample car parking. Open all year. All major credit cards accepted.

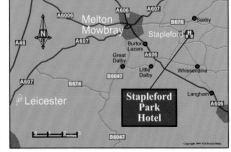

WASHINGBOROUGH HALL COUNTRY HOUSE HOTEL
Church Hill, Washingborough, Lincoln LN4 1BE

Telephone: 01522 790340   Fax: 01522 792936

Washingborough Hall is a charming Georgian manor house, peacefully situated on the edge of the village, just three miles from historic Lincoln. I received a warm welcome from the owners Brian and Mary Shillaker who are very congenial hosts. The Hall is furnished and decorated throughout to create a friendly and comfortable atmosphere. Each of the 12 bedrooms is different; all are most attractive, and equipped to a very high standard. Some have four-poster beds, some spa baths, and they are named according to the décor. Mary Shillaker is a first-class chef. In the Wedgwood dining room, I enjoyed a delicious dinner from the table d'hôte menu, which was cooked to perfection. However, there is also an interesting à la carte available, together with a very good choice of wines. After dining, the hall, with its huge fireplace, is a most comfortable and relaxing place in which to enjoy a drink. Mary must also be congratulated on the beautiful 3 acres of gardens for which she is responsible, her speciality being the wide variety of fuschias. Within the grounds, sheltered from the wind, is a small swimming pool which is heated in the summer months, and croquet can be played on the lawn when the weather is fine. A pleasant function room is also available to cater for up to 50 delegates. Washingborough Hall is an ideal base for the pretty Lincolnshire Wolds, a short drive away, and the walled medieval city of Lincoln is well worth the visit. Twin room and breakfast from £74.00 including VAT, no service charge. Weekend or midweek breaks available for stays of two nights or more from £42 per person per night.

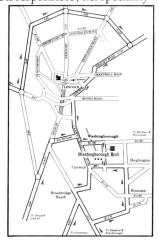

Lincoln 3, Hull 37, Peterborough 60, York 75, London 150.

F licence; 12 ensuite bedrooms, all with telephone, TV, hairdryer; trouser press; limited room service; last orders for dinner 8.30 p.m.; specialities; bar meals; children welcome; dogs accepted; conferences max. 50; croquet/boules; outdoor heated swimming pool (summer only); leisure centre & squash three miles; water skiing centre seven miles; golf, tennis, riding & fishing nearby; closed over Christmas; all major credit cards accepted.

THE BLAKENEY HOTEL
Blakeney, Nr. Holt, Norfolk NR25 7NE

Telephone: 01263 740797   *Fax: 01263 740795*

The Blakeney Hotel is a traditional privately owned and friendly hotel with magnificent views across the estuary and salt marshes to Blakeney Point, an area of outstanding beauty owned by the National Trust. North Norfolk is an ideal region for relaxation. There are lovely walks, birdwatching, cycling, sailing and fishing to enjoy. Other activities include shooting, tennis and golf which are all nearby. The lovely city of Norwich and the port of King's Lynn are each within an hour's drive, and close by are stately homes such as Sandringham, pretty villages, market towns and sandy beaches. The Blakeney offers a wide choice of accommodation. All rooms have private bathroom, colour TV and tea/coffee making facilities. There are suites, 4 rooms with four poster beds, a room with a balcony and a ground floor room suitable for wheelchairs . A few bedrooms are in an adjacent annexe, some with their own patios. The restaurant which serves a choice of good fresh food, and the cocktail bar both overlook the quay. There are comfortable lounges, fine south facing gardens in which to relax and new gardens overlooking the marshes. For the more energetic, the hotel has an indoor heated swimming pool, spa bath, sauna and mini gym. Two day **breaks** to include dinner, bed and breakfast from £54 per person, per night. Special four day holidays from £196; 7-day holidays from £343. Open all year.

London 127, Cambridge 60, Norwich 25, King's Lynn 30, Brancaster 15, Cromer 15.

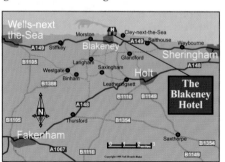

F licence, 60 en suite bedrooms (10 ground floor, 5 of which have own patio suitable for dogs and 1 for wheelchairs), all with telephone and TV; night service; diets; children welcome; baby listening; dogs accepted; banquet aad conference facilities; car parking; most credlt cards accepted.

SOUTH WALSHAM HALL
South Walsham, Norwich, Norfolk NR13 6DQ

Telephone: 01603 270378   *Fax: 01603 270378*

The first impression of South Walsham Hall is magnificent; having driven through a beautiful avenue of rhododendrons and yews, one suddenly sees this lovely building which stands back with lawns running down to the lake. This most attractive country mansion has been completely renovated and redecorated under the present Swiss management. The original part of the Hall is steeped in Norfolk's history, being Elizabethan with further additions up to Victorian times. The most impressive interior feature is the beautiful 17th century staircase which leads up to ten bedrooms all named after European cities, with one magnificent bridal suite opening up to the most sumptuous bathroom. Three of the rooms can be used for a family let, and the other seven are chalet-type rooms in the courtyard. The restaurant offers a wine list for the connoisseur and an extensive menu for the gourmet. In the garden behind the Hall is a rose garden and heated swimming pool with existing plans for future sporting improvements to the 34 acre surrounds. The Hall is nine miles from Norwich and within easy reach of Yarmouth, so is an ideal place to stay, away from the bustle of the city, where one can completely relax in a wonderful setting. Free to residents is the adjacent Fairhaven Garden Trust, a delightful, natural woodland and water gardens. Single room and breakfast from £40, double from £60 including VAT and service. **Weekend breaks** from £90 per couple one day; £170 two days. Special half board terms from £50 single, £80 double min. three nights and from £345 single, £490 double for any 7 days. Open all year. **Norwich 9, Great Yarmouth 11, Cromer 25, London 120.**

R & R licence; 17 en suite bedrooms all with colour TV and radio/alarm clocks; full central heating; meals to 10.00 p.m; bar meals; children welcome; ideal for weddings and conferences; outdoor heated swimming pool; 2 double tennis courts; 2 squash courts; horse-riding school; sea bathing 11 miles; sailing and boating on the Broads one mile; golf six miles; credit cards accepted.

LANGAR HALL
Langar, Nottinghamshire NG13 9HG

Telephone: 01949 860559   Fax: 01949 861045

I always love my visits to Langar Hall. The close proximity of Nottingham never ceases to amaze me, as Langar is beautifully situated overlooking the Vale of Belvoir. It is a lovely country house, built in 1837, which stands beside an early English church, with glorious views over the gardens, moat and parkland. The Hall is the family home of Imogen Skirving, where her father used to entertain famous cricketers of the 1930's. Langar Hall has delightful rooms, bursting with fine antiques and interesting pictures to be enjoyed by all. Imogen, a charming lady, and her excellent team, make every effort for their guests' happiness. Together with her chef Toby Garratt, she works to produce excellent, reasonably priced à la carte menus of French and English food. The menus, priced between £15 and £30 are kept small and varied, and include such dishes as chargrilled tuna steak with balsamic vinaigrette, local lamb, turbot, steak and chips with bernaise sauce or lobster. Recently, Imogen has extended one of her rooms to accommodate small conferences and private dinner parties. All the bedrooms are charming and uniquely furnished, and one has a four-poster bed. Family rooms are available in the stable block. This is a truly lovely place to stay, with a peaceful and relaxing atmosphere. Single room and breakfast, £60-£75, double room and breakfast from £80-£125. Licensed to hold marriages; exclusive house party booking. **Weekend breaks** - room and breakfast 2-night stay for 2 people from £150. Two nights for price of one - must include Sunday. **Nottingham 12, London 120, York 90.**

R licence; 10 en suite bedrooms, all with direct dial telephones, TV; room service; baby listening, last orders for dinner 9.30 p.m.; children welcome; dogs by arrangement; conferences 20 max; own coarse fishing - bring your own rod; golf four miles; Mastercard, Visa and Amex Credit Cards accepted.

THE OLD ENGLAND
Sutton-on-Trent, Nr. Newark, Nottinghamshire NG23 6QA

Telephone: 01636 821216   Fax: 01636 822347

The Old England is a real home from home. The Pike family have run the hotel since we first published Signpost and, more than 57 years later, we are still pleased to recommend it. You will find Sutton Village just off the A1, north of Newark. A "Hotel" sign on the main road points in the direction of the quiet village High Street, and approximately $^1/_2$ mile down on the left stands this most attractive country house. Situated in a large very well kept garden, which must be a haven of peace on a fine day, the house is continually being updated by its owners. All bedrooms have their own private bathrooms and are cheerful, cosy and well furnished. Those of you who appreciate good furniture, will be delighted with the beautifully polished antique tables and chairs in the dining room, and the many other interesting pieces and lovely old china throughout the hotel. The kitchen door is always open, for they have nothing to hide, and the food supervised by the Pike family, is really good British fare, such as steak, roasts and poached Scotch salmon, and always plenty of it. Later, I was assured by regular diners at the hotel that their high standard of food never varies. If you are travelling north or south, you can be assured of a very warm welcome at this lovely hotel. Single room and breakfast from £47.00, double from £57.00 including VAT.
Midweek breaks: £39.50 per person per night (min. stay two nights), including dinner, bed, breakfast & VAT. **London 128, Newark 8, East Retford 12, Leicester 41, Lincoln 24.**

R & R licence; 10 en suite bedrooms (1 ground floor), all with TV; room service; last orders for dinner 9. 00p.m.; special diets; children welcome; dogs accepted; conferences max. 45; grass tennis court; shooting/fishing four miles; golf 8 miles; open all year; Mastercard and Visa credit cards accepted.

CHIPPENHALL HALL
Fressingfield, Eye, Suffolk IP21 5TD

Telephone: 01379 586733 & 588180   *Fax: 01379 586272*

Approaching Chippenhall Hall up a long drive you are enveloped in rural peace. This Tudor building is a typical Suffolk Manor House mentioned in the Domesday Book and dating back even further than Fressingfield. The Hall, standing in seven acres of garden which includes an outdoor heated swimming pool, is the home of your host and hostess Jakes and Barbara Sargent. The rich scent of wood smoke greets you and I was assured that there are log fires even during cool English summer evenings. Amongst the mellow oaken beams the atmosphere is that of a home with drinks taken in a cosy bar area or outside by the pool and a superb candlelit dinner served at a refectory table. The menu, discussed in advance with guests, will consist of local fresh ingredients including game and vegetables from the garden. The bedrooms, named after their historic past, are beautifully furnished with the bath and shower rooms sympathetically integrated. Many country activities can be arranged and if you can tear yourself away

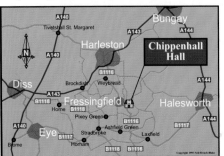

from the delights of Chippenhall. Some of Suffolk's most historic towns, villages and wildlife sanctuaries are but a short drive away. Single room rate including breakfast from £48.00; double room rate with breakfast from £55.00. **Ipswich 30, Norwich 23, London 103.**

F Licence. 3 en suite bedrooms (non-smoking) with radio, hairdryer, trouser press tea/coffee-making facilities. Last dinner orders 17.00 hrs. Croquet, jogging-track, outdoor swimming pool. Golf, riding, shooting - clay & game by arrangement. Parking 20 cars. Open all year. Some credit cards accepted.

■ Historic Houses, Gardens & Parks

GLOUCESTERSHIRE
Berkeley Castle
Bamsley House Garden
Buscot House, Nr. Lechlade
Hidcote Manor Garden, Hidcote Bartrim
Painswick Rococo Garden
Snowshill Manor, Nr. Broadway
Stanway House, Nr. Wmchcombe
Sudeley Castle & Gardens

HEREFORD & WORCESTER
Abbey Dore Court Gardens
Berrington Hall, Nr. Leominster
Burford House Gardens, Burford
Eastnor Castle, Nr. Ledbury
Eastgrove Cottage Garden Nursery, Nr. Shrawley
Hagley Hall, Nr. Stourbridge
H anbury Hall, Nr. Droitwich
Hergest Cloft Gardens, Kington
Hill Court Gardens, Nr. Ross-on-Wye
How Caple Court Gardens, How Caple
Moccas Court, Moccas
The Picton Gardens at Old Coust Nurseries, Colwall Village
Queenswood Country Park, Nr. Leominster
Spetchley Park, Nr. Worcester

SHROPSHIRE
Attingham Park, Nr. Shrewsbury
Benthall Hall, Broseley
Boscobel House, Nr. Albrighton
Goldstone Hall Garden, Market Drayton
Hawkstone Hall, Weston
Weston Park

STAFFORDSHIRE
Biddulph Grange Garden & Country Park,Biddulph
Chillington Hall, Codsall Wood
Greanway Bank Country Park, Nr. Biddulph
Hanch Hall, Lichfield
Shugborough, Milton
Trentham Gardens

WARWICKSHIRE
Arbusy Hall, Nr. Nuneaton
Baddesley Clinton House
Charlecote Park, Nr. Wellesboume
Coughton Court
Harthill Hayes Country Park, Nr. Nuneaton
Jephson Gardens, Leamington Spa
Kingsbury Water Park
Middleston Hall
Packwood House, Nr. Hockley Heath
Ragley Hall, Nr. Alcester
Ryton Organic Gardens, Coventry

WEST MIDLANDS
Aston Hall, Birmingham
Birmingharn Botanical Gardans
Clent Hills Country Park, Nr. Stourbndge
Coombe Abbey Country Park, Nr. Coventry
Moseley Old Hall, Fordhouses
Selly Manor & Minworth Greaves, Bourneville
Sutton Park, Sutton Coldfield
Wightwick Manor, Nr. Wolverhampton

GLOUCESTERSHIRE
Cotswold Water Park, South of Cirencester
Crickley Hill Country Park. Nr. Great Witcombe
Dean Heritage Centre, Nr. Cinderford
Great Western Railway Museum, Coleford
Forest of Dean Trails, starts at Cannop Ponds
Gloucester Guided Walks
Symonds Yat Forest Trail, SW of Ross-on-Wye

HEREFORD & WORCESTER
City of Hereford Guided Walks
Croft Garden Centre, Nr. Leominster
Kingsford Country Park, Wolverley
Malvern Hills Walks & Trails
Many short walks from Ross-on-Wye
The North Worcestershire Path
The Worcestershire Way

SHROPSHIRE
Broadway Tower Country Park
Cardingmill Valley, Long Mynd
Clee Hills, Cleobury Mortimer
Offa's Dyke, Clun Forest
Historic Hawkstone Park & Follies, Weston

STAFFORDSHIRE
Cannock Chase Country Park
Codsall Nature Trail
Deep Hayes Country Park, Nr. Longsdon
Manifold Valley, Nr. Waterhouses
The Wildlife Sanctuary, Nr. Cheadle

WARWICKSHIRE
Crackley Wood , Kenilworth
Edge Hill, Nr. Kineton
Hatton Locks, Nr. Warwick
Ufton Fields Nature Reserve

WEST MIDLANDS
Birmingham City Centre Canal Walk
Longmore Nature Trail
Wren's Nest National Nature Reserve, Dudley

■ Historical Sites & Museums

GLOUCESTERSHIRE
Chedworth Roman Villa, Nr. Cheltenham
Clearwell Caves, Nr. Coleford
Corinium Museum, Cirencester
Cotswold Motor Museum & Toy Collection, Bourton-on-the-Water
Gloucester Cathedral
Gloucester City Museum & Art Gallery
Gloucester Folk Museum
Holst Birthplace Museum, Cheltenham
Tewkesbury Abbey

HEREFORD & WORCESTER
Avoncroft Museum of Buildings, Nr. Bromsgrove
Cotswold Teddy Bear Museum, Broadway
Elgar's Birthplace, Lower Broadheath
Goodrich Castle, Nr. Ross-on-Wye
Hartlebury Castle State Rooms, Nr. Kidderminster
Hereford Cathedral
The Droitwich Spa Brine Baths
Worcester Cathedral
Worcester Royal Porcelain Dyson Perrins Museum

SHROPSHIRE
Acton Scott Historic Working Farm
Aerospace Museum, Cosford
Blists Hill Open Air Museum, Ironbridge
The Childhood & Costume Museum, Bridgnorth
Coalbrookdale Furnace & Museum of Iron
Ludlow Castle
Midland Motor Museum, Nr. Bridgnorth
Wroxeter Roman City, Nr. Shrewsbury

STAFFORDSHIRE
Bass Museum, Visitor Centre & Shire Horse Stables, Burton-on-Trent
The Brindley Mill & Museum, Leek
Gladstone Pottery Museum, Longton
Lichfield Cathedral
Samuel Johnson Birthplace Museum, Lichfield
Stafford Castle
Wall (Letocetum) Roman Site, Nr. Lichfield

WARWICKSHIRE
Anne Hathaway's Cottage, Shottery
James Gilbert's Rugby Football Museum, Rugby
Kenilworth Castle
Shakespeare's Birthplace, Stratford-upon-Avon
The Shakespeare Countryside Museum & Mary Arden's House, Wilmcote
Warwick Castle

WEST MIDLANDS
Bantock House Museum, Wolverhampton
Birmingham Cathedral
Birmingham Museum & Art Gallery
Birmingham Museum of Science & Industry
Black Country Museum, Dudley
Broadfield House Glass Museum, Kingswinford
Coventry Cathedral
Jerome K Jerome's Birthplace Museum, Nr Walsall
The Lock Museum, Willenhall
Midland Air Museum, Coventry
Museum of British Road Transport, Coventry
National Motor Cycle Museum, Bickenhill
Walsall Leather Museum

■ Entertainment Venues

GLOUCESTERSHIRE
Bibury Trout Farm
Birdland, Bourton-on-the Water
Cheltenham Hall of Fame, Cheltenham Racecourse
Cotswold Woollen Weavers, Nr. Lechlade
Gloucester Docks
House of Tailor of Gloucester
Model Village, Bourton-on-the-Water
National Birds of Prey Centre, Newent
The Wildfowl & Wetland Trust Centre, Slimbridge

HEREFORD & WORCESTER
Cider Museum & King Offa Distillery
The Hop Pocket Hop Farm, Bishop's Frome
The Jubilee Park, Symonds Yat West
Severn Valley Railway, Bewdley to Bridgnorth
West Midlands Safari Park, Nr. Bewdley

SHROPSHIRE
Dinham House Exhibition Centre
The Domestic Fowl Trust, Honeybourne
Lickey Hill Country Park
The Shrewsbury Quest, Shrewsbury
Twyford Country Centre, Nr. Evesham

STAFFORDSHIRE
Alton Towers, Alton
Drayton Manor Family Theme Park & Zoo, Nr. Tamworth
Stoke-on-Trent - many china factory tours

WARWICKSHIRE
Ashorne Hall Nicleodeon, Ashorne Hill
Heritage Motor Centre, Gaydon
Royal Shakespeare Theatre, Stratford
Stratford Open-top Bus Tours
Swan Theatre, Stratford
Twycross Zoo, Atherstone

WEST MIDLANDS
Birmingham Jewellery Quarter Discovery Centre
Cadbury World, Bourneville, Birmingham
Cannon Hill Park, Edgbaston, Birmingham
Royal Doulton Crystal, Amblecote

February 17-25   NATIONAL BOAT, CARAVAN & LEISURE SHOW
National Exhibition Centre, Birmingham

February 20   SHROVETIDE FAIR & PANCAKE RACE
Market Square, Lichfield, Staffordshire

March 7-12   WORLD FIGURE SKATING CHAMPIONSHIPS 1996
National Exhibition Centre, Birmingham.

March 12-14   GOLD CUP NATIONAL HUNT RACING FESTIVAL WEEK
Cheltenham Racecourse, Cheltenham, Glos.

March 14-17   CRUFTS DOG SHOW
National Exhibition Centre, Birmingham

March 16   HORSE RACING MIDLANDS GRAND NATIONAL
Uttoxeter Racecourse, Staffordshire.

March 20-26   WORLD INDOOR TARGET ARCHERY CHAMPIONSHIPS
National Indoor Arena, Birmingham.

April 27   SHAKESPEARE BIRTHDAY CELEBRATIONS
Town centre, Stratford-upon-Avon, Warwickshire.

April 25-30   BRITISH INTERNATIONAL ANTIQUES FAIR
National Exhibition Centre, Birmingham.

May 10-12   MALVERN SPRING GARDEN SHOW
Three Counties Showground, Malvern, Worcestershire.

May 4-6   BBC TOP GEAR CLASSIC & SPORTSCAR SHOW
National Exhibition Centre, Birmingham.

May 17-18   SHROPSHIRE & WEST MIDLANDS AGRICULTURAL SHOW
The Showground, Berwick Road, Shrewsbury, Shropshire.

June 11-13   THREE COUNTIES AGRICULTURAL SHOW
Three Counties Showground, Malvern, Worcestershire.

June 12-16   BBC GARDENER'S WORLD LIVE
National Exhibition Centre, Birmingham.

June 15-21   MIDSUMMER MUSIC FESTIVAL
Charlecote Park, Wellesbourne, Warwickshire.

June 16   RAF COSFORD OPEN DAY
Aerospace Museum, Cosford, Shropshire

June 23-25   UPTON JAZZ FESTIVAL
Throughout city, Upton-upon-Severn, Worcestershire.

July 16-21   CHELTENHAM INTERNATIONAL FESTIVAL OF MUSIC
Cheltenham Town Hall, Cheltenham, Glos.

June 29-July 14   WARWICK & LEAMINGTON FESTIVAL
Various venues throughout Warwickshire.

June 22-July 7   LUDLOW FESTIVAL
Ludlow Castle, Ludlow, Shropshire

July 1-4   THE ROYAL SHOW
National Agricultural Centre, Stoneleigh, Warks.

July 5-14   BIRMINGHAM INTERNATIONAL JAZZ FESTIVAL
Various venues around Birmingham.

July 5-14   LICHFIELD FESTIVAL
Various venues around Lichfield, Staffordshire.

July 8-22   STRATFORD-UPON-AVON FESTIVAL
Town Centre, Stratford, Warwickshire.

August 14-18   3rd INTERNATIONAL GILBERT & SULLIVAN FESTIVAL Buxton
Opera House, Buxton, Derbyshire

August 16-17   SHREWSBURY FLOWER FESTIVAL
Quarry Park, Shrewsbury, Shropshire.

August 16-18   BRITISH OPEN HORSE TRIALS CHAMPIONSHIP
Gatcombe Park, Minchin Hampton, Glos.

August 17-24   THREE CHOIRS FESTIVAL
Worcester Cathedral, Hereford & Worcestershire

September 3   31st ANNIVERSARY OF LAST STEAM TRAIN
G.W.R., Toddington, Glos.

September 11*   ABBOTS BROMLEY HORN DANCE
Abbots Bromley, Staffordshire.

September 14-
October 27   WALSALL ILLUMINATIONS
Walsall Arboretum, Walsall, West Midlands

September 21   DR. JOHNSON BIRTHDAY CELEBRATIONS
Market Square, Lichfield, Staffordshire.

October 7-8   DIVE - THE INTERNTIONAL SUB-AQUA WATERSPORTS SHOW
National Exhibition Centre, Birmingham.

October 11-20   *DAILY TELEGRAPH* CHELTENHAM FESTIVAL OF LITERATURE
Cheltenham Town Hall, Gloucestershire.

October 18-29   INTERNATIONAL BRITSIH MOTOR SHOW
National Exhibition Centre, Birmingham

November 10-12   HORSE RACING, THE MACKESON GOLD CUP
Cheltenham Racecourse, Gloucestershire.

Denotes provisional date

For further information contact:
The Heart of England Tourist Board, Larkhill Road, Worcester WR5 2EF. Tel: 01905 763436.

BIBURY COURT
Bibury, Gloucestershire GL7 5NT

Telephone: 01285 740337   *Fax: 01285 740660*

This gracious mansion started life in 1633, and it has preserved its lovely appearance and peaceful, charming setting in an $8\,{}^{1}/{}_{2}$ acre garden, bordered by the River Coln, to this day. The hotel is run by Anne and Andrew Johnston, and Anne's sister Jane, who give it a welcoming and friendly atmosphere. A most lovely panelled lounge with stone mullion windows leads from the flagstoned hall and the abundant fresh flowers and the attractive and comfortable furnishings make one feel really at home. Continental breakfasts, light lunches and light dinners are served in the oak beamed conservatory. In the evening, you can choose from a wide range of dishes made from only the finest ingredients in the restaurant. Bibury is such a pretty village and there are many beautiful walks from the hotel itself. You can walk down the River Coln to Coln St. Aldwyn, another charming village, in about 45 minutes and of course there are many other places of interest nearby—Bath, Oxford, Cirencester and Stratford-upon-Avon. If you are looking for good food, relaxation in a friendly home, and a warm welcome in a most beautiful part of the Cotswolds, then I highly recommend Bibury Court. Room and breakfast from £57.00 single, £78.00 double. Closed 23rd December-30th December. **Bargain breaks** available - £113 per person, 2 nights/2 dinners. **London 86, Burford 10, Cheltenham 17, Cirencester 7, Kemble Station 10, Stow 14**

F licence, 20 en suite bedrooms (3 single, 17 double/twin, 10 with four-poster beds), direct-dial telephone, hairdryer, colour TV; dogs welcome; small conferences; children welcome; river fishing; golf and watersports eight miles; hunting, shooting, riding, ballooning, aerial Cotswold trips available by arrangement; Amex, Diners, Mastercard and Visa accepted.

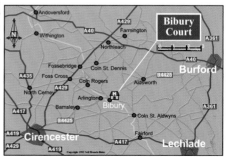

HOTEL ON THE PARK
Evesham Road, Cheltenham, Gloucestershire GL52 2AX

Telephone: 01242 518898   Fax: 01242 511526

At last, Cheltenham has an exclusive town house hotel. On the Park has been lovingly and caringly restored and refurbished by its enthusiastic owner, Darryl Gregory, who made me feel most welcome. Situated on the A435 Evesham road, just in Cheltenham (less than $^1/_2$ a mile from the main entrance to the famous Cheltenham Racecourse), and opposite Pittville Park, this elegant Regency house offers excellent accommodation in a very homely atmosphere. The bedrooms are beautifully appointed, and all have the most luxurious bathrooms, antique furniture, paintings and every little comfort required by today's guest. Darryl and Lesley-Anne have just added a superb extension to their hotel, which is equally elegant and blends in so well with the existing building. This includes four new bedrooms of which three are suites, a library, a reception area and cloakrooms. The restaurant is an important feature of this hotel. It is a very stylish room with a most unusual décor and lots of fresh flowers. Dinner was excellent and beautifully presented, and there is a selection of wines to complement every meal. On the Park was a very happy experience and I look forward to returning. Cheltenham is a splendid town, and whether you are on business, exploring the Cotswolds, a racing fanatic,

or you just feel like spoiling yourself, then I highly recommend this lovely hotel. Single room and continental breakfast £74.50, double room from £97.00. **Bargain breaks:** 2 nights / 2 people sharing, dinner, bed & breakfast from £64.25 per person per night. **London 96, Stratford-upon-Avon 30, Birmingham 49, M5 2, Bath 56.** *R & R licence; 12 en suite bedrooms (including 3 suites), all with direct dial telephone and TV, room service, last orders for dinner 9.30p.m.; special diets; children over 8 years welcome; dogs by arrangement; golf and riding two miles; tennis one mile; all major credit cards accepted.*

TUDOR FARMHOUSE HOTEL
Clearwell, Nr. Coleford, Gloucestershire GL16 8JS

Telephone: 01594 833046   *Fax: 01594 837093*

What a wonderful find! Nestling in the small village of Clearwell, almost touching the border of Wales, is the Tudor Farmhouse Hotel. It is a haven of warmth and charm, where you can be sure to find a friendly welcome from Richard and Deborah Fletcher. Whether you are looking to relax for a few days, are on business, or simply want to tour this wonderful area, the Tudor Farmhouse is a must. The cuisine at the hotel is outstanding, with two menus to choose from, and a good wine list to complement all dishes. The night I stayed, I enjoyed an excellent dinner of local salmon and scallops, with an abundance of fresh vegetables. You will certainly not leave the table feeling hungry, I promise! The actual house was built in the 13th century, and features oak beams and original wall panelling, and a large roughstone fireplace roars in the lounge in winter months. Some of the bedrooms are reached by an original oak spiral staircase, and they have all been refurbished to an extremely high standard, including two beautiful four-poster rooms. The other bedrooms are located in cider makers' cottages and barns, which are quietly situated in the garden and are suitable as family rooms. Clearwell Caves are just a few hundred yards away, and are definitely worth a visit . There is also a Midsummer and Halloween Ball held there, so why not make a weekend of it? But do make sure to book early so you don't miss out. Room and breakfast from £45 single/ £50 double; corporate business rate from £57.50 single, to include dinner, bed and breakfast and VAT.

London 125, Birmingham 55, Cardiff 50

R & R licence; 10 bedrooms (3 for the disabled), six with en suite bath and four with en suite shower, all with direct dial telephone and TV; baby listening; last orders for dinner 9.00 p.m.; children welcome; dogs accepted; mountain bikes, canoeing, abseiling, rock climbing and riding all by arrangement nearby; two golf courses within two miles; hotel open all year; all major credit cards except Diners accepted.

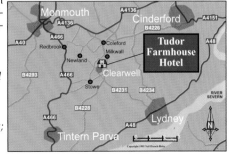

MANOR HOUSE HOTEL
Moreton-in-Marsh, Gloucestershire GL56 OLJ

Telephone: 01608 650501   Fax: 01608 651481

Here, in Moreton-in-Marsh, you will find a large Cotswold stone house which is steeped in history. The Manor House was originally built around 1545 and retains many of the 16th century features, such as a priest's hiding hole and a secret passage. Recently the majority of the bedrooms have been upgraded and totally redecorated to a high standard. They combine old world charm with all modern amenities. The small cosy bar looks over the well kept garden which was part re-modelled and planted in 1984 by Charlotte Evans. The restaurant offers both a fixed price and an à la carte menu. The cuisine is a combination of traditional and modern cooking, providing an excellent choice. Guests can enjoy good quality fresh produce that is supplemented by a wide variety of wines. The hotel has a custom built conference centre where the facilities do not interfere with the services of the other guests. For the more energetic, the swimmmg pool complex is a popular place. A relaxed atmosphere pervades the hotel, enhanced by the welcoming sight of log fires in the lounges. Duncan Williams and his staff do all they can to make sure your stay will be a memorable occasion. The Manor makes an excellent place to stay whilst visiting all the Cotswold villages and surrounding countryside.

Single room from £67, double from £87 including VAT and English breakfast. **Bargain breaks:** Two night stay £110 pp, dinner, b&b, weekend; £95 midweek. **Broadway 8, Bourton-on-the-Water 8, Stratford-upon-Avon 17, Cheltenham 22, Oxford 27, Birmingham NEC 30, London 90.**

F licence; 39 en suite bedrooms (4 with four posters), all with direct dial telephone and TV; room service; baby listening; night service; lift; last orders 9.30 p m; bar meals (lunch only), special diets; children welcome; conferences 70 max; indoor heated swimming pool; sauna; spa pool; golf 8 miles; open all year; all major credit cards accepted.

ORCHARD HOUSE
Aston Ingham Road, Kilcot, Nr. Newent, Glos. GL18 1NP
Telephone: 01989 720417

For those who enjoy peace and quiet, good food and wine, elegant surroundings and a picturesque area for exploration, Orchard House is the ideal venue. Wales, the Cotswolds, the Brecon Beacons and many historic towns are close by and guide books and maps are thoughtfully provided by your delightful hosts, Anne and Basil Thompson. A very warm welcome is extended to their visitors and an eye for detail, from the beamed lounge to the spacious dining-room, ensures a comfortable and relaxing holiday. The luxury bedrooms overlooking the garden are very comfortable, finely appointed and with well chosen and attractive fabrics. Returning guests testify to Anne's superb and original home cooking using only the best and freshest ingredients. Dinner is three courses, very reasonably priced and served in dinner party style with a well-chosen wine list to complement the menus. Five acres of grounds include well-stocked and lovingly tended gardens with a large conservatory overlooking the croquet lawn and fountain. Conveniently situated near to junction 3 of the M50 on the Aston Ingham road, Orchard House is the perfect place to unwind and relax away from the rigours of modern life. Double room rate including breakfast from £22.50.

Leisure Breaks: 1 or 2 nights from £22.50 pp b&b. 3 or more nights from £19.50 pp b&b.

Ross-on-Wye 9 , Cheltenham 20, Gloucester 9, Hereford 19 , Ledbury 8 , London 113.

R licence. 4 beautiful twin/double bedrooms of which two are en suite. Hairdryer, tea/coffee making facilities. Dinner at 20hrs. TV room. Croquet, fishing, clay pigeon shooting all in area; superb walking country. Ample parking. Visa and Mastercard accepted.

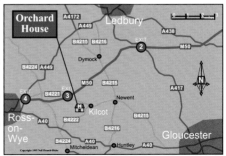

STONEHOUSE COURT HOTEL
Stonehouse, Gloucestershire GL10 3RA

Telephone: 01453 825155   Fax: 01453 824611

Privately owned until 1975, the 17th Century, mullion windowed Stonehouse Court is a superb Grade II listed manor wonderfully transformed into a modern hotel. Situated just outside the village of Stonehouse it is a premier location for local and more distant business visitors, with conference facilities second to none. The Caroline Suite is the venue for large occasions whilst the Crellin Room, once the library, can be used for smaller functions. A fully equipped business centre is also available . Bedrooms, which include a four poster suite, are all individually decorated and well stocked with luxuries for the comfort of guests. The views over Stroud Water and the rolling Gloucestershire countryside are outstanding. The fireplaces are a striking feature of the hotel especially the very fine carved example in the beautiful and spacious panelled lounge. The John Henry Restaurant, also panelled, enjoys a well deserved reputation for English cuisine, beautifully presented - and I can understand why rosettes have been awarded. Six acres of mature gardens include a pond with enormous carp and a croquet lawn. Slimbridge Wildlife Trust is close by. Golf is played at Stinchcombe Hill, fishing is on the River Stour and Regency Cheltenham is a few miles away for theatre and shopping. Altogether the hotel is a perfect venue for business or pleasure. Single room including breakfast from £55.00 Double room with breakfast from £80.00.

Leisure Breaks: From£55.00 d,b&b pppn. **Slimbridge Wildfowl Trust 9 miles, Berkeley Castle 10, Cheltenham 16, Bath 30, London 54.** *Full licence. 36 en suite bedrooms with colour TV, radio, direct-dial telephone; hairdryer, trouser press, laundry service, safety deposit box, tea/coffee making facilities. Last orders for dinner 21.45. Special diets available. Jogging track; Fishing nearby. Golf 9 miles. Watersports, riding, squash, tennis - all 5 miles. Full business services with 5 meeting rooms to total capacity of 150. Car parking for 200 cars. Open all year. Major credit cards accepted.*

THE GRAPEVINE HOTEL
Sheep Street, Stow-on-the-Wold, Gloucestershire GL54 1AU

Telephone: 01451 830344   *Fax: 01451 832278*

This award-winning gem of a hotel is set in the centre of Stow-on-the-Wold, renowned for its antique shops and galleries, mellow Cotswold stone houses and its wonderful position in the rolling hills of the Cotswolds. Much of the Grapevine's undoubted success lies with the staff, a loyal and happy team superbly led by Sandra (Sam) Elliott, attractive and energetic owner of the hotel. Bedrooms are beautifully decorated, some in the lovely old 17th Century building, others across the courtyard in the garden rooms. All have every modern facility and are well appointed and comfortable. I enjoyed a superbly presented dinner in the relaxed atmosphere of the romantic conservatory restaurant which is crowned by a magnificent historic vine. Excellent and inexpensive bar snacks are available in the characterful Gigot bar. The staff alone would guarantee a wonderful stay at the Grapevine and coupled with realistic prices, I can highly recommend it. Single room including breakfast from £77.00; double room from £114.00. **Leisure Breaks** are available for any two nights; d,b&b from £47.00 pppn on the basis of two people sharing a twin/double room.

Moreton-in-the-Marsh 5, Cheltenham 18, Cirencester 18, Oxford 23, Birmingham Airport 40, London Heathrow 80, London 84.

Full licence. 21 en suite bedrooms with colour TV; direct-dial telephone; hair-dryer; laundry/valet service; tea/coffee-making facilities. Room service until 23.30. Last orders for dinner 21.30. Golf by arrangement. Riding, clay-shooting and tennis in area; jogging track. One meeting room with capacity for 30 (+ boardroom 20). Full secretarial and AV services. Parking 23 cars. Car rental can be arranged. Safe deposit in reception. Closed 2 weeks in January. All major credit cards accepted.

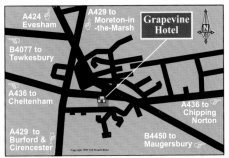

HARE AND HOUNDS
Westonbirt, Nr. Tetbury, Gloucestershire GL8 8QL

Telephone: 01666 880Z33   *Fax: 01666 880241*

This most attractive Cotswold stone Country House has been owned by the Price family for over forty years, and the two brothers, Martin and Jeremy, now run the hotel. The house, set in ten acres of garden and woodland, stands well back from the A433 which runs from the A40 near Burford towards Bath and Bristol. There are beautiful fresh flowers everywhere, which add a lovely personal touch to this elegant hotel. The spacious lounges are comfortable and relaxing, with views of the garden, and in the winter there are welcoming log fires as well as full central heating. The bedrooms are attractive and well furnished, with some particularly pleasant rooms in the adjacent garden cottage, including two on the ground floor. The restaurant offers daily menus with a good choice of varied and original dishes as well as à la carte. There is also Jack Hare's bar which serves excellent hot and cold food at lunchtime and evenings. Remember Westonbirt is the site of Britain's most famous arboretum and one of the country's best-known girls' schools, as well as the Hare & Hounds ! Single room from £58.00, doubles from £80.00. Dinner from £17.75. Always open. The family also owns the Amberley Inn, just a few miles away. Member of Best Western Hotels. **Bargain breaks:** 2 nights inc d,b&b Ist Nov '95-30 April '96 and 96/97 £102 pp; 1 May-31 Oct from £115.

London 100, Bath 19, Birmingham 78, Bristol 25, Cheltenham 26, Cirencester 13, Gloucester 22, Severn Wild Fowl Trust 15.

F licence; 30 en suite bedrooms, all with colour TV, radio and direct dial telephone; tennis; squash; snooker; croquet in summer; table tennis; golf one mile; children welcome; dogs welcome; drying room; conference rooms; large garden; snacks; diets.

THE SNOOTY FOX
Market Place, Tetbury, Gloucestershire GL8 8DD
Telephone: 01666 502436   Fax: 01666 503479

This 16th Century former coaching inn is situated at the heart of the ancient market town of Tetbury. Following a meticulous restoration programme it is now a most comfortable hotel with a strong feeling of a bygone age and the perfect base from which to explore the Cotswolds. There are 12 bedrooms, all delightfully furnished with English chintz and antiques. Toiletries, fresh fruit and home made biscuits are also supplied and you will find all the other facilities which go to provide for the highest standards of comfort. The rooms are quiet and on the hot day I visited, all were pleasantly cool on account of the thickness of the walls. The refurbished ground floor provides an attractive panelled public bar where light meals can be taken, a no-smoking lounge and a residents' and diners' lounge which also offer the use of the in-house board games. When you stay at The Snooty Fox the "must" is to dine in the oak-panelled restaurant with its mahogany tables, fresh flowers, portraits and superb menus devised by Stephen Woodcock. His inspired interpretation of British and French cuisine leads him to create meals for the modern palate which evoke memories of times past. A stay at The Snooty Fox is a guarantee of the finest hospitality in the most attractive surroundings. Single room including breakfast from £65.00. Double room with breakfast from £80.00.

Leisure Breaks: 2-night Scenechanger Break from £115.00 per couple per night; includes English breakfast, daily newspaper & residents' dinner. **Bath 23 , Bristol 26 , Cheltenham 24 , Gloucester 19 , Cirencester 10 , London 96.**

Full licence. 12 en suite bedrooms with TV and video; direct-dial telephone, hairdryer, laundry service, trouser press; tea/coffee making facilities. Fishing, golf, riding, tennis, watersports - all 8-10 miles. Squash nearby. Meeting room for up to 12 guests. Open all year. All major credit cards accepted.

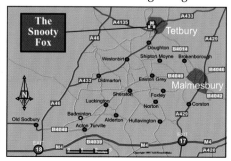

HATTON COURT HOTEL
Upton Hill, Upton St. Leonards, Gloucester, GL4 8DE

Telephone: 01452 617412 *Fax: 01452 612945*

This ivy-clad manor house with beautifully maintained gardens enjoys spectacular views across the Severn valley to the Malvern Hills and also relishes being de-luxe, for the pursuit of excellence is carried to great lengths here. The original 17th century building houses some bedrooms and the public rooms whilst the remaining bedrooms are nearby. All are individually decorated, offering a range of toiletries, bathrobes, fresh fruit and biscuits. Some have jacuzzis, all are home to a family of rubber ducks! The day rooms are comfortably furnished whilst open log fires and the oak panelled bar provide that added bonus of welcoming warmth. My thoughts turned to dining and I was not disappointed. The chef has a deserved name for serving the best of traditional cuisine created from fresh local produce. The setting is superb either by candlelight - or with those views by daylight. Later, guests may need to use sauna or exercise bike in the hotel's relaxation centre; an outdoor pool is also available. Another unusual feature is the acquisition of a wedding licence. It is an elegant venue for such even's and there are few places where you will be assured of such high standards and so frie idly a staff. Single room including breakfast from £88.00; double room with breakfast from £1 J0.00. **Leisure Breaks**: Two nights Scenechanger Break from £130.00 per couple per night, includes English breakfast, daily newspaper, residents' dinner. **Gloucester 3, Bristol 36, Cheltenham 10, Birmingham 52, London 106.**

Full licence. 45 en suite bedrooms with radio, TV with video films, direct-dial telephone, hairdryer, trouser press, laundry service, tea/coffee making facilities non-smoker bedrooms, 24-hour room service. Last orders for dinner 22.00 hrs. Fishing, watersports, shooting - 15/20 miles; golf, riding, squash, tennis - 5 miles. Croquet lawn, outdoor swimming pool. 6 meeting rooms with 60 guest capacity. Secretarial services. Car parking for 70 cars. Open all year. All major credit cards accepted.

BEAUMONT HOUSE HOTEL

Shurdington Road,
Cheltenham,
Gloucestershire GL53
OJE

Telephone: 01242 245986
Fax: 01242 520044
ETB ⌒⌒⌒ Commended

What a pleasure to find such a delightful hotel with such pleasant owners. This elegant Victorian edge-of-town hotel is ideally situated for those wishing to enjoy the delights of Cheltenham and the freedom of the Cotswolds. Many of the rooms have views of the Cotswold Hills and are furnished in a gentle, relaxing style which complements the light, friendly atmosphere. Cheltenham, well known for its gardens, parks, trees and splendid Regency architecture is home each year to a variety of musical, sporting and cultural festivals. Most of the treasures and secrets of the Cotswolds are within a 30-minute drive. Single from £24; double £38; twin £45; four-poster double £55.

R & R licence, 14 en suite bedrooms (some with four-poster beds), all with telephone, radio, hairdryer, tea/coffee making facilities, colour TV + satellite, full central heating throughout; baby listening; last orders for dinner 8 pm; no dogs; private parking; Amex, Mastercard & Visa accepted.

EDGEWOOD HOUSE

Churcham,
Gloucester, Glouces-
tershire GL2 8AA

Telephone: 01452 245986

Edgewood House is situated in Churcham, four miles from Gloucester and well placed for touring the Cotswolds, Malverns, Forest of Dean and many other places of interest. There are double, single and family rooms, all attractively decorated and mainly en suite. All have washbasins, shaver points and drinks trays. A spacious dining room and lounge with colour TV is provided for the comfort of guests. There is ample parking and two acres of garden and several excellent eating places nearby. Your hosts, Penny and Steve Stevens, will make you very comfortable in their charming home. Bed and breakfast £18.50 single; £19.50 double.

Family, double and single rooms, most en suite with tea/coffee making facilities; children over five welcome; sorry - no smoking or pets; open all year.

PRINCE OF WALES HOTEL
Berkeley Road, Berkeley, Gloucestershire GL13 9HD

Telephone: 01453 81047;
Fax: 01453 511370

The Prince of Wales hotel is conveniently located on the A38 between junctions 13 and 14 of the M5, in the heart of the Cotswolds, convenient for business people and holiday makers alike. Excellent conference facilities are offered with three differently sized suites: The Berkeley Suite accommodating 60 boardroom-style or 200 theatre-style; The Castle Suite 30 boardroom or 60 theatre-style and the Dursley 14 boardroom or 25 theatre-style. The hotel was recently expanded and refurbished to a high standard. A pretty restaurant offers varied and sensibly priced menus with bar meals available. Weekend breaks £22.50 per person per night sharing twin/£26 pppn single.
41 bedrooms, en suite; 14 twin, 9 single, 18 double from £39.00 per night (breakfast extra). Family rooms and bridal suite available. Lunch from £1.65 per head; dinner from 1900-2130 from £3.95 per head. TV, direct dial telephone, hairdryer, tea/coffee making facilities, ample parking.

CORSE LAWN HOUSE HOTEL
Corse Lawn, Nr. Tirley, Gloucestershire GL19 4LZ

Telephone: 01452 780771;
Fax: 01452 780840

In an attractive setting on the village green, the Corse Lawn House Hotel is an elegant Queen Anne building set in 12 acres of gardens and fields. It has been owned by the Hine family (of Cognac fame) for nearly 20 years and in that time has been extensively refurbished. Dining either in the restaurant or bistro; three drawing rooms, lounge bar, two conference rooms. Bed and breakfast from £65 (single); £72.50 (double). Short breaks available one night £130 per couple inc dinner, bed and breakfast; more than one night £115 per couple (exc. Cheltenham Race Week and Christmas/New Year).

19 en suite bedrooms, with colour TV, direct dial telephone, tea/coffee making facilities. Heated outdoor swimming pool, croquet lawn, tennis court. Golf, fishing and riding can be arranged locally. Conference room up to 40 persons.

THE SWAN AT HAY HOTEL
Church Street, Hay-on-Wye, Hereford HR3 5DQ

Telephone: 01497 821188   Fax: 01497 821424

Built round the old coaching yard this charming hotel in Hay-on-Wye is personally run by Rosemary and Colin Vaughan and their son Mark. The Swan's popularity is confirmed by many guests returning year after year. Well situated on the Welsh border, the hotel is ideally placed for excursions to view the Mappa Mundi at Hereford, the crystal factory at Rhayder, Blaenavon's Big Pit or the spectacular dams in the Elan Valley. There is also excellent local fishing on the Wye. Hay itself is a charming medieval town, famous for antique shops and antiquarian book shops which have won it the name of "the town of books". A stroll in the spacious flower garden of the hotel where you can enjoy a pre-dinner apéritif is a joy. The Cygnet restaurant offers à la carte menus beautifully cooked using fresh local ingredients. Bar meals are served in the Mallard Room, or you can join the locals in Drakes Bar. There are eighteen comfortable bedrooms with colour TV and all are individually furnished with some having special touches such as canopied beds. It is a pleasure to return to this friendly hotel after a day of exploring the wonderful surrounding area. Single room including breakfast from £45.00. Double room with breakfast from £60.00.
Leisure Breaks: Swan Special Breaks - £48.00 pppn incl. à la carte dinner, bed and breakfast.

Brecon16 , Hereford 21, Birmingham 51 , Cardiff 56 , London 154 .
Full licence. 18 en suite bedrooms with radio, colour TV, direct dial telephone. Hairdryer, trouser press, laundry service, tea/coffee making facilities, safety deposit box. Last orders for dinner 21.30 hrs. Special diets available. Billiards/snooker. Fishing, golf, watersports, shooting, massage - by arrangement nearby. Ballooning by arrangement 25 miles. Full business services include three conference rooms with total capacity for 160 guests. Car parking. Open all year. All credit cards accepted.

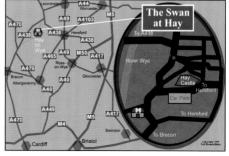

FOWNES HOTEL
City Walls Road, Worcester WR1 2AP

Telephone: 01905 613151   Fax: 01905 23742

If you are looking for the unusual you should visit Fownes Hotel which is a successful conversion from glove factory to elegant town house hotel in the centre of Worcester. The splendid proportions of the rooms have been retained and from the sumptuous marble in the large foyer to a sophisticated cocktail bar, all furnishings and fittings are of the highest quality. The bedrooms too are spacious and generously furnished with restful colour schemes complemented by luxurious en suite bathrooms and spa baths in the suites. Lovely sepia photographs show the hotel's original function and Spy prints adorn the attractive dining room. In it's award winning restaurant the hotel can be proud of excellent menus with a leaning to traditional English cooking. Royal Worcester bone china is on display in the tranquil library, where the collection can be viewed from deep green leather chairs in what is one of the most stylish rooms in an already very special hotel. The Fownes is situated near to a canal side walk and close to the city centre and cathedral. Single room with breakfast from £82.50. Double

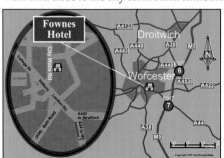

room including breakfast from £100.00. **Weekend breaks** all year from £37.50 pppn - dinner, bed & breakfast. **Evesham 16, Hereford 25, Bristol 61, Birmingham 26, London 114**

Full licence. 61 en suite bedrooms with radio & satellite TV. Direct-dial telephone. Hairdryer, trouser press, laundry service; non-smoker bedrooms, tea/ coffee making facilities. 24-hour room/meal service. Facilities for the disabled. Last orders for dinner 21.30 hrs. Special diets available. Full business services provided and 3 meeting rooms - capacity 175 guests. AV equipment available. Car rental. Car parking for 100 cars. Open all year. All credit cards accepted.

HAWKSTONE PARK HOTEL
Weston-under-Redcastle, Shrewsbury, Shropshire SY4 5UY

Telephone: 01939 200611   Fax: 01939 200311

For many years within these pages, Hawkstone Park has been described as a "golfer's and walker's paradise", and now has a great deal more on offer. The hotel's Grade 1 "walking centre" known as the Historic Park and Follies has already been host to over 5,500 visitors a month since its opening in April 1993. This attraction includes a gift shop, tea room, classroom and interpretation centre. Fascinating walks can be taken through the labyrinth of pathways containing antiquities and follies built in the 18th century. The mature "Hawkstone" golf course is set within this unique landscape, and the hotel's famous parkland now has a New Golf Centre, complete with extensive golf and leisure shop, hi-tech golf video training room, reception and changing facilities. Here, you will also find the Terrace Restaurant which offers grills and snacks all day, with balconies and terraces overlooking the golf courses and 13th century Redcastle. A Practice Range has been added to the complex together with an Academy course. Amidst this splendid scenic back-drop and with quiet efficiency, Hawkstone Park also accommodates business meetings and conferences for up to 200 delegates. For guests seeking total relaxation, a very warm and sincere atmosphere abounds and you will always be well looked after. The hotel's superb English cuisine is complemented by a competitively priced wine list. Bed and breakfast from £50.00. **"Breaks with Tradition"** from £48 pppn. 3-night Christmas & New Year Break from £225 pp. Golf Breaks - night, dinner, golf from £45 pppn. **Shrewsbury 14, Birmingham 50, Manchester 55, Chester 28, London 160.**

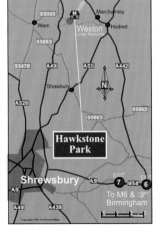

F licence, 65 en suite bedrooms (2 suites), all with every facility; dinner to 21.45; children welcome, conferences; billiards; croquet; Two Championship 18-hole golf courses, practice range, 6 hole par 3 Academy; course & golf centre with video room & golf shop, Shropshire's only English Heritage designated Grade 1 landscape - (Park with walks aad follies open 1st April-31st Oct.); helipad; clay shooting by prior arrangement; open all year; major credit cards accepted.

NUTHURST GRANGE
Hockley Heath, Warwickshire B94 5NL
Telephone: 01564 783972　　　　Fax: 01564 783919

Nuthurst Grange is found just off the A3400, between Birmingham and Stratford-upon-Avon, and is idyllically situated in $7^1/_2$ acres of well kept gardens. David Randolph and his wife Darryl bought Nuthurst as a private house, converted it into an hotel, and have built themselves an excellent reputation, not only as hoteliers, but restaurateurs as well. The food is imaginative and well presented and connoisseurs of gourmet cuisine will appreciate the large range of culinary treats, supported by a superb wine list. David and his team of chefs make sure only fresh, seasonal produce is used, and he makes a point of personally going to the markets. All the bedrooms are well proportioned and have views overlooking the garden and countryside. Each one is exquisitely furnished and provides you with all possible comforts, including the added personal touch of a fruit bowl, homemade biscuits and chocolates. Nuthurst Grange is the ideal place for business meetings as it is well placed at the heart of England's motorway network, and is also close to the International Airport and railway stations and the National Exhibition Centre. So whether on business or pleasure, treat yourself to some gracious living and self-indulgent luxury. Single room and continental

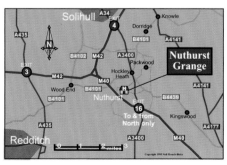

breakfast from £95.00, double from £115.00, all inc. VAT. **Weekend breaks** from £155 per person for two nights inc. dinner, bed,breakfast & VAT. **N.E.C. 8, Birmingham 11, Birmingham Int. Airport 8, Warwick 11, Coventry 15, Stratford-upon-Avon 13, London 104.**
R & R licence; 15 en suite bedrooms, all with spa baths, direct dial telephone, TV, hairdryer and trouser press; room service; night servce until 1.00 a.m.; last orders for dinner 9.30 p.m.; special diets; children welcome; conferences, classroom style max. 40 and theatre style max. 80; croquet, helipad; open all year; all major credit cards accepted.

BILLESLEY MANOR
Alcester, Nr. Stratford-upon-Avon, Warwickshire B49 6NF

Telephone: 01789 279955   Fax: 01789 764145

Billesley Manor is situated just off the A46 in the heart of England and it would be difficult to find a more agreeable place in the midst of Shakespeare country. Here you will come across the old blending with the new. There is a large oak panelled bar with a carved fireplace, usually burning logs in the winter months. The dining room is also panelled and I thoroughly enjoyed the Sunday table d'hôte lunch which was very well priced. The award winning restaurant which has received 3 AA Rosettes, has a good selection of wines which complement the excellence of its cuisine and service. All the public rooms are lavishly furnished and the bedrooms are all of the highest quality. Sixteen of these have been totally upgraded to a very high standard and all of these rooms overlook the well kept topiary which is a feature of the 11 acres of peaceful garden. Petra Billson, General Manager, oversees her friendly staff well and you can be assured of a warm welcome. The hotel is an ideal base for visiting the Royal Shakespeare Theatre and the many other historical sites that Warwickshire has to offer. However, if it is a quiet time you are looking for, Billesley is a perfect retreat for total relaxation. Twin or double room from £152.00 including VAT. **Weekend breaks** min. 2 nights £97 to end March '96; from 1st April £100, dinner, bed & breakfast or £76 b & b only. Open all year. **Stratford-upon-Avon 4, Birmingham 23, Oxford 40, London 95.**

F licence, 41 en suite bedrooms (9 ground floor), all with direct dial telephone and colour TV, full central heating; night service; last orders 9.30p.m.; diets; children welcome; baby listening by arrangement; conferences; large indoor heated swimming pool; tennis; croquet; pitch & putt; riding/shooting/ fishing by arrangement; Amex, Visa, Diners and Mastercard accepted.

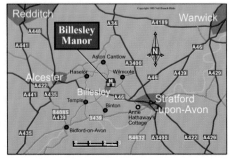

ASQUITH HOUSE HOTEL & RESTAURANT
19 Portland Road, Edgbaston, Birmingham B16 9HN

Telephone 0121 454 5282   *Fax 0121 456 4668*

What a surprise to discover this "Country House" hotel near Birmingham City Centre. Owned and run by Margaret Gittens, the ivy-clad house stands in lovely gardens in a pleasant part of Edgbaston. As a listed building, the mid-Victorian home is of architectural interest and much care has been taken in its restoration and decoration. Liberty wallpaper, Persian rugs, oil paintings, engravings, water colours and fresh flowers co-exist to make a delightful treasure-trove of a place. Bedrooms are all en suite , luxuriously furnished with colours and fabrics carefully co-ordinated. The best of fare is offered with constantly changing gourmet menus and a good wine list. Being so near to the City Centre, the hotel is ideal for mini-conferences, business meetings, and a must for private parties where guests can make use of the secluded gardens at the rear. The ICC is walking distance and the NEC a short drive away as are motorway exits and the City's excellent shopping. When you are in Birmingham, on business or pleasure, try The Asquith House Hotel which combines the relaxed atmosphere of a private

home with friendly and most efficient service. I know you will love it as I did. Single room with breakfast from £51. Double room inc. breakfast from £67.**Leisure Breaks:** Double room £48.00 Single rooms £38.00. Enquire for further details. **Birmingham City Centre 2, Stratford-upon-Avon 24 , Warwick 21 , Coventry 18, London 111.** *F licence. 11 en suite bedrooms with radio, colour TV, direct-dial telephone; hairdryer, trouser press, tea/ coffee making facilities. Last orders for dinner 21.00 hrs. Special diets available. 2 meeting rooms. AV equipment available. Car parking for 10 cars. Closed Christmas. Access, Mastercard, Amex accepted.*

■ **Historic Houses, Gardens & Parks**

CHESHIRE
Arley Hall & Gardens, Nr. Great Budworth
Bridgemere Garden World, Nr. Nantwich
Brookside Garden Centre, Poynton
Cholmondeley Castle Gardens
Dunham Massey, Nr. Altrincham
Gawsworth Hall Nr. Macclesfield
Little Moreton Hall, Nr. Nantwich
Ness Gardens Neston
Stapeley Water Gardens, Nantwich
Tatton Park, Knutsford

CUMBRIA
Acorn Bank Garden, Nr. Temple Sowerby
Brantwood House, Coniston
Dalemain Historic House & Gardens, Nr. Pooley Bridge
Graythwaite Hall Gardens, Newby Bridge
Holker Hall & Gardens, Cark-in-Cartmel
Hutton-in-the-Forest, 6 miles from Penrith
Larch Cottage Nurseries, Melkinthorpe
Levens Hall & Topiary Garden, Nr. Kendal
Lingholme Gardens, Linghholme, Keswick
Mirehouse, Underskiddaw
Sizergh Castle, Nr. Kendal

LANCASHIRE
All in One Garden Centre, Middleston
Astley Hall & Park, Nr. Chorley
Catforth Gardens & Nursery, Nr Preston
Gawthorpe Hall, Burley
Leighton Hall, Carnforth
Rufford Old Hall, Ormskirk
Williamson Park, Lancaster

MERSEYSIDE
Croxteth Hall & Country Park, Nr. Liverpool
Speke Hall, Liverpool

■**Walks & Nature Trails**

CHESHIRE
Jodrell Bank Science Ctre & Arboretum, Nr. Holmes Chapel
Styal Country Park
Walk the Walls, Chester
Wirral Peninsula

CUMBRIA
Cark to Cartmel Village
Dodd Wood
Dunnerdale Forest Nature Trail
Grange-over-Sands to Hampsfell
Grizedale Forest Park Visitor Centre, Hawkshead
Numerous fell walks and trails throughout Cumbria
Ulverston Town Trail

LANCASHIRE
Carnforth Canal Circuit, from Camforth Railway
  to Bolton-le-Sands
Pendle Way Walk at Pendle Heritage Centre, Nelson
The Weaver's Shuttle, around Pendle

■ **Historical Sites & Museums**
CHESHIRE
The Boat Museum, Ellesmere Port
Chester Cathedral
Experience Catalyst, Widnes
Macclesfield Silk Museum
Peckforton Castle, Nr. Tarporley
Quarry Bank Mill, Styal

CUMBRIA
Abbot Hall Art Gallery, Kendal
Appleby Castle, Appleby-in-Westmoreland
Birdoswald Roman Fort, Brampton
Brough Castle, Kirkby Stephen
Brougham Castle, Nr. Penrith
Carlisle Castle
Cartmel Priory
The Cumberland Pencil Museum & Exhibition Centre, Keswick
Dove Cottage, Grasmere
Furness Abbey, Barrow-in-Furness
Heron Corn Mill & Museum of Papermaking, Milnthorpe
Laurel & Hardy Museum, Ulverston
Museum of Natural History, Kendal
Penrith Museum
Rydal Mount, Nr. Ambleside
Stott Park Bobbin Mill, Newby Lake
Wordsworth Museum, Grasmere

GREATER MANCHESTER
Castlefield Urban Heritage Park, Manchester
Manchester Cathedral
Manchester United Football Museum
Museum of Science & Industry, Manchester

LANCASHIRE
Lancaster Castle, Lancaster

MERSEYSIDE
Liverpool Museum
Merseyside Maritime Museum, Albert Dock, Liverpool
Museum of Liverpool Life, Pier Head
Pilkington Glass Museum, St Helens

■ **Entertainment Venues**

CHESHIRE
Cheshire Candle Workshops, Burwardsley
Chester Zoo, Upton-by-Chester
Gulliver's World, Warrington
Port Sunlight Visitor Centre, Wirral
Wetlands & Wildfowl Trust Centre, Martin Mere

CUMBRIA
Cumbria Crystal, Ulverston
Fell Foot Park, Newby Bridge
Lake District National Park Visitor Centre, Windermere
Lakeland Bird of Prey Centre, Lowther
Ravenglass & Eskdale Railway, Ravenglass
Sellafield Visitors' Centre
South Lakes Wild Animal Park, Dalton-in-Furness
Ullswater Cruises
Webb's Garden Centre, Kendal
Windermere Lake Cruises
World of Beatrix Potter, Bowness-on-Windermere

GREATER MANCHESTER/LANCASHIRE
Alexandra Craft Centre, Saddleworth
Blackpool Tower & Pleasure Beach
Butterfly World, Bolton
Camelot Theme Park, Chorley
Frontierland, Morecambe Bay
Granada Studio Tours, Manchster
Lakeland Wildlife Oasis, Nr. Camforth
Life Centre, Blackpool
Noel Edmonds' World of Crinkley Bottom, Morecambe Sea

MERSEYSIDE
The Beatles Story, Albert Dock, Liverpool
Knowsley Safari Park, Prescot
Pleasureland Amusement Park, Southport
The Tate Gallery at the Albert Dock, Liverpool

February 4-9	WORDSWORTH WINTER SCHOOL
	The Wordsworth Trust, Dove Cottage, Grasmere, Cumbria.
February 23-25	BOOK COLLECTORS' WEEKEND
	The Wordsworth Trust, Dove Cottage, Grasmere, Cumbria.
February 25	HORSE RACING
	The Greenall Gold Cup - Victor Ludorum Hurdle. Haydock Park Racecourse, Newton-le-Willows, Merseyside.
March 29-31	HORSE RACING, GRAND NATIONAL MEETING
	Aintree Racecourse, Liverpool.
April 26-May 12	NORTH PENNINES SPRING FESTIVAL
	Various locations in the North Pennines, Allendale, Cumbria
May 9-11	HORSE RACING
	Chester Racecourse, Chester, Cheshire. May 9 - Chester Vase. May 10
-	Chester Cup. May 11 - The Ormonde Stakes.
May 11-14	REVELRY FLOWERS IN HOGHTON TOWER
	Hoghton Tower, Hoghton, Lancashire. Flower exhibitions/competitions, and craft stalls.
May 17-19	THE KESWICK JAZZ FESTIVAL
	Keswick, Cumbria.
*May 24/27/29	CARTMEL STEEPLECHASES
	Cartmel Racecourse, Cumbria.
May 25-27	THE LIVERPOOL SHOW
	Wavertree Playground, Liverpool
May 26-27	WIRRAL COUNTRYSIDE FAIR
	Wirral Country Park, Wallasey, Merseyside
May 24 -June 2	CONISTON WATER FESTIVAL
	Coniston Water, Cumbria.
May 31-June 2	GREAT GARDEN & COUNTRYSfDE FESTIVAL
	Holker Hall & Gardens, Cark-in-Cartmel, Grange-over-Sands, Cumbria
June 6-12	APPLEBY HORSE FAIR
	(Selling Day is on final day). Appleby-in-Westmorland, Cumbria.
June 15	COCKERMOUTH CARNIVAL
	Cockermouth, Cumbria
June 17-18	WEEKEND FOR PEOPLE WITH DISABILITIES
	Museum of Transport Manchester, Boyle Street, Cheetham, Manchester. An opening of the museum for people with disabilities. Extra guides available and free vintage bus rides.
June 18	KESWICK CARNIVAL
	Keswick, Cumbria.
June 18-19	CHESHIRE COUNTY SHOW 1996
	The Showground, Tabley, Cheshire.
June 29	WARCOP RUSHBEARING
	Warcop, Appleby-in-Westmorlamd, Cumbria. Ancient children's flower festival.
July 1	AMBLESIDE RUSE BEAPING
	Ambleside, Cumbria.
July 1-31	COCKERMOUTH FESTIVAL
	Cockermouth, Cumbria
July 2	MUSGRAVE RUSHBEARING
	Musgrave, Nr. Appleby-in-Westmorland, Cumbria.
July 6	ULVERSTON CARNIVAL & PARADE
	Ulverston, Cumbria
July 13-14	ANNUAL WIRRAL SHOW
	New Brighton, Merseyside
July 15	CUMBERLAND COUNTY SHOW
	Rickerby Park, Carlisle, Cumbria.

July 26-28	ROYAL LANCASHIRE SHOW
	Astley Park, Chorley, Lancs
July 28-30	CUMBRIA STEAM GATHERING
	Cark Airfield, Flookburgh, Cumbria.
July 29 to	LAKE DISTRICT SUMMER MUSIC FESTIVAL
August 11	Ambleside, Cumbria.
August 3	COCKERMOUTH AGRICULTURAL SHOW
	Cockermouth Farm, Greenlands, Cockermouth, Cumbria
August 22	GRASMERE SPORTS
	Geasmere, Cumbria.
August 4,5	CLASSIC MOTOR BOAT RALLY & 6
	From Windermere Steamboat Museum, Windermere.
August 7	CARTMEL AGRICULTURAL SHOW
	Cartmel, Cumbria
August 8	APPLEBY AGRICULTURAL SHOW
	Appleby-in-Westmoreland, Cumbria
August 9-11	LOWTHER HORSE DRIVING TRIALS & COUNTRY FAIR
	Lowther Castle, Lowther, Cumbria.
August 9-11	APPLEBY GREAT SUMMER FLOWER SHOW & CRAFT FAIR
	Ambleside, Cumbria
*August 20	CHESHIRE COUNTRY SPORTS FAIR
	Peover Hall, Peover Estate, Over Peover, Cheshire Gun dogs, ferrets, parade of hounds, birds of prey and trade stands.
August 21	THRELKELD SHEEPDOG TRIALS
	Threlkeld, Cumbria.
August 22-24	SOUTHPORT FLOWER SHOW
	Victoria Park, Southport, Merseyside.
August 22-26	CARLISLE CITY FESTIVAL
	Carlisle, Cumbria
*August 26 to	BOLTON FESTTVAL 1996
September 4	Locations Bolton, Victoria Square, Bolton, Lancs. Arts and commu nity festival, with international and street entertainment.
August 30 to	BLACKPOOL ILLUMINATIONS
November 3	Talbot Square, Blackpool Lancashire. Illuminations from 7 p.m. nightly.
September	KENDAL GATHERING AND TORCHLTGHT PROCESSION
(1st 2 weeks)	(Procession September 8th), Kendal, Cumbria.
September 12	WESTMORELAND COUNTY SHOW
	Westmoreland Co. Showfield, Crooklands, Cumbria
September 16	EGREMONT CRAB FAIR
	(World Gurning Championships) Egremont, Cumbria.
September 28	ESKDALE SHOW
	Brotherilkeld Farm, Boot, Cumbria
September 29	URSWICK RUSHBEARING
	Urswick, Ulverston, Cumbria
October 17-21	WINDERMERE POWER BOAT RECORD ATTEMPTS
	Lake Windermere, Cumbria.
*November	BIGGEST LIAR TN THE WORLD COMPETITION
	Bridge Inn, Wasdale, South Bridge, Cumbria.
November 3	GRAND TOWN FIREWORK DISPLAY
	Memorial Gardens, Cockermouth, Cumbria

*Denotes provisional date

For further information contact:

The Cumbria Tourist Board	The North West Tourist Board
Ashleigh, Holly Road	Swan House, Swan Meadow Road
Windermere, Cumbria LA23 2AQ.	Lancashire WN3 5BB.
Tel: 015394 44444	Tel: 01942 821222

BROXTON HALL COUNTRY HOUSE HOTEL
Whitchurch Road, Broxton, Chester CH3 9JS

Telephone: 01829 782321   Fax: 01829 782330

For readers looking for an historical sojourn, this hotel offers the ultimate experience. Broxton Hall is set in 3 acres of beautiful gardens, in the heart of the Cheshire countryside. This half-timbered Tudor house has been sympathetically furnished with antiques to create a warm and comfortable hotel. Add to this its proximity to Chester, famed for its Roman and medieval remains and buildings, and you have the perfect venue for the historian, tourist and country lover. But this is not all; Mr and Mrs Hadley, the owners, have built up a well deserved reputation for the food here, served in the elegant restaurant where menus consist of a mouth-watering array of dishes from traditional English to French cuisine. There is also a wine list to tempt the most sophisticated of palates and to match the varied and interesting meals. Each of the 10 bedrooms is tastefully furnished in keeping with the house, and all have every modern facility to add to your comfort. Imagine if you will, returning to Broxton Hall after a tiring day out exploring this wonderful area, and relaxing in front of a log fire in the glow of polished wood and the cosy décor. A gem of a country house and one to which I will return as often as I can. Single room and breakfast from £55.00. Double room with breakfast from £70.00. **Leisure Breaks:** 10% off room rate at weekends. **Chester 8, Liverpool 20, London 160.**

F licence. 10 en suite bedrooms with radio, Satellite TV and direct-dial telephone; hairdryer, trouser press, laundry service, tea/coffee making facilities, safety deposit box. Last orders for dinner 21.30. Special diets available. Golf, riding, shooting, fishing by arrangement. Indoor swimming pool - 5 miles. Meeting rooms with capacity for 30 guests. Car rental can be arranged. Car parking for 40 cars. Open all year. All major credit cards accepted.

ROWTON HALL HOTEL
Whitchurch Road, Chester, Cheshire CH3 6AD

Telephone: 01244 335262   Fax: 01244 335464

Rowton Hall, originally a country manor house standing on the site of the Battle of Rowton Moor 1649, in eight acres of gardens, is two miles from the historic city of Chester, just off the A41 Chester to Whitchurch road. The hotel is now owned by Stuart and Diana Begbie. The public rooms are comfortable and distinctive, particularly the Cavalier Bar, where light lunches are served, and the attractive oak-panelled Langdale Restaurant. The bedrooms are decorated, furnished and appointed to a high standard. Rooms are available for conferences and private parties. For those seeking healthy relaxation, or indeed, for those of a sporting nature, the new leisure centre offers ample opportunity, with its gymnasium, solarium, steam room and swimming pool. It should be noted, however, that children under six are not allowed in the leisure centre, and those aged 6-16 have their own special hours. An ideal centre for touring and there are many sporting activities in the area. Room and breakfast from £72.00 single, £88.00 double including VAT. Other terms on application.**Weekend breaks** - Friday to Sunday £58 per person per night, dinner bed & breakfast. Single room supp't £10.50 per night. **Chester 2, Liverpool 30, Manchester 40, Birmingham 80, London 200.**
F licence, 42 en suite bedrooms, 8 ground floor, all with radio, telephone and TV; full central heating; night service; meals to 9.30 p.m.; diets; children welcome; conferences and private parties; helicopter pad; leisure centre; heated indoor swimming pool, sauna; steam room; gym; tennis court; sea bathing and sailing 15 miles; tennis, squash, badminton, riding and fishing one mile. Mastercard, American Express, Diners Club, Visa cards accepted.

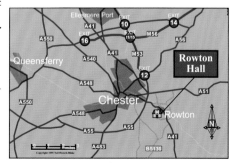

Hand Printed On Silk   Brocklehurst 1985

SUTTON HALL
Bullocks Lane, Sutton, Nr. Macclesfield, Cheshire SKll OHE

Telephone: 01260 253211   *Fax: 01260 252538*

If like myself you enjoy staying at an hotel of character, then Sutton Hall is one of the finest in which to indulge yourself. A wealth of beams, log fires and four poster beds are all in evidence, and the ales, conditioned in cask, are matched by the choice of food from an excellent menu. As with the inns of old, there is an atmosphere of warmth, hospitality and good cheer. This, married to such modern conveniences as en suite bathrooms and colour TV, makes a very happy amalgam of past and present. To travel, even from afar, is well worth while and this is made easy by the fact that the M6 and Manchester Airport are less than half an hour away. Also in the area are many other famous old houses as well as the scenic beauty of the Peak District. The hotel is personally run by Mr. and Mrs. Bradshaw. Room and breakfast from £68.95 single, £42.50 double, per person, inclusive of VAT and full English breakfast. Open all year.

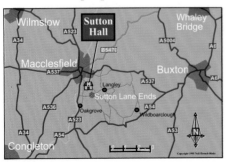

London 240, Macclesfield 1, M6 (J18/19) ¹/₂ hour, Manchester airport ¹/₂ hour.

F licence; 10 en suite bedrooms, all with four poster beds, colour TV, direct dial telephones, tea/coffee maker; trouser press; full central heating; late meals to 10 p.m.; diets; dogs welcome; conferences up to 20; golf, tennis, riding nearby; Peak National Park adjacent; most credit cards accepted.

NENT HALL
COUNTRY HOUSE
HOTEL
Alston, North Pennines,
Cumbria CA9 3LQ

Telephone 01434 381584
Fax 01434 382668

The 18th Century Nent Hall provides an excellent base from which to explore this area of outstanding natural beauty and beyond, and at the end of the day you receive a warm welcome back from Eric and Dorothy Peacock. Furnished to a high standard and with 17 comfortable en suite bedrooms the ambience here is relaxed. Lunch is a light bar meal, whilst diners have the choice of the gastronomic table d'hôte menu in the lovely dining room or the à la carte menu in the beamed restaurant; then coffee before the lounge's open fire. Single room including breakfast from £50.00. Double room with breakfast from £65.00. **Leisure Breaks:** 2/3 days £90.00 per day d,b&b 2 persons .
Carlisle 28 , Penrith 19 , Newcastle-upon-Tyne 45 , London 309 .
F licence. 17 en suite bedrooms with radio & colour TV; direct-dial telephone; hairdryer, laundry service, tea/coffee making facilities; safety deposit box. Last dinners 20.30 hrs. Special diets available. Fishing, golf, riding, game shooting nearby. Business services including two meeting rooms - capacity for 20 people. Hairdresser. Car parking for 40 cars. Major credit cards accepted. Open all year.

Signpost inspector Ronald Long (left) with Liz Hopwood, Ray Hopwood and John Barber outside the King's Arms Hotel, Askrigg in Wensleydale, North Yorkshire

KIRKSTONE FOOT COUNTRY HOUSE HOTEL
Ambleside, Cumbria LA22 9EH

Telephone: 015394 32232

I have known this hotel for many years, and it seems to improve each time I visit it. The Kirkstone Foot Hotel has further developed an already well deserved reputation for comfort and good food, and still represents some of the best value in the area. The stylish décor and furnishings are comfortable, warm and homely, and the food is superbly prepared, cooked and presented, and is complemented by an excellent wine list. There is always an air of friendly efficiency without the pomp and stuffiness of the many, often more expensive, pretentious hotels, which believe themselves to be of a similar standard. As its name suggests, the hotel is situated at the foot of Kirkstone Pass, tucked away in a quiet backwater, far from the holiday crowds. This location makes Kirkstone Foot Country House Hotel the ideal venue for taking part in the many pastimes and sports offered by the Lake District National Park. For guests who prefer self catering, there is a full range of cottages and apartments in the beautifully kept gardens, all of which are decorated to the same high standard of the hotel. Dinner, room and breakfast from £46.50 per person, per night. Closed for the first two weeks of December and all January.

Special Wine Weekends and low season tariff breaks. Prices & further details on application. **London 300, Kendal 13, Keswick 17, Penrith 30.** *R & R licence; 15 en suite bedrooms, all with direct dial telephone, TV, hairdryer and tea/coffee making facilities; full central heating; last orders for dinner 8.30 p.m.; special diets; children welcome; dogs in annexe only; sailing, boating golf, tennis, squash, riding and fishing nearby; 16 self-catering apartments; all major credit cards accepted.*

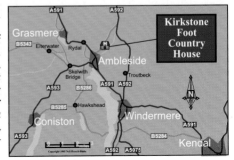

ROTHAY MANOR HOTEL
Rothay Bridge, Ambleside, Cumbria LA22 OEH

Telephone: 015394 33605   *Fax: 015394 33607*

If you believe, as I do, that one of the main ingredients of civilised life is good food and wines taken in comfortable surroundings, then Rothay Manor is, without a doubt, one of the finest venues in which to enjoy that life. The hotel has been voted top of the list by a publication on hotel breakfasts, and the excellence of the lunches and dinners complements the sumptuous surroundings. Antiques and fresh flowers are abundant, and the feeling of warmth and well-being are everywhere. The whole ambience is orchestrated by Nigel and Stephen Nixon and their wives, and the reputation that they have gained for all round excellence is more than justifiably deserved. These impressions were echoed by many of the other guests to whom I spoke, and even from the elegant brochure, you too will begin to feel the atmosphere of Rothay Manor. It seems unnecessary to add that the surrounding mountains, lakes and the air of the Lake District, make a superb backdrop and atmosphere in which to indulge these pleasures. Double room and breakfast from £114.00 for 2 people, and dinner, room and breakfast from £150.00 for 2 people.

Bargain breaks November-March, midweek, dinner, room & breakfast from £140 per night for 2 people; weekend break from £150 per night. **Kendal 13, Manchester 80, London 280.**

R & R licence, 18 en suite bedrooms (2 for the disabled) all with direct dial telephone and TV, room service; baby listening; last orders for dinner 9.00 p.m.;special diets; children welcome; conferences max. 20; free use of nearby leisure centre; tennis and fishing ¼ mile; sailing/boating ½ mile; open all year; all major credit cards accepted.

WATEREDGE HOTEL
Borrans Road, Ambleside, Cumbria LA22 OEP

Telephone: 015394 32332   *Fax: 015394 31878*

It is not often that one comes across a hotel that has excellent food, is immaculately and comfortably furnished and decorated, and yet is perfectly situated, but the Wateredge Hotel is exactly that. With its gardens running down to Lake Windermere, beautiful views from the public rooms, delightful bedrooms and delicious meals, it makes an idyllic venue for a holiday in the Lake District. Not only is there the peace and quiet of the hotel itself, but there is the tranquillity of a stroll on the nearby fells to be enjoyed. For those seeking a more active time, there is boating and fishing on the doorstep; there are sporting facilities of all kinds, both indoor and out, in the immediate vicinity. In addition, Ambleside is a lively and bustling town with everything that a holiday maker or tourist could need. The Wateredge is an unpretentious, "honest to goodness" hotel which makes any visit to the Lake District well worthwhile. Dinner, room and breakfast from £59.00 single, £102.00 double/twin. Closed mid-December to early February. 3-day midweek **breaks** £144 per person. 3-day weekend breaks £156 pr

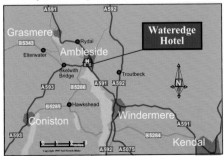

person including dinner, room and breakfast. Available 29 October - 16 December 1995 and 9 February-2 May 1996 (exc. Easter). Also Summer Breaks July and August.
London 300, Kendal 13, Keswick 17, Penrith 30
R licence; 23 en suite bedrooms (5 ground floor), all with radio, TV and telephone, complimentary morning tea and coffee tray; TV lounge; full central heating; diets, children over 7 welcome, dogs not allowed in public rooms or suites; small conferences; lake bathing; boating; fishing; private jetty for guest use; complimentary use of nearby leisure club; Mastercard, Amex and Visa credit cards accepted.

APPLEBY MANOR COUNTRY HOUSE HOTEL & LEISURE CLUB
Appleby-in-Westmorland, Cumbria CA16 6JB

Telephone: 017683 51571   Fax: 017683 52888

Appleby Manor stands high, commanding views of the historic little town, its romantic castle and the sweeping countryside and fells beyond. Within you will find relaxing and friendly courtesy, and most attractive and spacious public rooms. Facing south, the house gives shelter to its sunny gardens onto which some of the delightful rooms in the new wing have direct access. The bedrooms are comfortable and furnished in keeping with the period of the house. The recently refurbished coach house annexe is particularly comfortable. The award-winning dining room is informal and you can relax over a good table d'hôte menu, well presented and satisfying, or choose from one of the three other menus available. The wine list offers a selection of wines from 20 countries and the bar stocks a broad range of malt whiskies. There is plenty to see and do locally, there are walks to suit all abilities . Appleby is ideally situated for touring the scenic Lake District, and the Borders Hadrian's Wall, the Roman Camps, the high Pennines and the Yorkshire Dales are all within easy motoring distance. Prices per person start at £44 for bed and breakfast, £49.50 for dinner, bed and breakfast; weekly rates from £297, including dinner, bed and breakfast. **Bargain breaks:** min. 2 nights from £49.50 pppn; also "Flying Falcon" breaks, 2 nights from £156 and the "Cloud Nine Experience" from £127.50 and "Hangover Breaks" from £125 - all inc. dinner, b & b & VAT.

M6 (junctions 38 &40) 13, A1 Scotch Corner 37, Keswick 31, Kendal 25, Ullswater 15, Penrith 13
F licence; 30 en suite bedrooms (10 ground floor), all with telephone, hairdryer, colour TV, satellite and video film channels, last orders 9. 00 p.m.; diets; children welcome, baby listening; dogs in coachhouse bedrooms only; conferences 30 max; games room; snooker and pool; indoor heated swimming pool; jacuzzi; sauna, solarium, leisure centre, squash $\frac{1}{2}$ mile, fishing locally; riding 8 miles; golf 2 miles; hotel closed 3 days at Christmas only; all major credit cards accepted.

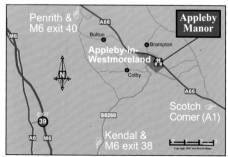

THE PHEASANT INN
Bassenthwaite Lake, Nr. Cockermouth, Cumbria CA13 9YE

Telephone: 017687 76234   Fax: 017687 76002

Dating from the 16th century, The Pheasant Inn has kept abreast of modern standards of comfort without losing any of its character and charm. Guests can enjoy bar snacks and real ale in the original bar, and there are a further three lounges in which to relax, all are tastefully decorated and furnished. The bedrooms, likewise, are comfortable and each has its own character and décor. It is heartwarming to return from any of the activities that may have brought you to this beautiful part of the Lake District, and to relax in front of a welcoming log fire. The fact that many non-residents come from far and near to dine here bears out that the food is prepared from the freshest ingredients, and cooked to the highest standards. The dining room is non-smoking, as is one of the resident's lounges. With pretty gardens and its own 60 acres of additional grounds and woodlands at the foot of Thornthwaite Forest, and with Bassenthwaite Lake only a few minutes walk away, The Pheasant Inn is a little step back into history - a nature lover's paradise and a gourmet's delight . Room and breakfast from £36.00. Dinner, room and breakfast from £54.00 including VAT. Winter breaks, midweek and weekends available from early November to March.

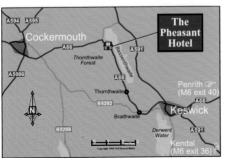

Cockermouth 5, Keswick 8, Carlisle 25, London 295.

F licence; 20 en suite bedrooms (no TV); room service; last orders for dinner 8.30 p.m.; bar meals at lunchtime; special diets; children welcome; dogs accepted in lounges and kennels; gardens and 60 acres of additional grounds and woodlands, fishing and riding nearby, golf locally; hotel closed on December 24th and 25th; Mastercard and Visa credit cards accepted.

GRAYTHWAITE MANOR HOTEL
Grange-over-Sands, Cumbria LA11 7JE

Telephone: 015395 32001/33755   Fax: 015395 35549

What first impressed me here was the courtesy and thoroughness with which one of the owners showed me round. As a result of what I saw and felt, I returned a few days later for a night's lodging and this is what I found. A largish and substantial house, beautifully appointed and with every indication that the detailed comfort of visitors had been most conscientiously achieved. The armchairs were cosy enough to go to sleep in. The dining room, an imposing affair, displays cut glass chandeliers and some fine oil paintings. There was a choice from the à la carte or table d'hôte menus at dinner, both excellently cooked and served. I made a special note, too, of how pleasant and attentive the staff were, obviously taking their cue from the owners. Bedrooms, all with private baths fulfilled the expectation of the downstairs comfort and elegance. Faithful guests return year after year for Graythwaite and Grange are within easy reach of the Lake District. Dinner, room and breakfast from £57.00 single, £99.00 twin.

Special breaks of two days or more available November to March; prices on request.

London 261, Lake District (Windermere) 15, Carlisle 58, Liverpool 76.

F 1icence; 22 bedrooms (some ground floor), 20 with private bathrooms and all with telephone, TV, tea/coffee making facilities, electric blankets; dryingroom; small conferences; billiards; attractive gardens; golf locally, putting green; hard court tennis; municipal sea water pool; riding nearby.

NETHERWOOD HOTEL
Grange-over-Sands, Cumbria LAll 6ET

Telephone: 015395 32552   *Fax: 015395 34121*

This imposing hotel, set in its own topiary gardens on a woodland slope, dominates the main road into Grange-over-Sands. The house dates back to 1893, and it retains all the original panelling, wood-carvings and fireplaces. However, modern conveniences also have their place here, and you will find a lift servicing the first floor bedrooms, and all the dining areas are air conditioned. There is a honeymoon suite with all its original furniture, to help you re-live the romance of days gone by, and there are ten new bedrooms, all non-smoking, furnished in harmony with the rest of the hotel. The food at the Netherwood is excellent, being prepared from the freshest ingredients with imagination and flair. It is easy to over-indulge in the dining room, but downstairs there is a heated swimming pool, spa bath, steam room and beauty salon where you can work off those extra inches gained, or simply relax after perhaps a tiring day touring this lovely area. The southern Lake District offers much for the nature lover and tourist alike, and the delights of Morecambe Bay and the Lune Valley are on the doorstep. Room and breakfast from £45 single, £90 double. Open all year.**Winter breaks** from 1st Nov. 1995-31st March 1996: 2 nights £110-£120; 3 nights £140-£150. Prices per person include dinner, bed & breakfast and VAT. Spring/Summer/Autumn breaks: 3 nights £174.75-£201 per person inclusive. **London 262, Lake District (Windermere) 5, Carlisle 58, Liverpool 82, Kendal 12, Keswick 41.**

F licence; 29 bedrooms (1 for disabled); all en suite , two pairs of intercommunicating bedrooms; all have radio, telephone, TV; night service; lift to 1st floor, late meals, special diets; children welcome; baby listening; dogs allowed, conferences; indoor heated swimming pool; spa bath; steam room; beauty area; parking for 160 cars; dancing; 11 acres of gardens; sea bathing and sailing 100 yds; tennis ¹/₂ mile; squash, badminton, riding, shooting and fishing all five miles; credit cards accepted.

STAKIS KESWICK LODORE SWISS HOTEL
Keswick, Cumbria CA12 5UX

Telephone: 017687 77285
Fax: 017687 77343

The Keswick Lodore Swiss, situated overlooking Derwent Water and at the foot of the famous Lodore Falls, is an hotel of international class and reputation. It caters superbly for all manner of guests and their families. One of the most impressive aspects is the way in which children are looked after by N.N.E.B. nurses, with their own playroom and kitchen, providing parents with a welcome rest. The public rooms are all bright and airy, the bedrooms are spacious and well appointed, and the whole hotel is beautifully decorated and cheerful. Many of the excellent dishes served are from original Swiss recipes, and the staff are all courteous and friendly. The gardens are a delight, and the immediate environs have the most imposing views, yet there is also a gentler beauty in the landscape. All the Lake District, with its sporting facilities, as well as its natural and historical features is easily accessible, so whether you are holidaying as a family or alone, there is something here to suit you. The hotel also has its own many and varied facilities for guests to enjoy. Dinner, bed and breakfast from £42.50 weekly rates (including dinner) from £287.00.

Bargain breaks - for a minimum of 2 nights, holiday rate from £42.50 per person per night applies, to include dinner, bed & breakfast.

Carlisle 42, Penrith 23, Keswick 3, London 285.

F licence; 70 bedrooms all with en suite bathroom, satellite TV and telephone; room and night service; baby listening; lift; last orders 9.30p.m.; bar lunches; special diets; children welcome; registered nursery with NNEB trained nannies; conferences up to 80; games room; outdoor/indoor heated swimming pool; leisure centre; sauna; gymnasium; sunbed; squash and tennis; sailing, boating and riding nearby; fishing by arrangement; free golf Mon-Fri (18 hole course), Sat-Sun £15. 00 per person; open all year; all major credit cards accepted.

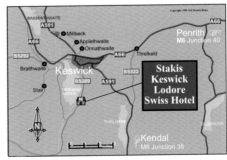

UNDERSCAR MANOR
Applethwaite, Nr. Keswick, Cumbria CA12 4PH

Telephone: 017687 75000   *Fax: 017687 74904*

Ranked as one of the best hotels in the North of England, it is surprising that we hear so little of Underscar Manor. This is because it is one of the most discreet hotels, and, hidden as it is up a secretive lane, it makes the perfect centre for discovering the Lake District, without encountering the crowds that so often mar such a visit. A guest here can wander in the hotel's own extensive and beautifully tended grounds, or up onto the fells without meeting a soul. The views are stunning. Inside, the décor can only be described as superb, the service is impeccable, and most importantly, the food is imaginative and delicious. For anyone contemplating a quiet break or a longer holiday, or for the businessman wanting to meet others without distractions, Underscar Manor is the perfect choice; the epitome of a country house hotel. Dinner, room and breakfast from £75.00 per person including VAT. **Bargain breaks** available - please enquire.

Keswick 2, M6 (Junction 40) 16, Manchester Airport 120, London 285.

F licence; 11 en suite bedrooms, all with direct dial telephone and TV; last orders for dinner 8.30p.m.; boardroom max. 16; riding 1¹/₂ miles; 18 hole golf course four miles; fishing nearby; open all year; credit cards accepted.

SCAFELL HOTEL
Borrowdale, Nr. Keswick, Cumbria CAl2 5XB

Telephone: 017687 77208   *Fax: 017687 77280*

It is not surprising that the Scafell is becoming one of Lakeland's leading hotels following its recent improvements and the consistent efforts of its management. Situated almost at the head of the beautiful Borrowdale Valley, its position is as outstanding as the service and comfort which it provides for all its guests. There is an excellent table d'hôte menu and for those wishing to dine later, a comprehensive à la carte supper menu. Both menus are accompanied by a well balanced wine list. Year after year guests return to walk and climb for they know that they are going to be comfortable and well looked after. For the less energetic, there are cosy and homely lounges. The bedrooms are comfortable and attractively furnished, all of them having their own private bathroom. Pleasant views are to be had of the sheltered garden ringed by mighty mountains on which internationally famous climbers have learned their craft. Yes, this is a home for the visitor seeking peace or exercise and wishing to 'get away from it all'. Hotel open all year except January. Dinner, bed and breakfast from £43.00 to £55.00. **Midweek breaks** are available : any two consecutive nights Sunday-Thursday inclusive £71.00 per person, dinner, bed and breakfast. Fell Break Weekends are available: Friday evening to Sunday lunch and include all dinners, packed lunches, breakfasts, afternoon tea and Sunday lunch - £103.75.
Penrith 24, Keswick 6, London 291, Carlisle 36, Kendal 36.
F licence; 24 en suite bedrooms (8 ground floor), all with direct-dial telephone, tea/coffee making facilities, TV; full central heating; children welcome and dogs accepted; bar meals; drying room; river bathing; boating; fishing; pony trekking; tennis six miles; golf ten miles.

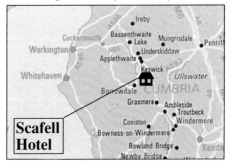

THE MILL
Mungrisdale, Penrith, Cumbria CA11 0XR

Telephone: 017687 79659

There are to my mind two main advantages to the location of the Mill. Firstly Mungrisdale is a secluded and little known part of the Lake District and therefore the crowds and traffic are almost non-existent. Secondly, as this picturesque area is on the Eastern edge of the national park, not only is the centre easily accessible but so are such interesting places as the Eden Valley, Hadrian's Wall, the Solway Firth and Carlisle. Even the border regions of Scotland and the Yorkshire Dales are within touring range. Having said this, I am sure that many people would be quite happy to wander no further than a mile or two from this charming hotel, which dates from 1651. The Mill stands at the foot of the fells, set in a pretty garden with a mill leat and waterfall and inside, it is cosy, cheerful and welcoming. The rooms in the Mill are not large but they are very well furnished and bright with flowers; the bedrooms are pretty and very comfortable, but it is the dining room that really excels. The food is nothing but delicious and beautifully presented, and this is borne out by the fact that the restaurant has been awarded an AA Rosette for its cuisine. I can wholeheartedly recommend this quiet family hotel, superbly run by resident proprietors, Richard and Eleanor Quinlan. Dinner, bed and breakfast from £59.00 inclusive. Hotel closed from November till mid February. **Bargain breaks:** Five nights or more - 10% discount. **Penrith 10, Keswick 10, London 290, Newcastle-on-Tyne 70.**

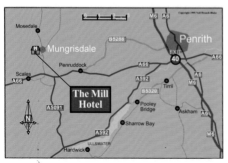

R & R licence; 9 bedrooms (2 ground floor) - 6 with private bath; all with TV; full central heating; dinner 7.00 p.m.; diets on request, with a vegetarian choice on offer each evening; baby listening; dogs allowed; snooker, darts and table tennis, sailing, boating and golf nearby, badminton in summer; riding; local fishing; clay pigeon shooting; no credit cards.

THE SWAN HOTEL
Newby Bridge, Nr. Ulverston, Cumbria LA12 8NB

Telephone: 015395 31681   Fax: 015395 31917

Set 'twixt the river and the lake in what must be one of the most superb situations in the Lake District, the Swan has all the facilities that a traveller or holiday maker could wish for. It has its own lovely marina, fishing in the river and is close to the steam railway at Newby Bridge; all this at the end of Lake Windermere. The hotel was originally a coaching inn but has now been completely modernised to provide every convenience. Special autumn breaks are offered and my only regret was that I could not stay longer to explore this lovely part of Cumbria. Room and breakfast from £58.00 single and £92.00 double. The Lonsdale Suite has a king size bed, luxurious drapes and crafstman-built mahogany furniture to luxury standard. Hotel open for 3-day Christmas Holiday Break and 1, 2 or 3 day New Year Break. 'Swan Breaks' - any two nights weekends only (Friday and Saturday or Saturday and Sunday) from £96 per person, dinner, bed and breakfast in double room with private bath. "Racing at Cartmel" - 2 day stay in May including breakfast and dinner and an afternoon at the Races in support of the "Swan at Newby Handicap Steeplechase". Spring to Autumn "Swan Break Superplus" - 4-day breaks - dinner, bed and breakfast, mini-cruise and "A Trip Down Memory Lane" from £192 per person. November 1995 saw the return of the now widely acclaimed "Weekend of Gilbert and Sullivan", starring principals of the world of operetta past and present. Extra Special Breaks will be offered January-March 1996 to celebrate 20 years of the hotel's trading under the current management team. Further details on application. **London 261, Manchester 83, Bristol 238, Edinburgh 155, Birmingham 159.**

F licence; 36 en suite bedrooms including shower, all with TV, radio, tea/coffee making facilities, hairdryer and telephone; central heating; night service; late meals by arrangement; diets; children welcome; baby listening; conferences up to 20; fishing; marina; riding two miles; golf 6¹/2 miles; most credit cards accepted.

SHARROW BAY COUNTRY HOUSE HOTEL
Ullswater, Howtown, Nr. Penrith, Cumbria CA10 2LZ

Telephone: 017684 86301 or 86483   Fax: 017684 86349

Away from the bustle of the holiday rush, in the most envied position in the Lake District, Francis Coulson M.B.E. and Brian Sack M.B.E. must be congratulated on their 48th year of service to the gourmets of the world, providing the most exquisite food and wines in the most comfortable of atmospheres. Reputed to be the first Country House Hotel in this country and to be approved by the Relais et Chateaux, only 21 being so included in Great Britain, is surely recommendation enough, but speak to anyone who has stayed here and you will hear nothing but superlatives as the owners believe in creating a home from home. The decor is superb, the service impeccable and the overall effect is the product of these two brilliant hoteliers. Add to all this the beauty of the Lake and mountains and you have total perfection. I should add there is now a beautiful converted farmhouse called Bank House, about a mile from Sharrow, which has seven superbly furnished bedrooms, all with private bathrooms and lake views. Breakfast is served in the magnificent Refectory dining room, which was converted from the seventeenth century barn. It has a striking Portland stone fireplace and overmantle, which came from Warwick Castle. It also has incredible English silk damask curtains, old English furniture and a specially made carpet, being a copy of that in the Royal Opera House. Lunch and dinner are served at Sharrow Bay. Some of the staff have been with the hotel for over 30 years, and Nigel Lawrence and Nigel Lightburn, who are now directors, will carry on Sharrow Bay's renowned traditions. Tariff on application. **London 289, Penrith 7, Kendal 33, Keswick 20, Windermere 25.** *R and R licence; 28 bedrooms; 24 with private bath and/or shower, including 6 cottage suites; TV; radio; antiques; peace; golf locally; lake bathing; boating; riding; fishing; small conference facilities; closed from end of November - end of February.*

CEDAR MANOR HOTEL
Ambleside Road, Windermere, Cumbria LA23 1AX

Telephone: 015394 43192   Fax 015394 45970

True lovers of the Lake District wishing to immerse themselves in everything that the beautiful area has to offer will naturally seek out a smaller, more intimate hotel. They need look no further than the Cedar Manor which is a traditional and very genuine Lakeland house, with some interesting architectural features, in a country garden setting. Moreover all that is within the hotel is a reflection of its peaceful and secluded location for it exudes an air of comfort, friendliness and quiet efficiency with the added bonus of immaculate decoration and elegant furnishings in the public rooms. The bedrooms too are very comfortable and some have lovely views towards Lake Windermere. The reputation of the restaurant had preceded it and is reflected in the many awards and accolades it has received from connoisseurs. The food was indeed excellent with fresh local produce and I enjoyed a roast leg of lamb Westmoreland style with Cumberland sausage stuffing and other trimmings. This homely country hotel, so close to Cumbria's beauties and not far from its many other attractions, is a place for the lover of good things in life. The Cedar Manor puts it another way: "Often sought, seldom found". Single room including breakfast from £29.50. Double room with breakfast from £59.00.
Leisure Breaks: Christmas & New Year Programmes; Golf Breaks - throughout the year.

Honeymoon Package. Details of all these are available upon request.

London 246, Kendal 8, Lancaster 28, Penrith 26.

Full licence. 12 en suite bedrooms with radio & colour TV. Direct-dial telephone. Hairdryer, laundry service; non-smoker bedrooms; tea/coffee making facilities. Last orders for dinner 20.30 hrs. Special diets available. Fishing, watersports, riding, tennis - all nearby. Golf, shooting - 20 miles. Hotel offers free use of local leisure facilities. Car parking for 16 cars. Open all year. All credit cards accepted.

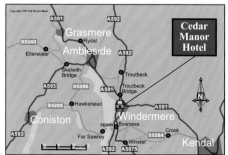

FAYRER GARDEN HOUSE HOTEL
Lyth Valley Road, Bowness-on-Windermere, Cumbria LA23 3JP

Telephone: 015394 88195   *Fax: 015394 45986*

With superb views over Lake Windermere, yet away from the bustle of the holiday makers in Bowness itself, Fayrer Garden House Hotel shares its 5 acres of grounds with not just its guests, but with deer, squirrels, badgers and the ubiquitous rabbits. Inside, the beautifully decorated rooms all offer warmth, comfort, tranquillity and a sense of well being. Iain and Jackie Garside, known for many years for the excellence of their previous hotel, are now bringing their skill and expertise to bear at Fayrer Garden. Dining here is an experience. With the Lake and the fells as a backdrop, the culinary creations, prepared by Jackie and her team, are delicious and lovingly presented. We here at Signpost wish them the same success in this venture that they previously enjoyed and so richly deserved. Room and breakfast from £27.50-£52.50 per person; dinner, room and breakfast from £37.50-£65.00 per person, including VAT. **Winter breaks.** 3 nights dinner, bed and breakfast from £99.50 per person. **Summer breaks.**

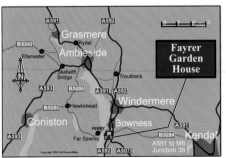

3 nights dinner, bed and breakfast from £125 per person. 4-poster Lake View rooms available at supplement. **Bowness 1, Kendal 7, Manchester 76, Newcastle 90, London 280.**

R & R licence; 14 en suite bedrooms (3 suitable for the infirm), all with direct dial telephone and TV; last orders for dinner 8. 00 p.m .; special diets; children welcome; dogs accepted; conferences max. 24; tennis; free use of nearby leisure centre with swimming pool and squash courts; sailing/boating and riding nearby; golf one mile; shooting/fishing and hot air ballooning by arrangement; open all year; all credit cards except Diners accepted.

LINTHWAITE HOUSE HOTEL
Crook Road, Bowness-on-Windermere, Cumbria LA23 3JA
Telephone: 015394 88600   Fax: 015394 88601

This hotel, situated on the B5284 Bowness to Kendal road, only a mile or so from Bowness, is surely the epitome of what every Signposter would like to find. It is set in 14 acres of superbly kept grounds with magnificent views of Lake Windermere and of every major peak in the Lake District. There is a well stocked tarn (in which 5 lb trout have been caught) and where one can while away the day with a picnic. The golf practice area is surrounded by lovely woodland walks. Naturally, within a very short distance are all the other amenities that one expects in the area, such as swimming, yachting and tennis. But enough of outside activities! Inside the hotel is immaculate, tastefully interior designed. A feature is the use of old trunks and suitcases. What more can I say, except that the food is superb and that so many of the guests return to Linthwaite again and again? Surely this must speak more eloquently than any words of mine. I am sure that any Signposter who visits here for the first time will, like others, keep coming back to the atmosphere of peace and tranquillity. Prices on application. **Romantic breaks** (minimum 2 nights) - including champagne in room on arrival, heart shaped chocolates, canopied king size double bed with lake view, breakfast and candlelit dinner.

London 208, Bowness 1, Kendal 7, Manchester 76. *R & R licence; 18 en suite bedrooms (5 ground floor rooms), all with direct dial telephone and satellite TV; room service; last orders for dinner 9.00 p.m., light lounge lunches; special diets; children over 8 years welcome; conferences 20 max; sauna, solarium, spa pool, gymnasium and golf 1 mile; lake bathing; mountain walking and riding 3 miles; sailing/boating and water-skiing 1 mile; golf practice hole par 3; own tarn brown trout; open all year; all major credit cards accepted.*

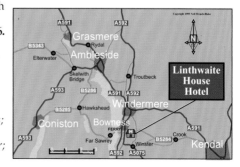

THE MORTAL MAN HOTEL
Troutbeck, Nr. Windermere, Cumbria LA23 1PL

Telephone: 015394 33193.   Fax: 015394 31261

Up on the hills on the long rise from Windermere to the summit of the Kirkstone Pass you'll spy a freshly painted, gabled, black and cream house a few hundred yards west. A sign at the entrance to a lane points the way to the Mortal Man, a hotel with a long, romantic and honourable history. It's just the place for a go-as-you-please holiday exploring the fells, lakes and passes . Under the capable management of Annette and Christopher Poulsom the hotel maintains the reputation that it has always enjoyed. As with so many hotels in the area, peace is the main attribute but with the Mortal Man this is accentuated by the fact that it stands on a little-used side road and, even in the height of the season, one can relax in comfort. Dinner, bed and breakfast from £55.00 single, £110.00 twin. Closed mid-November to mid-February.

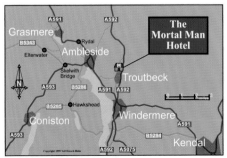

London 283, Windermere Station 3, Kirkstone Summit 3, Patterdale 9.

F licence, 12 en suite bedrooms, all with TV, telephone, trouser press, tea/coffee making facilities; last orders for dinner 9.00p.m.; bar meals; diets available; dogs welcome; no children under 5 years old; free membership to Leisure Centre including swimming pool, sauna, jacuzzi, squash and gym three miles; riding $^1/_4$ mile; fishing rights.

THE OLD VICARAGE COUNTRY HOUSE HOTEL
Witherslack, Cumbria LA11 6RS

Telephone: 015395 52381   *Fax: 015395 52373*

The Old Vicarage was recommended to me by one of the country's top hoteliers - and how right he was to do so. For those wishing to visit the Lake District, to remain in perfect peace and seclusion and yet to sample the art of cooking and service at their best, then here is the venue in which to do so to perfection. The hotel is set in a particularly beautiful valley and it offers the finest of food prepared only from the freshest of ingredients. It is indeed a haven. The atmosphere is of unhurried simplicity but the thought and energy expended to achieve this ambience is, I am sure, immeasurable. Mr. and Mrs. Burrington-Brown and Mr. and Mrs. Reeve have set a standard that many hotels will strive to match but which few will attain. I look forward to visiting this unique hotel again, and especially to staying in the "Celebration Suite", one of the new bedrooms in the Orchard House, with its terraces overlooking unspoilt woodland. Room and breakfast from £49.00 per person, inclusive of VAT. No service charges. Open all year. **Bargain breaks** - near to the lakes, far from the crowds. Any two nights midweek or weekends, fully inclusive from £55 per person, dinner, bed and breakfast per night.

M6 Junction 36 10 mins., Sea 4, Kendal 8, Lake Windermere 6, Lancaster 19, London 263.

R & R licence; 10 en suite bedrooms and 5 in the Orchard House, all with telephone, colour TV, full central heating; dinner 7.30 p.m. for 8.00 p.m.; diets; children by arrangement; dogs by arrangement; all weather tennis court for guests' use; sailing, golf, squash, badminton, riding, shooting, fishing all nearby; all major credit credit cards accepted.

GEORGIAN HOUSE HOTEL
Manchester Road, Blackrod, Bolton, Lancashire BL6 5RU

Telephone: 01942 814598   Fax: 01942 813427

Few hotels today can be described as exciting but this is one of those few that can offer both excitement and relaxation. It is sophisticated but not pompous, it is interestingly and well furnished and decorated, it is very comfortable and it has a list of amenities to keep the most bored of guests occupied. There is a large billiards room, a swimming pool, gymnasium, jacuzzi and there are sauna and massage facilities to name but a few. Add to this list 5 conference suites and a superb restaurant and you have a four star hotel that makes business a pleasure and holidays in the area a delight. For the former, all modern teaching aids are available and for the latter, the district has a host of attractions all within a few miles. Have you been to Camelot or Wigan Pier for example? They are not to be missed, and the Pennines, Morecambe Bay and even the Lake District are not far away. For excellent service, food and comfort the Georgian House Hotel represents all that is best in the area. Room and breakfast (midweek) from £80.00, double room from £92.00. **Mini break** - Saturday dinner dance, à la carte dinner, accommodation, Sunday lunch and use of the leisure facilities £60 per person inc.

VAT. **Maxi break** - Friday and Saturday dinner dances, two nights as above £94 per person inc. **Manchester 22, London 186, Cumbria 110, Liverpool 50, Blackpool 38.**
F licence; 101 en suite bedrooms (4 for the disabled), all with direct dial telephone and TV; room service; baby listening; night service; lift; last orders for dinner 10.00 p.m., bar meals; diets; children welcome; dogs accepted; conferences 300 max; snooker/billiards; indoor swimming pool; leisure centre; sauna; solarium; spa pool; gymnasium; dianer dances on Fridays and Saturdays; open all year; all major credit cards accepted.

CHADWICK HOTEL
South Promenade, Lytham St Annes, Lancashire FY8 1NP

Telephone: 01253 720061   *Fax: 01253 714455*

I was most impressed with this hotel. It is owned and run by the Corbett family and every detail has been carefully thought out and provided. The staff are particularly charming and helpful and they immediately make you feel at home. the décor is bright and airy and all the rooms are well decorated and comfortable. Here are all the facilities of a large international hotel, but without the pomposity sometimes associated with them. There are rooms for the disabled; there is a health club with an indoor heated swimming pool, spa bath, solarium, and the bedrooms have every convenience including in-house movies and satellite TV. The Chadwick Hotel's newly refurbished restaurant serves excellent food and has a good wine list. The Bugatti Bar features over 100 malt whiskies. The Chadwick is situated right on the sea front of this pretty town and there are particularly good rates for families with children and also for the keen golfer with many superb courses within a very short distance. Double/twin room and breakfast from £24 per person, including VAT. **Bargain breaks**. From November until mid-April our midweek winter breaks with two persons sharing a room are £34.20 for dinner, bed and breakfast. Alternatively our popular dinner dance and speciality weekends include entertainment on Friday and 7-course banquet with dancing on Saturday for £77.50 per person for the complete weekend. **London 224, Preston 14, Lancaster 30, Blackpool 7.**

R & R licence; 72 en suite bedrooms (2 for the disabled), some with 4-poster beds, some with spa baths, all with direct dial telephone and TV; room service; baby listening; night service; 24-hour food service; lift; last orders for dinner 8.30 p.m., bar meals; diets; children welcome; conferences max. 50; childrens' soft adventure playroom; indoor heated swimming pool; leisure centre; sauna; solarium; spa pool; sea fishing; golf ¹/₂ mile; sailing/ boating, tennis and squash courts 1 mile; riding 3 miles; open all year; all major credit cards accepted.

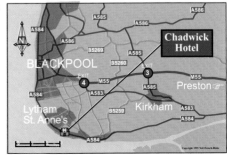

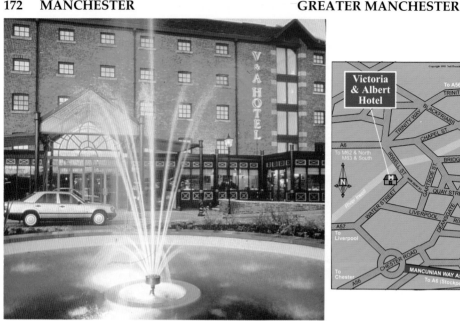

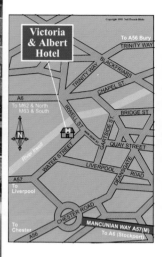

THE VICTORIA AND ALBERT HOTEL
Water Street, Manchester M3 4JQ

Telephone: 0161 832 1188   *Fax: 0161 834 2484*

Of the few great international hotels in the North of England. the Victoria and Albert in Manchester city centre is possibly the newest and one of the best. Converted from a Victorian warehouse on the River Irwell, no expense has been spared in the design, materials or workmanship of the building, and the same applies to the décor and furnishings. It is a fabulous concept, well executed and representing the ultimate in comfort. Recent developments include an extension to the John Logie Baird function suite and 20 extra bedrooms will be in service by June 1996. The staff have been chosen from the best in this country and abroad and the overall result is an hotel which should be a yardstick to others in the category. The food, served in the Sherlock Holmes Restaurant and the Café Maigret, is superb and the hushed atmosphere of the hotel fills one with a sense of serenity. For those wishing to hold a meeting or large conference in Manchester, there is a variety of meeting rooms and suites, all with the most modern visual and audio aids. All the public rooms and bedrooms are named after Granada Television programmes, and this is hardly surprising as the hotel was built by one of the Granada Group companies and is situated only yards from their famous studios. Also within a short walking distance are the Science Museums and the G-Mex Centre. For anyone planning to visit this most interesting and exciting city, the Victoria and Albert must be the obvious choice. Special weekend rates are offered from £90 per night for a twin/double room including English breakfast and VAT, midweek from £130 room only.
Piccadilly Station 1, M62 Motorway 2, M65 3, Manchester Airport 10, London 201.

F licence; 132 en suite bedrooms (2 for the disabled, 17 executive rooms, 4 lounge suites & 6 rooms in the Ladies' Wing), all with direct dial telephone, tea/coffee making facilities and TV; 24-hour room service; night service; 2 lifts; last orders for dinner 10.30 p.m., bar meals; special diets; conferences 400 max; snooker/billiards; curio shop; indoor swimming pool 200 yards; leisure centre; sauna; solarium; gymnasium; indoor car park; adjacent to Granada Studios Tour; open all year; most major credit cards accepted.

■ **Historic Houses, Gardens & Parks**

CLEVELAND
Burn Valley Gardens, Hartlepool
Fairy Dell, Middlesbrough
Ormesby Hall, Ormesby, Middlesbrough
Ward Jackson Park, Hartlepool

COUNTY DURHAM
Eggleston Hall Gardens, Eggleston
Hardwick Hall Country Park, Stockton-on-Tees
Houghall Gardens, Durham

HUMBERSIDE
Burton Agnes Hall, Driffield
Burton Constable Hall & Country Park, Nr. Hull
Sledmere House, Driffield

NORTHUMBERLAND
Alnwick Castle
Belsay Hall, Castle & Gardens, Belsay
Cragside House & Country Park, Rothbury
Hexham Herbs, Chollerford
Howick Hall Gardens, Alnwick
Hulne Park, Alnwick
Lady Waterford Hall, Berwick on-Tweed
Meldon Park, Morpeth
Otterburn Hall
Paxton House, Berwick on-Tweed
Seaton Delaval Hall, Blyth
Shaw Garden Centre Cramlington
Wallington House Walled Garden & Grounds, Morpeth

TYNE & WEAR
Bessie Surtees House, Newcastle-upon-Tyne
Bolam Lake Country Park, Newcastle-upon-Tyne
Kirkley Hall Gardens, Ponteland, Newcasde-upon-Tyne
Rising Sun Country Park & Countlyside Centre, Benton
Saltwell Park, Gateshead

YORKSHIRE
Allerton Park, Knaresborough
Beningbrough Hall, York
Bramham Park, Wetherby
Burnby Hall Gardens, Pocklington
Castle Howard, Coneysthorpe
Constable Burton Hall Gardens, Leyburn
Duncombe Park, Helmsley
East Riddlesden Hall, Keighley
Epworth Old Rectory, Doncaster
Fairfax House ,York
Golden Acre Park, Bramhope
Harewood House, Leeds
Harlow Carr Botanical Gardens, Harrogate
Japanese Garden, Horsforth
Kiplin Hall Richmond
Land Farm Garden, Hebden Bridge
Lotherton Hall, Leeds
Margaret Waudby Oriental Garden, Upper Poppleton
Newburgh Priory, York
Newby Hall Gardens, Ripon
Normanby Hall, Scunthorpe
Nostell Priory, Wakefield
Nunnington Hall, York
Parceval Hall Gardens, Skipton
Ripley Castle, Harrogate
St Nicholas Gardens, Richmond
Sheffield Botanical Gardens, Sheffield
Sheriff Hutton Park, Nr. York

Stockfield Park, Wetherby
Sutton Park, Nr. York
Temple Newsam House, Leeds
Thorp Perrow Arboretum, Bedale

■ **Walks & Nature Trails**

CLEVELAND
Bilingham Beck Valley Country Park

COUNTY DURHAM
Allensford Park, Consett
Blackton Nature Reserve, Teesdale
Derwent Walk, Consett
Durham Coast, Peterlee
Hamsterley Forest, Bishop Auckland

HUMBERSIDE
Elsham Hall Country & Wildlife Park, Brigg
Humber Bridge Country Park, Hessle
Normanby Hall Country Park, Scunthorpe

NORTHUMBERLAND
Allen Banks Woods, Hexham
Bedlington Country Park
Carlisle Park & Castle Wood, Morpeth
Fontburn Nature Reserve
Hareshaw Dene, Bellingham, Hexham
Ingram National Park Visitor Centre
Northumberland Coast, Newton-by-the-Sea, Alnwick
Plessey Woods Country Park
Scotch Gill Wood Local Nature Reserve, Morpeth

TYNE & WEAR
Derwent Walk Country Park, Rowlands Gill
The Leas & Marsden Rock, South Shields
Thornley Woodlands Centre, Rowlands Gill

YORKSHIRE
Anglers Country Park, Wintersett
Barlow Common Nature Reserve, Selby
Bretton Country Park, Wakefield
Bridestones Moor, Pickering
Brimham Rocks, Harrogate
Cannon Hall Country Park, Barnsley
Chevin Forest Park, Otley
Dalby Forest Drive & Visitor Centre, Pickering
Hardcastle Crags, Hebden Bridge
Howstean Gorge, Pateley Bridge
Malham Tarn, Settle
Millington Wood Local Nature Reserve
Marston Moor, Huddersfield
Newmillerdam Country Park, Wakefield
Ogden Water, Halifax
Ravenscar Coastline, Scarborough
Rother Valley Country Park, Sheffield
Sutton Bank Nature Trail - between Helmsley & Thirsk
Ulley Country Park, Sheffield
Worsbrough Country Park, Barnsley

■ **Historical Sites & Museums**

CLEVELAND
Guisborough Priory, Guisborough
Gray Art Gallery & Museum, Hartlepool
Guisborough Museum, York
Saltburn Smugglers Heritage Centre
PSS Wingfield Castle, Hartlepool

COUNTY DURHAM
Barnard Castle
Beamish - The North of England Open Air Museum
Durham Cathedral
Durham Castle
Raby Castle, Staindrop

HUMBERSIDE
Burton Agnes Manor House, Driffield
Maister House, Hull
Wilberforce House, Hull

NORTHUMBERLAND
Aydon Castle
Bamburgh Castle
Berwick Castle, Berwick on-Tweed
Brinkburn Priory, Longframlington
Chesters Roman Fort, Hexham
Chillingham Castle
Dunstanburgh Castle
Edlingham Castle
Etal Castle, Etal, Cornhill-on-Tweed
Grace Darling's Museum, Bamburgh
Hadrian's Wall
Hexham Abbey
House of Hardy Museum & Country Store, Alnwick
Lindisfarne Castle, Holy Island, Berwick-on-Tweed
Marine Life Centre & Fishing Museum, Seahouses
Norham Castle, Berwick-on-Tweed
Prudhoe Castle
Warkworth Castle
Wine & Spirit Museum & Victorian Chemist Shop,
  Berwick-on-Tweed

TYNE & WEAR
Castle Keep, Newcastle-upon-Tyne
Hatton Gallery, Newcastle-upon-Tyne
The Laing Art Gallery, Newcastle-upon-Tyne
Newbum Hall Motor Museum, Newcastle-upon-Tyne
The Shipley Art Gallery, Gateshead
South Shields Museum, South Shields

YORKSHIRE
Aldborough Roman Town, Nr. Borougbridge
Assembly Rooms, York
BardenTower, Bolton Abhey
Barley Hall, York
Beverley Minster, Beverley
Bishops House, Sheffield
Bolling Hall, Bradford
Bolton Castle, Leyburn
Borthwick Institute of Historical Research, York
Bronte Parsonage Museum, Haworth
Captain Cook Memorial Museum, Whitby
Clifford's Tower, York
Dales Countryside Museum, Hawes
Eureka! The Museum for Children, Halifax
Fountains Abbey a Studley Royal, Ripon
Fulneck Moravian Settlement & Museum, Nr. Pudsey
Gainsthorpe Deserted Medieval Village
Georgian Theatre Royal & Museum, Richmond
Jervaulx Abbey, Ripon
Jorvik Viking Centre & Brass Rubbing Centre, York
Kirstall Abbey, Leeds

King's Manor, York
Marmion Tower, Ripon
Mount Grace Priory, Northallerton
National Museum of Photography, Film & Television,
  Bradford
National Railway Museum, York
Red House, Gomerad
Rievalulx Abbey, Rievaulx
Sion Hill Hall & Birds of Prey Centre, Kirkby Wiske
Skipton Castle, Skipton
The Old Smithy & Heritage Centre, Owston Ferry
Tetleys Brewery Wharf, Leeds
Treasurer's House, York
York Castle Museum, York
York Story, York
York Minster, York

■ **Entertainment Venues**

CLEVELAND
Botanic Centre, Middlesbrough
Cleveland Craft Centre, Middlesbrough
Margrove South Cleveland Heritage Centre, Boosbeck,
  Saltburn-by-Sea
Stewart Park, Middlesbrough

COUNTY DURHAM
Bowlees Visitor Centre, Middleton-in-Teesdale

HUMBERSIDE
Bondville Miniature Village, Sewerby
Fosse Hill Jet Ski Centre, Driffield
Humberside Ice Arena, Hull
Sewerby Hall, Park & Zoo, Bridlington

NORTHUMBERLAND
Belford Craft Gallery
Tower Knowe Visitor Centre, Kielder Water,
  Hexham

TYNE & WEAR
Bowes Railway Centre, Gateshead
Predator Paintball, Newcastle-upon-Tyne

YORKSHIRE
Catterick Indoor Ski Centre, Catterick Garrison
Flamingo Land Family Funpark & Zoo, Malton
Harrogate Ski Centre, Yorkshire Showground
Hemsworth Water Park & Playworld
Hornsea Pottery Leisure Park & Freeport Shopping
  Village
Kinderland, Scarborough
Lighwater Valley Theme Park, North Stainley
North of England Clay Target Centre, Rufforth
Piece Hall, Halifax
Sheffield Ski Village, Sheffield
The Alan Ayckbourn Theatre in the Round,
  Scarborough
Tockwith (Multi-Drive) Activity Centre, Tockwith
Thybergh Country Park
Turkish Baths, Harrogate
Watersplash World, Scarborough
The World of Holograms, Scarborough

January 20	YORK COIN AND STAMP COLLECTIONS FAIR York Racecourse, Tadcaster Road, York. Largest event of this kind outside London.
February 10-17	JORVIK VIKING FESTIVAL Various venues, York. Viking themed - combat, feasts, fireworks, torchlit procession and boatburning, crafts and music.
March 1-16	BRADFORD FILM FESTIVAL National Museum of Photography, Pictureville, Bradford
March 8-10	ILKLEY LITERATURE FESTIVAL Craiglands Hotel and various venues, Ilkley
March 10-12	WORKING DAYS Abbeydale Industrial Hamlet, Abbeydale Road, South Sheffield. Working demonstration of traditional metal crafts plus home-based crafts.
*March 23-25	HORSE RACING, THE WILLIAM HILL LINCOLN FESTIVAL Doncaster Racecourse, Doncaster, South Yorkshire.
*March 25	24th IAAF/SNICKERS WORLD CROSS COUNTRY CHAMPION-SHIPS Maiden Castle, Off A177, Durham City. Races in junior and senior men's and women's category. 80 nations - the elite of the world's distance runners.
*March 25-26	MOTORSPORTS '96 Sheffield Arena, Sheffield, South Yorkshire.
March 29-31	EAST OF ENGLAND KNITTING & NEEDLECRAFT EXHIBITION Exhibition Centre, Freightliner Rd, Hull
April 1	12TH SPRING SHOW INCLUDING ALPINES Youth Centre, Grammar School Road, Brigg, Humberside.
April 9	MICKLEGATE SINGERS EASTER CONCERT Chapter House, York Minster, York.
April 5-12	HARROGATE INTERNATIONAL YOUTH MUSIC FESTIVAL Various venues, Harrogate
*April 14-30	EMBASSY WORLD CHAMPIONSHIP SNOOKER Crucible Theatre, Norfolk Street, Sheffield.
April 15-17	EASTER EXTRAVANGANZA Beningbrough Hall, Shipton-by-Beningbrough, North Yorkshire.
April 25-28	SPRING FLOWER SHOW Valley Gardens, Harrogate, North Yorkshire.
May 4-12	LEEDS INTERNATIONAL MUSIC FESTIVAL College of Music, Institute Building, Gorridge St, Leeds
May 9-12	BEVERLEY EARLY MUSIC FESTIVAL Various venues, Beverley, Humberside
May 18	OTLEY SHOW Otley Showground, Otley, West Yorkshire
May 25-27	MAYFAIR Various venues throughout Berwick-on-Tweed, Swaledale and
May 27	NORTHUMBERLAND COUNTY SHOW (agricultural) Overdean Park, Craigton, Northumberland.
June 1	ALLENDALE FAIR Market Square, Allendale, Northumberland.
June 8	SWALEDALE MARATHON Arken Garthdale Rd, Reeth, North Yorkshire
June 15-16	DURHAM REGATTA River Wear, Durham
June 21 to July 6	BRADFORD FESTIVAL Various venues, Bradford, West Yorkshire.
June 30 to July 7	ALNWICK FAIR Alnwick Market Place, Alnwick, Northumberland.

July 1-2	SOUTH TYNESIDE SHOW
	Coast Road, South Shields
July 5-7	EVENING CHRONICLE NORTH OF ENGLAND MOTOR SHOW
	The Links, Whitley Bay, Tyne & Wear
July 5-7	WHITLEY BAY TRADITIONAL JAZZ FESTIVAL
	Park Hotel, Grand Parade, Tynemouth
July 5-14	YORK EARLY MUSIC FESTIVAL
	Various venues, York, North Yorkshire.
July 6-7	NORTHERN ELECTRIC INTERNATIONAL KITE FESTIVAL
	Northern playing fields, Washington, Tyne & Wear
July 9-11	GREAT YORKSHIRE SHOW
	Great Yorkshire Showground, Wetherby Road, Harrogate.
July 14	JAGUAR RALLY
	Harewood House, West Yorkshire
July 14-15	DURHAM COUNTY SHOW (agricultural)
	Clondyke Garden Centre, Lambton Park, Chester-le-Street, Durham.
*July 23	BRASS BAND COMPETION & CONCERT
	Burton Constable Hall, Nr. Hull, Humberside.
July 26-28	PICKERING TRACTION ENGINE RALLY
	The Showfield, Pickering, North Yorkshire
July 27	CLEVELAND COUNTY SHOW
	Stewart Park, Middlesbrough, Cleveland
August 3-4	SUNDERLANDS INTERNATIONAL AIR SHOW
	Coast Road, Sunderland
August 3-10	ALNWICK INTERNATIONAL MUSIC FESTIVAL
	Market Square, Alnwick
August 31 to	INTERNATIONAL SEA SHANTY FESTIVAL
September 3	Hull Marina, Hull, Humberside.
September 15	GREAT NORTH RUN (Official World Half Marathon)
	Various venues throughout Tyneside
September 4-9	SCARBOROUGH OPEN GOLF WEEK
	North Cliff & South Cliff Courses, also Filey Golf Course, N Yorks.
September 6-7	HORSE RACING, ST. LEDGER
	Doncaster Racecourse, Ledger Way, Doncaster, South Yorkshire.
September 13-15	GREAT AUTUMN FLOWER SHOW
	Great Yorkshire Showground, Harrogate, North Yorkshire.
September 21-29	SCARBOROUGH ANGLING FESTIVAL
	Scarborough
October 7-10	YORKSHIRE THREE CHOIRS FESTIVAL
	Ripon Cathedral, Ripon, North Yorkshire.
October 10-26	LEEDS FILM FESTIVAL
	Various venues, Leeds
December 31	ALLENDALE BAAL FESTIVAL
	Market square, Allendale

Denotes provisional date

For further information contact:

Yorkshire & Humberside Tourist Board
312 Tadcaster Road
York YO2 2HF.
Tel: 01904 707961

Northumbria Tourist Board
Aykley Heads
Durham DH1 5UX
Tel: 0191 384 6905

ROYAL COUNTY HOTEL
Old Elvet, Durham, County Durham DHl 3JN

Telephone: 0191 386 6821   *Fax: 0191 386 0704*

The historic city of Durham is surely the ideal location for the holidaymaker from which to explore the delightful north eastern corner of England. The beautiful scenery of the counties of Durham, Yorkshire, Northumberland and even Cumbria, are all within easy reach, and the city itself is a must on any tourists itinerary. For the businessman, Durham also makes an ideal centre for meetings and conferences, as the industrial areas of the north east are all easily accessible by road or rail. Situated right in the heart of Durham, on the very banks of the River Wear, is this gem of an hotel. Originally a coaching inn, but now extended and modernised, The Royal County offers everything that the discening guest could hope for. The comfort is superb, the service excellent but discreet, and the ambience warm and friendly. There is a restaurant offering the most delicious food from well thought out menus, and a Brasserie for more informal meals. After indulging in all this luxury, the hotel has a super leisure centre to suit all moods, with an indoor heated swimming pool, gymnasium, sauna and solarium. I cannot recommend the Royal County too highly - it is a hedonist's delight! Room and breakfast from £85.00 single, £120.00 double/twin, weekly rates on application. **Swallow Breakaway Packages** : 2 nights, half board plus one lunchon the day of your choice. **Newcastle 15, Edinburgh 115, London 265.**

F licence; 150 en suite bedrooms (1 for the disabled), all with direct dial telephone and TV; room service; baby listening; night service; 3 lifts; last orders for dinner (Mon-Sat) 10.15p.m.; diets; children welcome; dogs accepted; conferences 140 max; Brasserie; indoor heated swimming pool; leisure centre; sauna; solarium; steam room; spa pool; gymnasium; open all year; all major credit cards accepted.

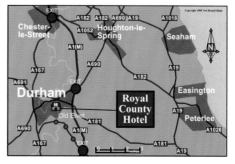

WAREN HOUSE HOTEL
Waren Mill, Bamburgh, Northumberland NE70 7EE

Telephone: 01668 214581   *Fax: 01668 214484*

The North-East coast offers few hotels of distinction, but Waren House is one of those which can boast exceptional quality. After battling with the traffic on the Al, a sign points you to Waren Mill. Follow 2 miles of peaceful back roads and signposts will direct you up the tree lined drive to the house. Having been quietly shown to your room where sherry awaits you, perhaps before doing anything else, you will complete the unwinding by enjoying a hot tub in a superb bathroom. Throughout the hotel the furnishings, mostly beautiful antiques, and the immaculate and well chosen décor, exude a warm and friendly atmosphere. But this is not all. Waren House is a haven for the gastronome. Delicious repasts prepared from the freshest of ingredients are tastefully presented and a most thoughtfully chosen wine list is provided with a large selection of half bottles. Discreet service completes the air of peace and well-being and Anita and Peter Laverack, the owners, are to be congratulated on the ways they constantly find to improve this delightful hotel. I should add, that a visit to this area is more than worthwhile, not only to stay at Waren House, but to visit such castles as Bamburgh, Alnwick, Dunstanburgh and Warkworth. For the ornithologist, there is a wealth of bird life at Budle Bay and the Farn Islands Bird Sanctuaries and for the tourist, Lindisfarne and the Cheviot Hills are but a short distance away. Room and breakfast from £52.00 per person, double occupancy and two suites are also available. No smoking except in the library. Bargain breaks: From 18.10.95-4.5.96 dinner, room and breakfast for £55 pppn sharing (min. 2 nights). *Signpost* readers will be upgraded to a superior room or suite subject to availability. Please mention *Signpost* when booking. £25 pp extra for Xmas Day and New Year's Eve. RAC ★★★, ETB ❤❤❤❤ CrownHighly Commended. Open all year. **Berwick 14, Alnwick 14, Newcastle 45, London 350.**

F licence; 7en suite bedrooms (all no smoking), with telephone and colour TV; last orders 8.30 p.m.; special diets; no children; croquet lawn; tennis court; sea bathing; riding; birdwatching; local sailing/boat-ing; seven golf courses within 12 miles; shooting/fishing by arrangement; major credit cards accepted.

KINGS ARMS HOTEL
Hide Hill, Berwick-upon-Tweed, Northumberland TD15 1EJ

Telephone: 01289 307454   Fax: 01289 308867

Historical links and geographic location are the main attractions of the 18th-Century Kings Arms Hotel and also, by virtue of its reputation, it is a natural venue for business people, farmers, anglers and tourists alike. The welcome here is warm, the standard of service high and the bedrooms, including family rooms, private suites and three four posters have recently been refurbished to a high standard. The chandeliered lounge and the pleasant cocktail bar allow plenty of room to relax whilst the oak-panelled Kings Room restaurant offers extensive table d'hôte and à la carte menus with fresh local specialities such as Tweed salmon. Simpler meals, but of the same quality, are available in the Cafe Pizzazz Italian style restaurant or the Garden Terrace Self Service Restaurant. The border town of Berwick has changed hands thirteen times but now it is more peacable: favoured by artists, distinguished by its mediaeval walls and its three famous bridges, it is truly picturesque as well as being near to a wealth of attractions, including the wool, cashmere and mohair towns of Melrose and Kelso, famous golf courses, Holy Island, The Tweed itself and Edinburgh - but an easy journey by rail or road. The Kings Arms provides an ideal and most comfortable base. Single room including breakfast from £53.50. Double room with breakfast from £69.50. **Leisure Breaks:** £59.50 - 2 nights d,b&b incl. 3-course dinner in Cafe Pizzazz or £15.00 allowance against Kings Room Brasserie Menu. Based on twin occupancy. **Edinburgh 57 , Alnwick 30 , Newcastle -upon Tyne 63 , Haddington 39, London 337 .**

F licence; 36 en suite bedrooms with colour TV; Direct-dial telephone, hairdryer, trouser press, laundry service, tea/coffee making facilities. 24-hour room service. Last orders for dinner 22.00 hrs. Fishing, golf, squash, tennis and riding all nearby. Business services provided and two conference rooms with total capacity for 200 guests; AV facilities. Open all year. Major credit cards accepted.

WARKWORTH HOUSE HOTEL

16 Bridge Street, Warkworth, Northumberland NE65 0XB

Telephone 01665 711276 ;
Fax 01665 713323

Dominated by its 15th Century castle and nestling by the River Cognet, Warkworth is an important landmark in the Northumbrian coastal region. Warkworth House Hotel, built in 1830, situated in the picturesque main street, offers the charm of a listed building and every comfort. In the beautiful dining-room - cum conservatory - the tempting menu combines a choice of local dishes with international ones, complemented by an excellent wine list. Meals are also available in the attractive bar. Mr and Mrs Duncan Oliver make their guests very welcome in this well appointed hotel. Single room including breakfast from £50.00. Double room with breakfast from £75.00. **Leisure Breaks:** 4 nights d,b&b £159.00. Special winter rates available plus Christmas & New Year rates.

Berwick 39, Edinburgh 96 , Alnwick 9 , Newcastle-upon-Tyne 32 , London 298 .

Full licence. 14 en suite bedrooms, including 2 family rooms, with radio, Colour TV; direct-dial telephone. Hairdryer, trouser press, laundry service, non-smoker bedrooms, tea/coffee making facilities. Last orders for dinner 8.30 pm. Special diets available. Facilities for the disabled. Fishing, golf, riding nearby. Shooting 9 miles. Car parking for 14 cars. Open all year. Main credit cards accepted.

APPLETON HALL HOTEL

Appleton-le-Moors, N. Yorkshire YO6 6TF

Telephone: 01751 417227 / 417452 ;
Fax: 01751 417540

If you are looking for peace and tranquillity away from the usual tourist routes, then Appleton Hall is the hotel for you. The Hall is an English country house which has been converted to form a most comfortable hotel with all its bedrooms en suite. There are magnificent views especially from the elegant lounge with its comfortable furniture and log fire. The Hall is situated at the end of the picturesque and historic village of Appleton-le-Moors. Inside, there is a cosy bar serving over 80 brands of whisky. Mrs. Davies uses the freshest of ingredients and produces a delicious range of English dishes which are available throughout the day and evening. One day is hardly enough time to enjoy this hotel and its lovely surroundings, and special breaks are available for those wishing to stay longer. Dinner, bed and breakfast from £48.00, £3.00 supplement per person for suites or four-poster room. Open all year round. **London 232, York 33, Whitby 26, Scarborough 24, Thirsk 24.**

R & R licence; 10 en suite bedrooms, including 2 suites and a four-poster, all with TV, full central heating; lift; meals to 8.30p.m.; diets; dogs welcome; golf 1 1/2 miles, riding three miles, fishing by arrangement; Mastercard, Amex, Visa credit cards accepted.

GEORGE AND DRAGON HOTEL

17 Market Place, Kirkbymoorside, North Yorkshire YO6 6AA

Telephone/Fax: 01751 433334

The ambience of a coaching inn with the comforts of a modern hotel, with good food and wine, and an ideal venue for exploring the North Yorkshire moors and the many famous homes, abbeys and castles of the area. The George and Dragon is situated in the centre of the small market town of Kirkbymoorside, and thus virtually all of North Yorkshire, including York, is within easy drive of the hotel. All the rooms are decorated and furnished to a high standard are are in two separate buildings around a lovely walled garden. Room and breakfast from £40 single; £34 twin/double per person.

Bargain breaks: 2 nights dinner, bed and breakfast £89 per person (sharing); Golf midweek breaks - 2 days' free golf + 2 nights dinner,b&b - £119 per person.

A1 - Thirsk 20, York 30, Scarborough 28, London 244.

F licence; 19 en suite bedrooms, all with direct dial telephone, TV and hospitality tray; room service; last orders for dinner 9.00 p.m.; bar meals; special diets; dogs accepted; conferences max. 25; golf and shooting nearby; open all year; Mastercard, Amex and Visa credit cards accepted.

ALDWARK MANOR GOLF HOTEL

Aldwark, Alne, Nr. York, North Yorkshire YO6 2NF

Telephone 01347 838146/7 Fax 01347 838867

Aldwark Manor is a country house hotel with its golf course spanning the River Ure. The Manor provides every comfort for its guests including four posters. This is a friendly place from which to explore the varied countryside or simply to play golf on the superb course. The food is excellent too. This is a great place to stay for the sports enthusiast, the bon viveur or simply for a relaxing holiday. Single room including breakfast £45.00. **Leisure Breaks:** Golf Break mid-week £130.00 pp 2 nights; £150.00 pp weekend. Yorkshire Break mid-week £95.00 pp 2 nights; £110.00 pp weekend.

York 14, Boroughbridge 7, Thirsk 12, Easingwold 3, London 212.

Full licence. 20 en suite bedrooms (one for the partially disabled) all with TV and direct dial telephone; hairdryer, trouser press, laundry service, tea/coffee making facilities, non-smoker bedrooms. 24-hour room service. Last orders for dinner 21.30. Bar meals, special diets. Conferences max 80. Hairdresser. 18 hole golf course, fishing, riding by arrangement. Car parking. Airport pick-up. Hairdresser. Open all year. All major credit cards accepted.

THE MILBURN ARMS HOTEL
Rosedale Abbey,
Pickering, North
Yorkshire YO18 8RA
Telephone: 01751 417312
Fax: 01751 417312

This country hotel set in a village in
the North York moors is a delight of
comfort and cuisine. The lounge with its books is homely, the bedrooms, some overlooking the
cedar graced garden, are individually decorated and my hosts, Terry and Joan Bentley, proved
experts on walks and places to visit. You can dine in the oak-beamed bar with log fire, or in
the dining-room where the award -winning chef specialises in English cuisine with fresh local
produce. In these surroundings the cares of the world fall away. Single rooms including
Breakfast from £41.00; double room with breakfast £68.00.
Leisure Breaks: "Mid-Week" and "Romantic Week-End" breaks - enquire for further details.
Scarborough 16 , Whitby 20, Malton 8, York 25, Middlesbrough 43, London 213.
*Full licence. 11 en suite bedrooms with radio & colour TV. Direct-dial telephone, hairdryer, laundry
service, tea/coffee making facilities. Last orders for dinner 21.30 hrs. Riding and golf 5-8 miles. Busi-
ness services, typing, photocopying. Car parking 50 cars. Open all year. Credit cards accepted.*

PARK HALL HOTEL AND UPLANDS MANOR RESTAURANT
Spinkhill, Sheffield,
South Yorkshire S31
9YD

Telephone 01246 434897
Fax 01246 436282

This lovely 14th Century Manor House set in eight acres of grounds is close to Sheffield for the
business traveller, yet located in quiet countryside for the tourist. Jan and Tony Clark give a
friendly welcome to their peaceful retreat where modernisation provides all comforts, but
without detriment to open fires, panelled halls and mullioned windows. Cultivated gardens,
a croquet lawn and ancient walls recall a more leisurely past. Single room with breakfast from
£56.50. Double room including breakfast from £75.00. Weekend Breaks available on application. **Leeds 36 , Manchester 41, M1 Junction 30 - 3 , Nottingham 44 , London 174.**

*F licence. Eight en suite bedrooms with radio & colour TV; direct-dial telephone, hairdryer, trouser
press, laundry service; non-smoker bedrooms, tea/coffee making facilities. Last orders for dinner
21.30 hrs. Special diets available. Croquet. All other main leisure activities within 5 miles. Business
services include 3 meeting rooms with capacity for 75 and some AV facilities. Car parking for 75
cars. All major credit cards accepted.*

DEVONSHIRE ARMS COUNTRY HOUSE HOTEL
Bolton Abbey, Skipton, North Yorkshire BD23 6AJ

Telephone: 01756 710441   Fax: 01756 710564

The Devonshire at Bolton Abbey, for many years renowned as one of the best hotels in York-shire, is a contrast in styles. On the one hand there is the original coaching inn with the warmth and atmosphere of days gone by, and on the other, is the new extension with all the light and space created by a modern building. The superb furnishings and décor have been most tastefully chosen by the Duchess of Devonshire herself using many paintings and an-tiques from her home at Chatsworth. Seven of the bedrooms have four-poster beds made by the craftsmen at Chatsworth Carpenters, and six rooms have been designated non-smoking. However, this is no old-fashioned hotel and the service is impeccable, earning it the coveted Yorkshire and Humberside Tourist Board "Hotel of the Year Award", for the past 3 years . The food, acclaimed by all in the county, is delicious, well presented and served by willing and attentive staff. It need hardly be added that the hotel is situated in one of the most envi-able of positions, in the heart of Wharfedale close to Bolton Abbey and within easy motoring distance of Yorkshire' s many other attractions. Here is the ideal venue for a business meeting or conference, visual aids and secretarial services, fax etc. being available. To sum up, this is a charming, stylish hotel, thoroughly modern in its approach to comfort and efficiency. Room and breakfast from £105 single, £140 double. **York 40, Leeds 23,Ilkley 6, Harrogate 17,London 214.** *F licence; 41 en suite bedrooms (18 ground floor), all with telephone, TV; night service, last orders 10.00 pm; bar meals; diets; children welcome; baby listen-ing; dogs accepted; conferences max. 150; golf nearby; riding, helicopter tours & tailor-made team building activity events can be arranged; classic car motoring; shooting; fishing; leisure, health & beauty therapy cen-tre. Open all year. All major credit cards accepted.*

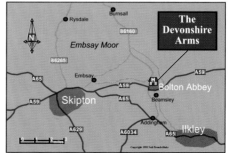

THE BALMORAL HOTEL AND HENRY'S RESTAURANT
Franklin Mount, Harrogate, N. Yorks. HGl 5EJ

Telephone: 01423 508208   Fax: 01423 530652

What a delightful surprise it was to discover this superb hotel! It is situated in its own award winning gardens, away from the centre of town and yet within walking distance of all the amenities that Harrogate provides - conference centre, shops and wonderful surrounding countryside. The Balmoral is unique - beautifully furnished, mostly with antiques and tastefully decorated to create a warm, luxurious and welcoming atmosphere. The bedrooms are all individual, many having four poster beds and again are extremely comfortable with thoughtfully chosen décor. Everything that you could possibly need is provided and to stay in one of these rooms is an experience in luxury. The food here is not only imaginative but is prepared from the finest ingredients, cooked to perfection and served by friendly and attentive staff.   Room and breakfast from £69.00 single, £92.00 double and weekly rates on application. Short breaks are also available throughout the year as are pampering and relaxing Spa breaks. E.T.B. ≈≈≈≈ Highly Commended.

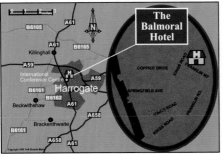

York 20, London 200, Yorkshire Dales 15, Leeds/ Bradford Airport 18.

R & R licence; 20 en suite bedrooms (9 four poster rooms), all with direct dial telephone and TV; room service; baby listening; limited night service; last orders for dinner 9.00 for 9.30 p.m.; diets; children welcome; dogs accepted; conferences (boardroom) 20 max/(theatre style) 30 max; solarium; indoor heated swimming pool and leisure facilities 100 yards away; 4 golf courses and riding stables nearby; tennis by arrangement; open all year; major credit cards accepted.

KIMBERLEY HOTEL
11-19 Kings Road Harrogate North Yorkshire HG1 5JY

Telephone: 01423 505613;   Fax: 01423 530276

There is a new way to stay in the heart of Harrogate, that delightful spa town at the centre of scenic North Yorkshire. It is called The Kimberley Hotel, which opened it's doors only recently to welcome guests to the beautifully renovated interior. The public areas are elegant and relaxing and the spacious bedrooms are designed for comfort and convenience, with some even providing additional points for personal computers. The location is brilliant: for the tourist it is a short walk from the town's many attractions and residents can also visit the hotel's family estate at Kilnsey Park where every type of entertainment is offered. The hotel's facilities are superb for the executive and the International Conference Centre is practically next door. The day begins with a sumptuous breakfast buffet in the large dining room, but despite having state of the art kitchens the hotel produces an informative brochure of recommended places which offer a range of cuisine for guests to savour in the excellent restaurants nearby. The day finishes with a quiet drink in the cosy bar. The "new way" is a formula of quality hospitality and comfort which I am sure will continue to work for other guests as it did so well for me. Single room with breakfast and newspaper from £55.00. Double/Twin with breakfast and newspaper from £59.50. **Leisure Breaks:** Short breaks for a two night stay from £32.00 pppn with breakfast and newspaper to include a Saturday night. Enquire for other special offers during year.
York 22 , Leeds 15 , Bradford 18 , Newcastle-upon-Tyne 76, London 211 .
Full licence. 60 en suite bedrooms with radio & satellite TV; direct-dial telephone; hairdryer, trouser press, laundry service; tea/coffee making facilities. Fishing, golf, watersports, riding, shooting, squash and tennis by arrangement nearby. Facilities for disabled. Car rental. Car parking for 58 cars. Open all year. All major credit cards accepted.

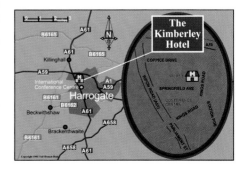

FEVERSHAM ARMS HOTEL
Helmsley, North Yorkshire YO6 5AG

Telephone: 01439 770766   Fax: 01439 770346

Originally a coaching inn where candles and beer were made and sold, this hotel has been elegantly modernised and improved to a high standard not often found in this country. The bedrooms. intimate rather than large, are individually decorated and well appointed with every modern convenience. The reception rooms are relaxing and there is an all-round friendly and welcoming atmosphere. The award winning candlelit Goya restaurant displays a very comprehensive menu including seafood, shellfish and some game specialities and the awarded wine list is truly incredible. The extensive bar snack menu would put many restaurants à la carte menu to shame and, on a hot day, a meal on the besutiful Spanish style patio by the swimming pool is my idea of heaven. Helmsley is an excellent centre for sporting activities, for visiting historical buildings, abbeys and stately homes and for exploring the unique North York Moors National Park. Room and breakfast £55 single, £70 twin/double and £80 four-poster or suite. "Bonanza Breaks" available all year round. Ask for a brochure and you will not be disappointed. Open all year. **York 20, Thirsk 14, Teeside Airport 35, London 222.**

L licence, 18 en suite bedrooms (6 ground floor, 5 four-posters), all with hairdryer, trouser press, tea/ coffee making facilities, safe, radio, direct-dial telephone and TV + satellite. Full central heating. Last orders 9.30 p.m.; diets; bar snacks; children welcome; baby listening; dogs welcome; conferences up to 30 (18 residential); swimming pool; patio; tennis court and gardens in hotel grounds; riding and golf near-by; Visa, Amex, Mastercard and Diners cards accepted.

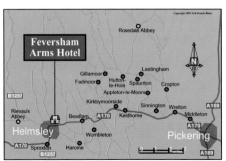

THE PHEASANT
Harome, Helmsley, N. Yorkshire YO6 5JG

Telephone: 01439 771241

The Pheasant was recommended to me by another hotelier of note in Yorkshire and how right he was to guide me to it. Set in a pretty village, overlooking the village pond, it has been imaginatively created from a group of buildings on two sides of a courtyard. Inside, the log fires, the antiques and the numerous beams lend an air of warmth and comfort to the tastefully decorated rooms. Old fashioned in atmosphere the hotel might be, but the best of all the modern conveniences are also there where needed. The bedrooms, for example, all have colour television, telephone, tea/coffee making facilities, etc. Mrs 'Tricia Binks provides the most delicious food and many of the ingredients come from the hotel's own large garden and paddock. Holly Cottage is also available - this is a charming, thatched 16th century cottage just 350 yards from the hotel, with two double bedrooms and two sitting rooms, all attractively furnished to the same high standard as the hotel. It is serviced by the hotel staff and meals are taken in the hotel. A quiet and peaceful haven with a delightful atmosphere. Having said all this, The Pheasant makes an ideal base from which to explore this most beautiful part of England, where there is so much to see and do. Dinner, room and breakfast from £51.50 (1st Nov-mid-May); £57.50-£59.95 (high season) including VAT. Closed January and February. **Helmsley 3, York 22, Scarborough 28, Leeds 48, Edinburgh 160, London 220.**
R & Rlicence, 14 en suite bedrooms (1 ground floor), all with telephone, colour TV, tea/coffee making facilities; full central heating; last orders 8. 00p.m; bar meals (lunch); diets; children over 14 welcome; dogs by arrangement; conferences max. 12; own heated indoor swimming pool; golf, tennis, riding, fishing all nearby; credit cards not accepted.

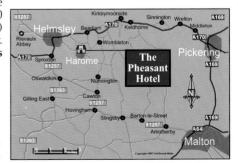

RYEDALE LODGE
Nunnington, Nr. Helmsley, North Yorkshire YO6 5XB

Telephone: 01439 748246; Fax: 01653 694633

What a delghtful find! In what used to be a country railway station, Jon and Janet Laird have created a superb little hotel. Where trains once ran, you can now stroll and listen to the evening bird song and the distant lowing of cattle. It is an idyllic setting. However, Ryedale Lodge is exceptional not only for its situation, but for its comfort; inside, every room is tastefully and beautifully furnished, and an air of warmth and serenity pervades throughout. As the reader can no doubt deduce, I find this hotel particularly inviting, but it is for its food that I shall be most tempted to return. Not only is Janet Laird a good cook, but she chooses the finest and freshest ingredients to produce the most varied and imaginative menu. The results are stupendous! I look forward eagerly to visiting this hotel again and again. If you look at a map of Yorkshire, Nunnington is almost in the middle and as such Ryedale is truly the centre of all that is best in this lovely and historic county.   Room and breakfast from £41.50 (double per head)/£47.50 single; weekly rates from £330.00 per person. **Bargain breaks:** 2 consecutive nights between 1/10/95 and 31/5/96 £128 per person inc. room, breakfast and dinner. Summer 2-day break between 1/6/96 and 30/9/96 £134. 3 nights or more - tariff on application. **Helmsley 5, York 20, East coast 30, Edinburgh 160, London 230.**

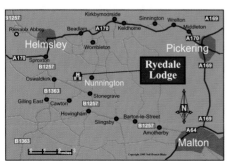

R licence; 7 en suite bedrooms (one ground floor), all with colour TV, hairdryer, telephone and full central heating; last orders 9 p.m.(table d'hôte £26.75); diets; children welcome; baby listening; no dogs; conferences up to 20; swimming pool; fishing; golf and riding five miles; Visa and Access cards accepted.

LASTINGHAM GRANGE HOTEL
Lastingham, Nr. Kirkbymoorside, Yorkshire YO6 6TEI

Telephone: 01751 417345 or 417402

You can discover this delightfully situated, elegant country house by leaving the A170 at Kirkbymoorside and making for Hutton-le-Hole. The Grange is stone-walled and built round a courtyard. It is set within 10 acres of well-kept gardens and fields, on the edge of the moors, in the historic village of Lastingham, a peaceful backwater in the heart of the National Park. Lastingham Grange is owned and personally run by Mr. and Mrs. Dennis Wood. The atmosphere, even during the height of the season, is unhurried and peaceful, the south-facing terrace providing a pleasant setting in which to relax and enjoy the beautiful rose garden, noted for the variety and rarity of its many flowering shrubs and trees. The spacious and homely lounge, with its open fire, and the comfortable bedrooms with their impressive views, are all tastefully furnished. The food is excellent - speedily and cheerfully served. Room and breakfast from £59.00 single. Short breaks available.

Open March to the beginning of December.
Bargain breaks: Dinner, bed & breakfast from £83.75 for 2 days or more; £77.75 one week or more, per person per night.
London 232, Malton 15, Scarborough 24, Thirsk 24, Whitby 26, York 33.

R and R licence, 12 en suite bedrooms, four with bath, eight with bath and shower; all with telephone, trouser press, hairdryer; children welcome; baby listening in all rooms; drying room; diets; golf five miles; riding one mile.

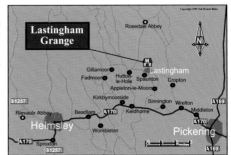

THE KING'S ARMS HOTEL AND CLUBROOM RESTAURANT

Market Place, Askrigg in Wensleydale, Leyburn, N. Yorkshire DL8 3HQ

Telephone 01969 650258   Fax 01969 650635

Beamed ceilings, richly panelled rooms, roaring log fires, and cosy bars where the locals meet: these are features you associate with quality English country hotels and at the King's Arms in the heart of the Dales all of them are to be found. Liz and Ray Hopwood are welcoming hosts to this lovely Georgian Manor House Hotel where the guests are first shown to the comfort of beautifully appointed period bedrooms whose original features are in character with the hotel, with antique furnishings, oak beams and choice of bed from brass ornamental to four-poster. Then there are the pleasures of award winning food and John Barber, the chef, uses prime quality local foodstuffs such as grouse, fresh fish from Whitby,and locally grown vegetables to create dishes blending traditional Yorkshire food with continental cuisine - the Restaurant, Grill and Bar meals enjoy a great reputation as a result. Surrounding Askrigg is the magnificent Dales scenery, which delighted Turner when he stayed in the King's Arms, as it does so many people today. Single room with breakfast from £50. Double room including breakfast from £75. **Leisure Breaks**: Special tariff with dining in Two-Rosette restaurant. Min. 2 nights stay mid-week discount and upgrade for *Signpost* readers subject to availability. **Leeds 70, York 63 , Kendal 32 , Leyburn 12 , Skiton 31 , London 245.**

Full licence. 10 en suite bedrooms with radio & colour TV; direct-dial telephone; tea/coffee making facilities. Last orders for dinner 21.00 hrs. Diets. Fishing, riding, shooting nearby. Golf 20 miles. Full business services including 3 meeting rooms with capacity for 8-40 guests. Car parking for 14 cars. Open all year. Major credit cards accepted.

MONK FRYSTON HALL
Monk Fryston, Nr. Leeds, North Yorkshire LS25 5DU

Telephone: 01977 682369   Fax: 01977 683544

This is surely the epitome of a country house hotel. In a superb house, with a history going back to the Middle Ages, you can enjoy every modern comfort and convenience whilst wining and dining in a style reminiscent of those former times. The richly panelled rooms are lit by stone mullioned windows and, in winter, are warmed by open fires creating a glowing ambience of well being. Outside, with the splendid stone elevations of the house as a backdrop, you can stroll by the lake or on the terraces of the gardens, both formal and informal. If motoring up the A1, visiting the races at either Doncaster or York, holding a small conference or simply touring in this lovely area, then Monk Fryston makes an excellent place to stay and indulge oneself. Room and breakfast from £68.50-£72.00 (single); £95.00-£102.00 (double), VAT. included. **Weekend breaks** until 31st March 1996 - £116 per person for 2 nights; £174 per person for 3 nights. From 6 April 1996 - £120 per person for 2 nights; £180 per person for 3 nights. Includes Bank Holidays except Christmas and New Year. Open all year.
York 18, Harrogate 25, Selby 7, Al -2, London 184.

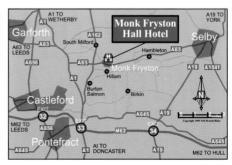

F licence; 28 bedrooms (6 ground floor) all with private bathroom, radio, telephone and TV; central heating; late meals to 9.30 p.m.; diets; children welcome, baby listening; dogs welcome; conferences up to 16 residential, day conferences up to 50; credit cards accepted.

EAST AYTON LODGE COUNTRY HOTEL & RESTAURANT

Moor Lane, East Ayton, Nr. Scarborough, N. Yorkshire YO13 9EW

Telephone: 01723 864227   *Fax: 01723 862680*

The North Yorkshire Moors are, to me and to others, one of the most beautiful parts of Britain, and a visit to them is essential for any lover of the countryside. Where better then, than to stay at an hotel on the edge of these moors, with its own 3 acres of gardens in which to relax. With both sea and river fishing close by, lovely walks in the Forge Valley, and the whole of historic Yorkshire all around East Ayton Lodge, it is an ideal centre for a holiday, a bonus being the proximity of Ganton Golf Club located a few miles from the hotel. Having relaxed, after what can often be a strenuous day of exploring, dinner can be chosen from either the comprehensive table d'hôte, or the interesting à la carte menus, and enjoyed in the large, comfortable dining room. There is a well chosen wine list from which to indulge yourself, and finally the inviting bedrooms beckon one to a well-earned rest. It should, perhaps, be mentioned that the hotel offers conference facilities to companies who are looking for a peaceful

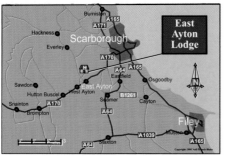

setting, and an "out of town" venue . Room and breakfast from £27.50, dinner, room and breakfast from £37.50, including VAT. **Scarborough 3, Whitby 24, York 36, Leeds 65, London 213.**

F licence, 31 en suite bedrooms (9 for the disabled and including four bridal suites), all with direct dial telephone aad TV, room service; baby listening; night service; last orders for dinner 9. 00 p.m.; bar meals; special diets; children welcome; dogs accepted; conferences max. 100; shooting/fishing nearby; golf and tennis three miles; riding five miles; open all year; all major credit cards accepted.

WREA HEAD COUNTRY HOTEL
Barmoor Lane, Scalby, Scarborough, North Yorkshire YO13 0PB

Telephone: 01723 378211   *Fax: 01723 355936*

Set in fourteen acres of wooded, landscaped grounds, near the sea and the North York Moors National Park, Wrea Head is ideal for the tourist seeking peace or to explore the rich heritage of this lovely region: Whitby, a picturesque former whaling port and home of Captain Cook; Robin Hood's Bay; York, home of the National Railway Museum and the Jorvik Centre and Goathland with its spectacular waterfalls are some of the fascinating places close by. Wrea Head has retained the charm and character of a traditional Victorian English Country House, with its magnificent panelled hall and lounge, minstrel's gallery, ingle-nook fireplace and bow-windowed library. Fine pieces of original furniture, antiques and paintings grace the beautiful interior. The bedrooms are well appointed and individually decorated, very comfortable and with attractive views. Cuisine is predominantly English using fresh local produce from the garden and the dining room is welcoming and spacious; its windows looking out over a vista of lawns and woodland. A comfortable bar lounge with adjoining conservatory and sunny terrace, serving light refreshments throughout the day, enhance the restorative attributes of this excellent hotel. Single room with breakfast from £57.50. Double room with breakfast from £115.00. **Scarborough 2¹/₂ , Whitby 17 , Pickering 18, York 36, London 216.** *Full licence. 21 en suite bedrooms with colour TV & direct-dial telephone. Hairdryer, trouser press, laundry service, tea/coffee making facilities. Last orders for dinner 21.15. Special diets available. Indoor swimming pool one mile. Full business services including two conference rooms and AV equipment. Open all year. Major credit cards accepted.*

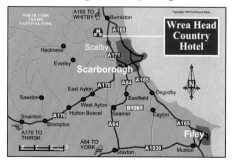

THE JUDGES LODGING HOTEL
9 Lendal, York, North Yorkshire YO1 2AQ

Telephone: 01904 638733   *Fax: 01904 679947*

Imagine yourself in York in the early 1 8th century. You are arriving at your grand house in the city centre. There is a glow from the windows and the servants await you. Now, retaining that ambience in your mind, transport yourself to the present day; add the comforts that we have all come to expect, and you will begin to sense the flavour of a stay at The Judges Lodging. The house has been impeccably kept to its original plan and atmosphere, and yet it has been cleverly transformed into a small, warm and intimate hotel. The furnishings and decor are beautifully in keeping with the building. There is a lovely candlelit restaurant serving delicious food, and a wine list to suit all palates. Now, when you visit York, you cannot only see all the historical sites such as the Minster, the Jorvik Viking Centre and the National Railway Museum, but you can stay in one of the most historic houses in the city. It is an experience in itself, and it can set the scene for exploring the many other houses and abbeys with which Yorkshire abounds and the wild and exciting Yorkshire Moors. Room and breakfast from £67.50 single, £90.00 double, including VAT. **Bargain breaks** available from November-Easter. Tariff on application.

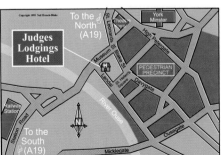

Leeds 24, Manchester 72, Edinburgh 192, London 209.

F licence; 12 en suite bedrooms (two with spa baths), all with direct dial telephone and TV; room service; baby listening; night service; last orders for dinner 9.30 p.m; bar meals, special diets, children welcome, dogs by arrangement; conferences max. 20; sailing/boating 200 yards; four major golf courses within five miles; open all year; all major credit cards accepted.

■Historic Houses, Gardens & Parks

CLWYD
Chirk Castle, Bodelwyddan
Bodrhyddan Hall, Rhuddlan
Bodnant Garden, Tal-y-Cafn
Erddig Hall, Wrexham
Colwyn Leisure Centre

DYFED
Manor House Wildlife & Leisure Park, Tenby
Tudor Merchant's House, Quay Hill, Tenby

GWYNEDD
Bryn Bras Castle, Llanrug, Nr. Llanberis
Parc Glynllifon, Nr. Caernarfon
Plas Newydd, Llanfairpwll, Anglesey

GWENT
Bryn Bach Park, Tredegar
Caldicot Castle & Country Park, Nr. Newport
Tredegar House, Newport

GLAMORGAN
Castell Cochi, Tongwynlais, Cardiff
Cosmeston Lakes Country Park & Medieval Village
Dyffryn House & Gardens, St. Nicholas, Nr. Cardiff
Llanerch Vineyard, Pendoylan
Margam Park, Port Talbot

■Walks & Nature Trails

CLWYD
Greenfield Valley Heritage Park, Holywell
Llyn Brenig Visitor Centre, Corwen
Logger Heads Country Park, Nr Mold
Ty Mawr Country Park, Cefn Mawr, Nr. Wrexham

DYFED
Bwlch Nant Yr Arian Forest Visitor Centre, Ponterwyd
Gelli Aur Countly Park, Llandeilo
Llysyfran Reservoir & Country Park, Nr. Haverfordwest
Pembrey Country Park, Pembrey

GWYNEDD
Bryntirion Open Farm, Dwyran, Anglesey
Coed-y-Brenin Forest Park & Visitor Centre, Ganllwyd, Dolgellau
The Greenwood Centre, Port Dinorwic
Parc Padarn, Llanberis
South Stack Cliffs Reserve & Elfins Tower Information Centre, Holyhead
Tyn Llan Crafts & Farm Museum, Nr. Porthmadog
'Ý Stablau', Gwydyr Forest Park, Llanrwst

GWENT
Festival Park, Ebbw Vale
Llandegfedd Reservolr, Pontypool

POWYS
Brecon Beacons Mountain Centre, Nr. Libanus
Gigrin Farm & Nature Trail, Rhyader
Lake Vyrnwy RSPB Reserve & Information Centre
Ynys-Hir Reserve & Visitor Cenne, Machynlleth

GLAMORGAN
Alan Forest Park & Countryside Centre, Port Talbot
Bryngarw Country Park, Nr. Bridgend
Garwnant Visitor Centre, Cwm Taf, Merthyr Tydfil
Gnoll Country Park, Neath

■ Historical Sites & Museums

CLWYD
Bodelwyddan Castle
Denbigh Castle
Flint Castle & Town Walls
Valle Crucis Abbey, Llangollen
Rhuddlan Castle, Nr. Rhyl

DYFED
Castell Henllys Iron Age Hillfort, Crymych
Carreg Cennen Castle, Trapp, Llangollen
Museum of the Welsh Woollen Industry, Llandysul
Castle Museum & Art Gallery, Haverfordwest
Kidwelly Castle
Manorbier Castle, Nr. Tenby
Milford Haven Museum, The Docks, Milford Haven
Picton Castle, Haverfordwest
Pembroke Castle
St Davids Bishop's Palace

GWENT
Chepstow Castle, Chepstow
The Nelson Museum & Local History Centre
Penhow Castle, Nr. Newport
Raglan Castle
Tintern Abbey, Tintern

GWYNEDD
Beaumaris Castle
Caernarfon Castle
Conwy Castle
Cymer Abbey, Dolgellau
Dolwyddelan Castle
Harlech Castle
Llanfair Slate Caverns, Nr. Harlech
The Lloyd George Museum, Llanystumdwy, Criccieth
Penrhyn Castle, Bangor

POWYS
Powys Castle & Museum, Welshpool
Tretower Court & Castle, Crickhowell

GLAMORGAN
Aberdulair Falls, Vale of Neath, Neath
Caerphilly Castle
Cardiff Castle
Castell Coch, Cardiff
Cefn Coed Colliery Museum, Crynant, Neath
National Museum of Wales
Welsh Folk Museum, Cardiff

■ Entertainment Venues

CLWYD
Afonwen Craft & Antique Centre, Nr. Mold
Llyn Brenig Visitor Centre, Cerrigydrudion

DYFED
Alice in Wonderland Visitor Centre, Llandudno
Anglesey Bird World, Dwyran/Sea Zoo, Brynsiencyn
Butlins Starcoast World, Pwllheli
Felin Isaf Water Mill, Glan Conwy
Ffestiniog Railway, Porthmadog
James Pringle Weavers of Llanfair P.G.
The Llywenog Silver-Lead Mines, Nr Aberystwyth
Maes Artro Tourist Village Llanbedr
Oakwood Park Theme Park, Narberth
Penmachno Woollen Mill, Nr. Betws-y-Coed
Portmeirion Village, Nr. Porthmadog
Sygun Copper Mine, Beddgelert

GWYNEDD (continued)
Snowdon Mountain Railway, Llamberis
Trefriw Woollen Mills, Trefriw
Welsh Gold, Dolgellau
Welsh Highland Railway, Porthmadog

POWYS
Welshpool & Llanfair Light Railway
Welsh Whisky Visitor Centre, Brecon

GLAMORGAN
Dan-yr-Ogof Showcaves, Abercraf
Margam Park, Port Talbot
Penscynor Wildlife Park, Cilfrew, Nr. Neath
Rhondda Heritage Park

WALES DIARY OF EVENTS 1996

January 1	BBC NATIONAL ORCHESTRA OF WALES NEW YEAR CONCERT St. David's Hall, Cardiff.
February 17	INTERNATIONAL RUGBY UNION, WALES v SCOTLAND Cardiff Arms Park, Cardiff.
February 26-28	LLANDUDNO BEER FESTIVAL Aberconwy Centre, Llandudno
March 1-3	35TH PORTMEIRION ANTIQUES FAIR Hercules Hall, Porthmeirion, Gwynedd
March 16	INTERNATIONAL RUGBY UNION, WALES v FRANCE Cardiff Arms Park, Cardiff.
May 25-June 1	ST. DAVIDS CATHEDRAL FESTIVAL St. Davids, Dyfed. Week long festival of the best classical music.
May 26-June 3	BEAUMARIS FESTIVAL Various venues in Beaumaris, Gwynedd
June 21-23	GWTLIFAN WELSH FOLK & DANCING FESTIVAL Various locations in Cardiff and surrounding areas
June 22-28	THREE PEAKS YACHT RACE - BARMOUTH TO FORT WILLIAM The Quay, Barmouth, Gwynedd.
July 9-14	LLANGOLLEN INTERNATIONAL MUSICAL EISTEDDFOD The Pavilion, Llangollen, Clwyd.
July 13-14	MIDWALES FESTIVAL OF TRANSPORT Powys Castle Showground, Welshpool
July 21-28	IAN RUSH INT'L SOCCER TOURNAMENT UCW Playing Fields, Llanbadarn Fawr, Aberystwyth, Dyfed
July 24-27	ROYAL WELSH SHOW Royal Welsh Showground, Llenelwedd, Builth Wells. Wales' Premier Agricultural Show.
July 22-28	GWYL CONWY FESTIVAL Streets around Conwy, Gwynedd.
July 25-28	BRITISH TRANSPLANT GAMES, CARDIFF 1996 Various locations in Cardiff & surrounding area
August 1	GOWER AGRICULTURAL SHOW Fairwood Airport, Swansea, West Midlands
August 3-10	ROYAL NATIONAL EISTEDDFOD OF WALES Bro Dinefwr, Llandeilo, Dyfed
August 9-11	BRECON JAZZ FESTIVAL Various venues, Brecon, Powys.
August 17-25	LLANDRINDOD WELLS VICTORIA FESTIVAL Various venues in and around Llandrindod wells, Powys
August 21-23	LADIES BRITISH OPEN AMATEUR STROKEPLAY CHAMPIONSHIP Conwy Golf Club, Morfa, Gwynedd

August 24	MONMOUTHSHIRE SHOW
	Monmouth Vauxhall Field, Monmouth, Gwent
September 14	USK SHOW
	Gwernesney, Nr. Usk, Gwent
September 16-22	NORTH WALES MUSIC FESTIVAL
	The Cathedral, St Asaph, Clwyd
September 20-28	TENBY ARTS FESTIVAL
	St Mary's Church & other venues in Tenby, Dyfed
November 1-3	36th PORTMEIRION ANTIQUES FAIR
	Hercules Hall, Portmeirion, Gwynedd
December 3	ROYAL WELSH AGRICULTURAL WINTER FAIR
	Royal Welsh Showground, Llanalwedd, Powys

For further information contact:
Wales Tourist Board Brunel House 2 Fitzalan Road Cardiff CF2 lUY. Tel: 01222 499909

LLANWENARTH HOUSE
Govilon, Abergavenny, Gwent NP7 9SF
Telephone: 01873 830289
Fax: 01873 832199
This fine house, home of the Weatherill family, stands in its own beautiful and tranquil grounds within The Brecon Beacons National Park. The house dates from the 16th Century and is historically linked with Captain Henry Morgan, the privateer, and King Charles I. Dinner is beautifully cooked and presented by Amanda, who makes full use of organically home grown produce and fine local meat, fish & game, complemented by a comprehensive wine list. Bedrooms are spacious and elegantly furnished. You will be as enchanted by Llanwenarth House as I was! Double room inc. breakfast £74 (single occupancy £20 discount off room rate). **Bargain breaks**: £66 per room 2 people sharing for 2 nights or more; 3 or 4 night Christmas package available. **Cardiff 35, London 165** m approx. Directions: A 40 from Monmouth, A 465 from Hereford or A 4042 from Newport, east of Abergavenny, follow A 465 towards Merthyr Tydfil for $3^1/2$ miles to next roundabout. Take first exit to Govilon and the $^1/4$ mile drive is 150 yds on right-hand side. *R & R licence. Five en suite bedrooms (one ground floor) with colour TV, hairdryer on request, tea/ coffee making facilities. Smoking discouraged in bedrooms & not allowed in dining room. Superb walking in the mountains. Fishing, golf, riding and other country pursuits all within 10 miles; Car rental by arrangement. Parking for six cars. Open March to mid-January.*

GLEN-YR-AFON HOUSE
Pontypool Road, Usk Gwent, Wales NP5 1SY

Telephone: 01291 672302/673202   Fax: 01291 672597

One of the first things that the visitor will notice about the Glen-Yr-Afon is the friendliness and efficiency of owners Jan and Peter Clarke who believe in a "hands on" approach. This is reflected in their staff who cheerfully anticipate the guests' every need. Only five minutes' walk from the pleasant market town of Usk, the hotel is situated on the Pontypool road with an agreeable river walk opposite. An excellent base from which to explore South Wales and only half an hour from the motorway. Glen-Yr-Afon is an imposing and elegant Victorian house retaining many original features, yet sympathetically updated by Jan and Peter. Bedrooms, which include a bridal suite, are large and tastefully decorated, with wonderfully large baths. The oak-panelled restaurant offers an excellent choice of à la carte or table d'hôte menus, imaginatively presented with generous helpings and a well-chosen wine list. Business people and wedding parties are well cared for with a function suite seating 140, whilst the charming library is the venue for anniversaries, dinner parties and smaller functions for up to 20 people. I noticed many guests return year after year and so shall I. Single room including breakfast from £46 + VAT. Double room with breakfast from £56 + VAT. **Leisure Breaks:** Any two days sharing room d,b&b £75. Cardiff 22 , Monmouth 13 , Newport 10 , Bristol 30 , Gloucester 39, Monmouth 13 , London 136 .

Full licence. 26 en suite bedrooms with satellite TV, radio, direct-dial telephone, laundry service, non-smoker bedrooms, tea/coffee making facilities. Facilities for disabled. Last orders for dinner 21.00. Special diets available. Croquet, fishing, golf, gliding, grass skiing - nearby. Full business services and 2 conference rooms for total of 120 guests. AV equipment available. Car parking for 87 cars. Open all year. Most credit cards accepted.

TREFEDDIAN HOTEL
Aberdovey, (Aberdyfi) LL35 OSB

Telephone: 01654 767213   Fax: 01654 767777

The Trefeddian Hotel stands in its own grounds, away from the main road, and is one mile from the middle of Aberdovey, a village with many attractions and which is becoming a centre where everyone, particularly the young, can pursue many outdoor activities. For example, supervision and special instruction can be arranged for sailing. The Directors, Mr. and Mrs. John Cave and Mr. Peter Cave, are responsible for the running of this first class family hotel, which has all the amenities that are part of a splendid holiday. The lounges are spacious, relaxing and peaceful and have recently been beautifully refurbished. The bedrooms, with views of Cardigan Bay, are comfortable and elegantly decorated. The menus offer a good choice of interesting and nicely presented dishes, complemented by a well chosen wine list. The Trefeddian is in the immediate vicinity of a four mile stretch of sandy beach and overlooks the golf course with the ever changing view of the sea beyond. The courtesy and efficiency of the staff create a happy atmosphere. Dinner, bed and breakfast from £44 per person, inclusive of VAT. Weekly terms, mini breaks (from £46 pppn, d,b&b), golf breaks, reductions for children, all shown on tariff sent, with brochure, on application. Open March to January (inc. Christmas and New Year), but office always open. **London 215, Birmingham 111, Manchester 110, Dolgellau 24, Barmouth 34, Harlech 45, Machynlleth 11, Talyllyn & Cader Idris 14.** *F licence; 46 en suite bedrooms, all with colour TV; lift; drying room; children welcome; baby listening; dogs welcome by arrangement but not in public rooms; games room with snooker table, pool table, table tennis; indoor heated swimming pool and solarium; putting green; tennis court; golf; sea bathing; boating; fishing nearby; garage.*

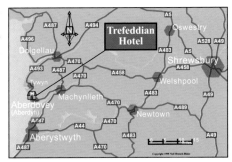

BORTHWNOG HALL COUNTRY HOUSE HOTEL & RESTAURANT
Bontddu, Dolgellau, Gwynedd LL40 2TT

Telephone 01341 430271   Fax 01341 430682

Idyllically poised on the shores of the Mawddach estuary with views stretching six miles to the coast, this gem of a hotel dates back to the late 17th Century. Six hundred feet of peaceful gardens with many unusual plant varieties, run alongside the water, and this also provides for a good mix of woodland and estuary birdlife. Based here you are well placed to enjoy the myriad wonderful walks that the Mawddach area is famed for. Bedrooms, some with superb views of the Cader Idris range of mountains, are pretty, spacious and comfortable with beautiful furniture and fabrics. The personalities of your hosts, Vicki and Derek Hawes are reflected in the abundance of interesting and original antiques and objets d'art and their pride in their home is self evident. Within the hotel there is also an Art Gallery with an excellent range of paintings, pottery and other works of art. The intimate and characterful restaurant offers both à la carte and table d'hôte menus on which you will find some unusual dishes complemented with excellent wines. Borthwnog has been described as a "little gem" and with the highest accolades from the AA & RAC. I too can highly recommend it to any Signposter. Double room rate including breakfast from £42.00.

Barmouth 6, Dolgellau 4, Aberystwyth 38, Caernarfon 42, Birmingham 110, London 235.

F licence. Three en suite bedrooms with radio, colour TV and direct-dial telephone; hairdryer; tea/coffee making facilities; safe; Last orders for dinner 20.30 hrs. Special diets available. Art gallery in hotel. Golf and riding nearby. Parking for eight cars. Open all year. Most credit cards accepted.

BONTDDU HALL HOTEL
Bontddu, Nr. Dolgellau, Gwynedd LL40 2SU

Telephone: 01341 430661   Fax: 01341 430284

Bontddu Hall, wonderfully situated in 14 acres of landscaped grounds, overlooks fine views of the Mawddach Estuary and famous Cader Idris range of mountains. The unspoilt charm of this attractive Victorian mansion has always made it a favourite of mine, and the owners Margaretta and Michael Ball, know what is good. You will enjoy excellent food from an interesting country house evening dinner menu, dishes are varied and nicely served. Salmon and lobster are a speciality when available. In the Garden Restaurant an appetizing lunch is served and a Special Carvery lunch on Sundays. The furniture, pictures, colour schemes and flowers are all reminiscent of a country house and the hotel has been completely refurbished. All rooms are very comfortable and the "Princess of Wales" Bar extends a warm welcome. Nearly all bedrooms are with estuary and mountain views. In the Lodge, above the main drive are some additional rooms with balconies and exceptional views. I can only recommend a visit and you will want to come again and again. Room and breakfast from £62.50 (single), £90.00 (double/twin), inclusive of VAT. Weekly demi-pension £399.50 per person; four-poster suites for romantics £150. Open Easter to October. **Bargain breaks:** Any 2 consecutive nights half board from £120 per person inc. service & VAT. (excluding Bank Holidays). Extra nights pro rata. **Barmouth 5, Dolgellau 5, Aberystwyth 35, Caernarfon 50, Birmingham 110, London 235.**

F licence; 20 en suite bedrooms, all with telephone, colour TV, clock radio, hairdryer, tea/coffee making facilities; central heating; night service to midnight; late meals to 9.30p.m.; diets; children welcome; dogs welcome; sea bathing, golf and riding all five miles; gold mine nearby; Access, Amex, Visa credit cards accepted.

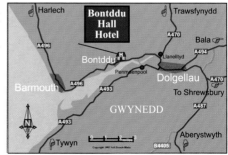

WARPOOL COURT HOTEL
St. Davids, Pembrokeshire SA62 6BN

Telephone: 01437 720300   *Fax: 01437 720676*

The Warpool Court is sited in a wonderful position overlooking the wild Atlantic and within a few minutes' walk of the famous St. David's Cathedral. This splendid country house hotel, with its unique collection of antique tiles, has been recommended by Signpost for a long time. It is owned by Peter Trier and through his expertise you can be assured of good food, gracious living and a warm welcome. The colour schemes are soft and restful and the staff cheerful and efficient. The hotel has a high reputation for good food and a fine selection of well chosen wines. Four course table d'hôte menus are excellent and whenever possible local produce is used. Salmon is smoked on the premises, crab and lobster are caught at the nearby village of Solva. These are supported by an interesting vegetarian menu. The lounge bar provides a relaxed atmosphere for diners, and the residents' lounge ensures peace and comfort. There are numerous outdoor activities available, the most popular being walking, bird watching and surfing. Room and breakfast from £69 (single), £98 (twin) inclusive of VAT. **'Country House Breaks'** (2 nights out of season d,b&b from £65; 7 nights from £59 pppn). Full Christmas and New Year packages. Open Feb-December inclusive.**London 264, Birmingham 177, Severn Bridge 130, Carmarthen 46, Fishguard 16, Haverfordwest 16.**

F licence; 25 en suite bedrooms all with telephone, colour TV + satellite, baby listening, tea/coffee making facilities; family rooms; full central heating; meals to 9.15 p.m.; diets; children welcome; dogs accepted; leisure facilities: table tennis, gymnasium and sauna, pool table, heated covered swimming pool (Apr-Oct), all weather tennis court, 9 hole golf course nearby (2 miles); sea bathing; sandy beaches; lovely walks; major credit cards accepted.

GLIFFAES COUNTRY HOUSE HOTEL
Crickhowell, Powys NP8 1RH

Telephone 01874 730371   Fax: 01874 730463

Romantically situated in the lovely valley of the River Usk, Gliffaes is midway between the Black Mountains and the Brecon Beacons. 32 acres of grounds are planted with rare trees and shrubs, some dating from the nineteenth century. There is plenty to see and do in the area and the hotel also offers a hard tennis court with practice wall, putting green and croquet lawn. Over two miles of the river are reserved primarily for guests to fish for salmon and trout in the beautifully tranquil setting. For the less energetic there is a full sized billiard table. The sitting room and the drawing room are most relaxing and French windows lead from the latter into an attractive and spacious sun room, which opens onto the terrace, as do the dining room and newly refurbished bar. The food at Gliffaes is excellent, breakfast including scrambled eggs garnished with smoked salmon. Light lunch dishes may be ordered from the bar and home made afternoon tea is best described as a trencherman's dream! An extensive dinner menu includes plenty for vegetarians, using only the freshest ingredients and supported by a sensibly priced wine list. The bedrooms are priced according to size and views, all are comfortable, characterful and en suite. Having owned the hotel since 1948, the Brabner family are experienced, charming and informal hosts, as a result of which many guests return year after year. Room and breakfast from £34.50-£51 per person. **Bargain breaks:** Short stay and weekly rates on application. **Crickhowell 3¹/₂, Abergavenny 10, Brecon 10¹/₂, London 160.**

F licence; 22 en suite bedrooms all with direct-dial telephone, colour TV, tea/coffee making facilities and baby listening; children welcome; dogs (but not in hotel); late meals by arrangement; diets; TV room; small conferences; receptions; salmon & trout fishing; tennis; putting & practice net; croquet; billiards; golf, riding, shooting, sailing & boating all nearby; Amex, Diners, Access & Visa accepted.

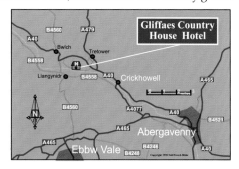

BODFACH HALL COUNTRY HOUSE HOTEL
Llanfyllin, Powys SY22 5HS

Telephone: 01691 648272　　　　　*Fax: 01691 648272*

Bodfach Hall Country House Hotel can be found at the end of the A490 just $^1/_4$ mile off the Oswestry to Lake Vyrnwy Road. Four acres of mature and sheltered gardens contain many interesting trees and shrubs. Parts of the house date back to the 17th century, although there has been a building on the site since the 12th century. There are many fine stained glass windows, and all periods of the building are sympathetically interwoven in this lovely old house. The morning room, where breakfast is served, has a spectacular painted relief ceiling, and the drawing room, an 18th century moulded ceiling and fine marble fireplaces. There is a sun room with terrace and a large lounge bar. Most bedrooms have wonderful views and all are en suite, with either bath or shower. The dining room is oak panelled, and a four course table d'hôte dinner is offered, as well as a choice of à la carte and vegetarian dishes . The interesting wine list is reasonably priced. There is plenty to see and do - walking, climbing, sketching, and there are three golf courses to choose from, as well as tennis courts and a sports centre in nearby Llanfyllin. The Gray family feel that peace and comfort are important for their guests, and this, they easily achieve. Room and breakfast is sensibly priced from £33.50 per person. **Bargain breaks:** Any two consecutive nights, dinner, b&b from £46.50 pppn. One week (7 nights) from £275 per person. **London 3-3$^1/_2$ hrs, Leeds 3-3$^1/_2$ hrs, Liverpool 1$^1/_2$ hrs, West Midlands 1$^1/_2$ hrs.**

F licence; nine en suite bedrooms, all with direct dial telephone and TV, room service; last orders for dinner 8.45 p.m.; bar meals; special diets; children welcome; dogs accepted; leisure centre, golf and tennis nearby; open all year; all major credit cards accepted.

THE MILL AT GLYNHIR
Llandybie, Ammanford Dyfed SA18 2TE

Telephone: 01269 850672

The Mill at Glynhir was originally a XVIth century water-driven corn mill. Imaginatively converted, the houise is at several levels. Free golf is offered from a choice of courses; fishing, horse riding and magnificent walks are at hand. The Mill can be found by turning down by a sign marked "Golf Club" in the village of Llandybie.Cuisine is very reasonably priced and offers the best of British home cooking. Choice of packages, from £99 for 2 nights to £365 for 7 nights dinner, bed and breakfast combined with golf and fishing. **Bargain breaks** from £36.50 per person per day dinner, bed and breakfast, min. two nights.

All 11 bedrooms, including a luxury suite with its own private sitting room, have whirlpool baths, tea/ coffee making facilities, colour TV, hairdryer, trouser press, hospitality tray. Most have south-facing terraces. Small heated indoor swimming pool.

CAERLEON HOUSE HOTEL
Caerau Road, Newport NP9 4HU

Telephone: 01633 264869

AA QQ. WTB ⌐⌐⌐

The Caerleon House Hotel is convneinetly situated off junction 2 of the M4, close to the centre of Newport. It is a quiet area, yet close to Newport's shops and restaurants. Evening meals are available 6 pm to 7.30 from £4.50 per head and there is a licensed bar. Residents have use of a large enclosed rear garden and there is ample parking at the front. Rooms are attractively decorated. Single £23.00; double £36.00; family room £46.

2 singles, 2 twins, 1 family room, all en suite with colour TV and tea/coffee making facilities.

WILLOWS HOTEL
128 Cathedral Road, Cardiff, South Glamorgan CF1 9LQ

Telephone & fax: 01222 230122

WTB ☁☁☁

You will find the Willows Hotel (previously known as The Briars) friendly, informal and cheerfully run by the owner Mrs Jan Pottinger. The hotel is within walking distance of Cardiff Castle, Cardiff Arms Park, modern shopping precincts and many good restaurants, although dinner is available at the hotel (from 6.30-7.30 pm at £8.95 per head). There is a licensed bar and small functions are catered for. Décor throughout is French cottage style and bedrooms are prettily decorated. Single from £18; double from £32; family room from £45.

5 singles, 9 double, most en suite and all with colour TV, direct-dial telephone and tea/coffee making facilities. Children welcome, ample parking.

JANE HODGE HOTEL
Trerhyngyll, Nr. Cowbridge, South Glamorgan CF7 7TN

Telephone: 01446 772608;
Fax: 01446 775831
WTB ☁☁☁

Catering especially for the disabled, the Jane Hodge Hotel loses none of its warmth to modernity. All on one floor, it is ideal for the physically disabled as well as for the able bodied. Amenities are extremely comprehensive with an outstanding range of sporting activities (see below). Bedrooms and family suites are excellent and there are three lounges, a spacious dining room and a low-level bar. The hotel has its own minibuses for excursions to the Gower peninsula, several castles in the vicinity or to Cardiff or Cowbridge. Bed and breakfast from £24 (winter) to £38 (mid-summer); half board £32-46. **Bargain breaks** include Valentine Special (£59 per head for two nights), Family Activity Holidays (seven nights from £110 children/£220 adults) and Turkey and Tinsel wekends (2 nights from £55 per person per night).

R & R licence; 22 bedrooms, all en suite and with radio, colour TV, tea and coffee making facilities. Indoor swimming pool, jacuzzi, badminton, bowls, volleyball, boardgames, sauna, tennis courts, gym. No dogs (except guide); conferences welcomed. ♿

RAISDALE HOUSE HOTEL
Raisdale Road, Penarth, South Glamorgan CF6 2BN

Telephone & fax: 01222 707317

Situated high on the cliffs at Penarth, the Raisdale House enjoys a quiet situation and wonderful sea views. Only four miles from Cardiff and close to the M4, the hotel is ideal both for holiday makers and business people. The house dates from 1870 and retains many original features. There is a lounge, comfortable licensed bar and the restaurant provides excellent meals using the freshest of ingredients. Wedding parties and conference delegates are very welcome. Your genial host is David Wheeler. Single from £22.50 bed & breakfast; double from £26.

5 singles, 13 double, all en suite and all with colour TV, radio, direct-dial telephone and tea/coffee making facilities.

CRESCENT GUEST HOUSE
132 Eaton Crescent, Uplands, Swansea, West Glamorgan SA1 4QR

Telephone: 01792 466814

AA listed. RAC acclaimed.
WTB ⌒⌒ Highly Commended

Enjoy a friendly atmosphere at this warm and inviting guest house situated in a residential are in the Uplands area of Swansea. The house is approximately one mile wset of Swansea, close to the main Swansea-Gower road A 4118, the leisure centre, marina, St Helen's rugby and cricket ground, university. Patti pavilion, Brangwyn Hall and several parks. There is a large and comfortable lounge with panoramic views and a separate dining room. Bed & breakfast £20 per night; weekly rate £133.Your hosts are Mr & Mrs Convey.

2 twin bedrooms, 3 double, 1 family, all en suite and with colour TV, clock radio and tea/coffee making facilities. Ample parking. Dogs accepted. Children welcome. No restaurant.

■ **Historic Houses & Gardens & Parks**

BORDERS
Bowhill, 3m W of Selkirk
Dawyck Botanic Garden, Stobo
Floors Castle, Kelso
Kailzie Gardens, 2m E of Peebles

DUMFRIES & GALLOWAY
Drumlanrig Castle & Country Park, 3m N of Thornhill
Galloway House Gardens, Garlieston
Maxwelton House, 13m NE of Dumfries
Meadowsweet Herb Garden, Castle Kennedy, Stranraer
Threave Garden, 1m W of Castle Douglas

LOTHIAN
Dalmeny House, By South Queensferry
The Georgian House, Charlotte Sq., Edinburgh
Gladstone's Land, Royal Mile, Edinburgh
House of the Binns, l5m W of Edinburgh
Hopetoun House, W of South Oueensferry
Inveresk Lodge Garden, 6m E of Edinburgh
Malleny Garden, Balerno, W of Edinburgh
Royal Botanic Gardens, Edinburgh
Suntrap (Garden) Gogarbank, 6m W of Edinburgh

■ **Walks & Nature Trails**

BORDERS
Jedforest Deer & Farm Park, Camptown
Pease Dean, Nr. Cockburnspath

DUMFRIES & GALLOWAY
Caerlaverock National Nature Reserve, S of Dumfries

LOTHIAN
Cammon Estate, NE off Queensferry Road, Edinburgh
John Muir Country Park, Dunbar

■ **Historical Sites & Museums**

BORDERS
Dryburgh Abbey, 5m SE of Melrose
Robert Smail's Printing Works, Innerleithen
Hermitage Castle 5m NE of Newcastleton
Jedburgh Abbey

Jim Clark Memorial Trophy Room, Duns
Melrose Abbey
Smallholm Tower, 6m W of Kelso

DUMFRIES & GALLOWAY
Burns House, Dumfries
Caerlaverock Castle, 8m SE of Dumfries
Carlyle's Birthplace, Ecclefechan
Dumfries Museum & Camera Obscura, Dumfries
Maclellan's Castle, Kirkcudbright
Mill on the Fleet Heritage Centre, Gatehouse of Fleet New
Abbey Cornmill, 8m S of Dumfries
Sweetheart Abbey, New Abbey
Threave Castle, 3m E of North Berwick

LOTHIAN
Craigmillar Castle, 2.5m SE of Edmburgh Stranraer
Dirleton Castle & Garden, 7m W of North Berwick
Edinburgh Castle
Linlithgow Palace
Palace of Holyrood House, Edinburgh
Preton Mill a Phmtassie Doocot, 23m E of Edinburgh
Tantallon Castle, 3m E of North Berwick
The Heritage of Golf, Gullane

■ **Entertainment Venues**

BORDERS
Borders Wool Centre Nr. Galashiels
Peter Anderson of Scotland Cashmere Woollens Mill &
Museum, Galashiels
St. Abb's Head, 2m N of Coldingham

DUMFRIES & GALLOWAY
Old Blacksmith's Shop Centre, Gretna Green
Robert Burns Centre, Dumfries

LOTHIAN
Edinburgh, Camera Obscura, Castlehill
Edinburgh Clan Tartan Centre, Leith
Edinburgh, Crabbie's Histonc Winery Tour, Great
Junction Street
Edinburgh Crystal Visitor Centre, Penicuik BORDERS
Edinburgh, Kinloch Anderson Heritage Room, Leith
National Gallery of Scotland, The Mound, Edinburgh
The Scottish Whisky Heritage Centre, Royal Mile,
Edinburgh

Signpost Scottish hotels inspector David Mc Murtrie (right) with David Webster, General Manager, in front of Sunlaws House Hotel, Borders.

March 10	BERWICKSHIRE CROSS - COUNTRY TEAM EVENT
	Duns Castle, Borders.
March 27	BUCCLEUCH HUNT POINT-TO-POINT
	Friars Haugh, Kelso.
April 6	GALA RUGBY SEVENS
	Melrose, Borders
April 18-20	HORSE RACING: THE SCOTTISH GRAND NATIONAL MEETING
	Ayr Racecourse, Ayr, Strathclyde.
May 25-26	BEER FESTIVAL
	Innerleithen, Peeblesshire
May 24-June 2	DUMFRIES & GALLOWAY ARTS FESTIVAL
	Various venues, Dumfries & Galloway
June 14	SELKIRK COMMON RIDING
	Selkirk, Borders.
June 15-16	EYEMOUTH SEAFOOD FESTIVAL
	Eyemouth, Borders
June 17-22	PEEBLES BELTANE FESTIVAL
	Peebles, Borders.
July 13	JEDBURGH BORDER GAMES
	Jedburgh, Borders.
July 20-21	HORSE RACING: THE GLASGOW FAIR MEETING
	Ayr Racecourse, Ayr, Strathclyde.
July 14-20	KELSO CIVIC WEEK
	Kelso.
July 26-27	BORDERS UNION SHOW
	Kelso.
August 25	MASSED PIPE BANDS
	Floors Castle, Kelso.
August 31-	SCOTTISH FESTIVAL OF WALKING
Sepember 13	Hawick, Borders
September 19-21	HORSE RACING: THE WESTON MEETING
	Ayr Racecourse, Ayr - The Gold Cup on the 21st.

For further details contact:
The Scottish Tourist Board, 23 Ravelston Terrace, Edinburgh EH4 3EU. Tel: 0131 332 2433

SUNLAWS HOUSE HOTEL
Kelso, Roxburghshire TD5 8JZ

Telephone: 01573 450331   *Fax: 01573 450611*

Sunlaws House is owned by the Duke of Roxburghe who lives at the impressive Floors Castle (well worth a visit in itself), supervised its conversion into an hotel, and continues to take a keen interest in the success of this once family house. The hotel is situated 3 miles south west of Kelso through Heiton on the A698 turning right with a signposted lane. Fishing on its own beat of the river Teviot and shooting in the Roxburghe Estates are both very popular. Leaflets on fishing breaks and shooting breaks are available. Hearty breakfasts are the order of the day and I certainly enjoyed one during my stay. Emphasis is on Scottish cooking and there is a good selection of wines - some of the older wines coming, no doubt, from His Grace's cellar. Accommodation is of a high standard, as you would expect, the bedrooms being comfortable and relaxing. The conservatory, where I enjoyed a pre-dinner drink, is delightful and bar lunches and afternoon teas can be served here. The Roxburghe Suite is available for private parties or conferences. Mr. David Webster ably manages this small country house hotel of character. Dave Thomas is currently designing a championship 18-hole golf

course, due to open in 1997. Single £90-95; double £140; 4-poster £165 b & b.Open all year. **Bargain breaks**: Special themed or relaxing 2-day breaks available from Jan-May. Tariff on application. **Edinburgh 50, Newcastle 60, Berwick 24, Jedburgh 9, Kelso 3, Hawick 20, London 338.** *F licence; 22 en suite bedrooms (9 on ground floor), all with radio, direct dial telephone, satellite TV; full central heating; night service; meals to 9.30 p.m.; diets; children welcome; baby listening; dogs welcome; conferences up to 20; tennis; riding; shooting; fishing; new health and beauty salon; golf three miles; major credit cards accepted.*

CRINGLETIE HOUSE HOTEL
Peebles, Borders EH45 8PL
Telephone: 01721 730233   *Fax: 01721 730244*

I have been visiting this fine turreted hotel for 20 years and each year on my return I notice certain improvements. Bedrooms over the years, for instance, have been re-arranged, individually styled and attractively decorated. One aspect that does not change is the cooking. Aileen Maguire is in charge of the kitchen and she prepares consistently good, well presented dishes at very good value and this also applies to the varied selection of wines. The walled kitchen garden, well stocked with vegetables and fruit, provides the freshest possible produce. Not surprisingly the restaurant has won wide acclaim. Cringletie was designed by David Bryce, the well known Scottish architect, and built in 1861. The hotel stands in 28 acres of well kept gardens and woodlands with marvellous views overlooking the Eddleston valley 2 miles north of Peebles on the A703 Edinburgh to Peebles road. As Edinburgh is only half an hour's drive away, this hotel is ideal both for shopping in that lovely city or for touring the Border country with its spectacular scenery. You will be well cared for by the Maguire family during your stay. Room and breakfast from £52.50 single, double as single £65 and £98-£104 for 2 people in double/twin room. Dinner £24.50, Sunday lunch £15 .00 and weekday lunch from £5.50. Closed 2nd January to 8th March 1996 inclusive; open for Christmas and New Year. Enquire about 2 day Spring/Autumn breaks. **Edinburgh 20, Glasgow 50, Galashiels 19, Lanark 28,London 360.**

F licence; 13 en suite bedrooms all with telephone, remote control colour TV; lift to 1st and 2nd floors only, children welcome; comfortable residents' lounge and also non-smoking lounge; dogs permitted, but not in public rooms, or left unaccompanied in bedrooms; golf three miles; tennis; riding three miles; putting; croquet; fishing by permit on Tweed; Mastercard, Visa & Amex credit cards accepted.

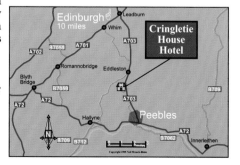

CAIRNDALE HOTEL AND LEISURE CLUB
English Street, Dumfries DG1 2DF

Telephone: 01387 254111   Fax: 01387 250555

The Cairndale Hotel has a position close to the centre of Dumfries, high standards of service and superb leisure club facilities, so the Scottish Tourist Board's five crown commended award is well deserved. It is an ideal base for exploring the Solway Coast with its fishing ports, castles and gardens, and for activities such as fishing, shooting, watersports and residential golf packages offered by the hotel. The Cairndale is privately owned by the Wallace family who understand what guests need for an enjoyable stay. This is a welcoming place from the hotel's comfortable dining room, which has an award too and runs a Saturday evening dinner dance and a Sunday Taste of Scotland dinner, to the 76 comfortable en suite bedrooms. There is a wide choice of traditional food with the Sawney Beans Bar and Grill serving hot roasts and light snacks in the Forum Café Bar overlooking the heated indoor swimming pool. The Barracuda Leisure Club has as good facilities as I have seen and now includes Cloud Nine Beauty salon. To stay here is to be entertained in style, with special breaks adding further variety. Single room including breakfast from £55.00-£75.00. Double room with breakfast from £75.00-£95.00. **Leisure Breaks**: Db&b £55 pppn. Murder Mystery £59.00 pppn db&b. 3-nights Ceilidh weekends £99.000 db&b pp. Special rates for over 60's. Golf Inclusive Breaks £55.00 db&b pppn. Dinner Dance, Bed & Breakfast from £40.00 pp. **Carlisle 33, Edinburgh 71, Glasgow 73, Ayr 59, London 327.**

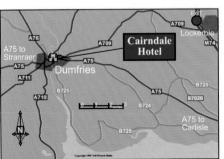

Full licence. 76 en suite bedrooms with satellite TV, radio, direct dial telephone, hairdryer, trouser press, laundry service, non-smoker bedrooms, tea/coffee making facilities, safety deposit box. 24-hour room service. Last orders for dinner 21.30 hrs. Special diets available. Facilities for the disabled. Jacuzzi, sauna, massage, indoor swimming pool, steam room, gym, toning tables, beautician. Golf nearby. Full business services and six meeting rooms with capacity for 200 guests. AV equipment. Car rental. Car parking for 60 cars. Open all year. Credit cards accepted.

MOFFAT HOUSE HOTEL
High Street, Moffat, Dumfries and Galloway DGl0 9HL

Telephone: 01683 220039   *Fax: 01683 221288*

Moffat is one of those delightful small towns which lures travellers by its charm and environs. It has won both the 'Best Kept Village in Scotland' and the 'Scotland in Bloom' awards and is surrounded by some of the best hill walking country and beautiful scenery in southern Scotland. Set in the very heart of the town, Moffat House is an Adam building which has been skilfully converted into a most comfortable hotel, within $2^1/2$ acres of landscaped gardens. The public rooms are warm and inviting and the bedrooms are immaculately decorated, comfortably furnished, and have all the amenities that we now expect of a good modern hotel. The owners, the Reid family, have been here for twenty years, and in that time they have constantly improved it, so that it is without doubt the best hotel for miles around. It is only minutes from the A74 (M) and yet it nestles in relatively unknown and beautiful countryside. For anyone wishing to take a holiday in this lovely area or breaking a journey between England and Edinburgh or Glasgow and beyond, Moffat House is the ideal choice. Room and breakfast from £54 single, £80 double. Dinner, room and breakfast from £59.50 per person, including VAT. **Bargain Breaks**: 3 days, d,b&b £160; 2 days £110; Winter breaks Nov-March exc Xmas/New Year - 3 days d,b&b £120 pp; 2 days £80 pp. **A74 (M) 1, Carlisle 40, Edinburgh 55, Perth 110, Oban 140, London 335.** *F licence; 20 en suite bedrooms (including one deluxe with four-poster bed and three rooms for the partially dIsabled), all with telephone, TV and hospitality tray; baby listening; last orders for dinner 8. 45 p.m.; bar meals, special diets with an extensive vegetarian selection; children welcome; dogs accepted in bedrooms only; conferences max. 20; good hill walking; leisure centre nearby; golf one mile; tennis $^1/_2$ mile; riding two miles; major credit cards accepted; open all year.*

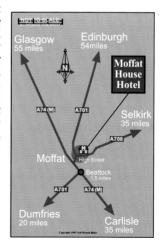

■ Historic Houses, Gardens & Parks

CENTRAL
Culcreuch Castle & Country Park, Fintry

FIFE
Balcaskie House & Gardens, 2m W of Pittenweem
Cambo Gardens, 1 m S of Kingsbarns
Earlshall Castle & Gardens, 1 m E of Leuchars
Falkland Palace & Gardens, 11 m N of Kirkcaldy
Hill of Tarvit Mansionhouse & Garden, 2m S of Cupar
Kellie Castle & Garden, 3m N of Pittenweem
Sir Douglas Bader Garden for the Disabled, Duffus Park
  Cupar

STRATHCLYDE
Ardanaiseig Gardens, 22m E of Oban
Arduaine Garden, 20m S of Oban
Barguillean Garden, 3m W of Taynuilt
Brodick Castle, Garden & Country Park, Isle of Arran
Culzean Castle & Country Park, 4m W of Maybole
Dean Castle & CountryPark, Kilmarnock
Greenbank Garden, Clarkston, Glasgow

TAYSIDE
Bell's Cherrybank Gardens, Perth
Blair Castle, 7m NNW of Pitlochry
Branklyn Garden, Perth
Cluny House Gardens, 3 ^{1}/2m from Aberfeldy
Edzell Castle & Garden, 6m N of Brechin
Duntrune Demonstration Garden, Dundee
House of Dun, 3m W of Montrose
Magginch Castle Gardens, 10m E of Perth
Scone Palace, 2m NE of Perth

■ Walks & Nature Trails

CENTRAL
Gartmorn Dam Country Park & Nature Reserve, By
  Sauchie

FIFE
Scottish Deer Centre, 3m W of Cupar

STRATHCLYDE
King's Cave, shore, 2m N of Blackwaterfoot
Lauder Forest Walks, 3m S of Strachur, Glenbranter
Muirshiel Country Park, 9m SW of Paisley
Puck's Glen, 5m W of Dunoon

TAYSIDE
Monikie Country Park, 10m N of Dundee
Queen's View Centre, Loch Tummel, 6m NW of
  Pitlochry
St. Cyrus National Nature Reserve, Nether Warburton

■ Historical Sites & Museums

CENTRAL
Blackness Castle, 4m NE of Linlithgow
Doune Castle, 8m S of Callander
Inchmahoune Priory, Lake of Mentieth
National Wallace Monument, 1^1/2 m NNE of Stirling
Stirling Castle

FIFE
Aberdour Castle
Balgonie Castle, by Markinch
Inchcolm Abbey (via ferry from South Queensferry)
St Andrew's Cathedral
St Andrew's Castle

STRATHCLYDE
Bachelor's Club (re: Robert Burns), Tarbolton
Bonawe Iron Works, Nr Taynuilt
Dumbarton Castle
Doon Valley Heritage, 2m S of Patna
Gladstone Court Museum, Biggar
The Hill House, Helensburgh
John Buchan Centre, 6m E of Biggar
Burns Cottage & Museum, 2m S of Ayr
Coats Observatory, Paisley
David Livingstone Centre, Blantyre
Inverary Castle & Gardens
Kilmory Castle Gardens, Lochgilphead
Rothesay Castle, Isle of Bute
Souter Johnnie's Cottage, Kirkoswald
The Tenement House, Garnethill, Glasgow
Weaver's Cottage, Kilbarchan, 12m SW of Glasgow

TAYSIDE
Angus Folk Museum, Glamis
Arbroath Abbey
Atholl Country Collection, Blair Atholl
Barrie's Birthplace, Kirriemuir
Black Watch Regimental Museum, Balhousie Castle,
  Perth
Glamis Castle, 5m SW of Forfar
Killiekrankie Visitor Centre, 3m N of Pitochry Loch
Leven Castle, via Ferry from Kinross

■ Entertainment Venues

CENTRAL
Bannockburn Heritage Centre, 2m S of Stirling
Blair Drummond Safari & Leisure Park
Rob Roy & Trossachs Visitor Centre, Callander
Village Glass, Bridge of Allan

FIFE
Deep Sea World, North Queensferry

STRATHCLYDE
Ardnamurchan Natural History & Visitor Centre, Nr.
  Glenborrowdale
Antartex Village, Balloch
Balloch Castle Country Park, at S end of Loch Lomond
The Burrell Collection, Glasgow
Glenbart Abbey Visitor Centre, 12m NW of Campbeltown
Glenfinart Deer Farm, Ardentinny
Inverawe Smokery, Bridge of Awe
Kelburn Country Centre, between Lairgs & Fairlie
The Time Capsule, Monklands, Coatbridge

TAYSIDE
Beatrix Potter Garden & Exhibition, Brinham
Caithness Glass (Perth), Inveralmond
Crieff Visitors's Centre
Discovery Point, Dundee

February 3	SCOTLAND v. FRANCE RUGBY UNION
	Murrayfield, Edinburgh.
March 2	SCOTLAND v. ENGLAND RUGBY UNION
	Murrayfield, Edinburgh.
March 22-24	ANTIQUES FAIR
	Hopetoun House, South Queensferry, Fife
March 29 to	EDINBURGH INTERNATIONAL SCIENCE FESTIVAL
April 16	Edinburgh.
May 2-6	9TH ISLE OF BUTE JAZZ FESTIVAL
	Isle of Bute
May 2-25	MAYFEST
	Glasgow.
May 18-June 1	FALKIRK DISTRICT FESTIVAL
	Falkirk, Stirlingshire
May 21-June 23	PERTH FESTIVAL OF THE ARTS
	Perth, Tayside
May 25 to	CHARLES RENNIE MACINTOSH EXHIBITION
	Glasgow
May 27-June 2	1996 SCOTTISH INTERNATIONAL CHILDRENS FESTIVAL
	Edinburgh
May 28*	BLAIR ATHOLL HIGHLAND GAMES
	Blair Atholl, Nr. Pitlochry.
June 20-23	ROYAL HIGHLAND SHOW
	Ingleston, Edinburgh.
July 6-7	THE GAME CONSERVANCY SCOTTISH FAIR
	Perth, Tayside
July 7	STIRLING HIGHLAND GAMES
	Stirling, Central
July 9-13	SCOTTISH OPEN GOLF CHAMPIONSHIP
	Carnoustie, Angus, Tayside
July 20-22	DUNDEE SUMMER FESTIVAL
	Dundee, Tayside
August 2-24	EDINBURGH MILITARY TATTOO
	Edinburgh Castle.
August 10-25	DRAMBUIE EDINBURGH FILM FESTIVAL
	Edinburgh
August 11-31	EDINBURGH INTERNATIONAL FESTIVAL & FRINGE
	Various locations, Edinburgh
August 17	WORLD PIPE BAND CHAMPIONSHIP
	Glasgow
August 21-22	ARGYLLSHIRE HIGHLAND GATHERING
	Oban
August 30-31	COWAL HIGHLAND GATHERING
	Dunoon, Strathclyde
September 14	RAF BATTLE OF BRITAIN INTERNATIONAL AIRSHOW
	Leuchars, Fife
October 11-18	ROYAL NATIONAL MOD
	Blairgowrie, Perthshire
November 30	ST ANDREWS DAY CELEBRATIONS
	St Andrews, Fife

* = provisional dates

For further information contact:
The Scottish Tourist Board, 23 Ravelston Terrace, Edinburgh EH4 3EU. Tel: 0131 332 2433

THE LAKE HOTEL
Port of Menteith, Perthshire FK8 3RA

Telephone: 01877 385258   Fax: 01877 385671

The Lake Hotel stands on the shore of the Lake of Menteith, with the most romantic of views spread before it. Owned and supervised by Mr. and Mrs. Leroy, who also own The Manor House at Oban and Killiechronan House, Isle of Mull, you can expect high standards of hospitality, service, cuisine, comfort and housekeeping. The hotel has recently been renovated and refurbished throughout, with a sympathetic eye to the age and style of the building. The bedrooms are comfortable and attractive, with two suites (bedroom, dressing room and large bathroom) overlooking the lake. There is a smart cocktail lounge which leads to the lakeside conservatory restaurant. The mood created here by the view, quiet music - often a live pianist - and discreet service, is perfect for the appreciation of the dishes from the well planned menu of Head Chef, Stuart Morrison. He uses fresh local fish meat and game, with vegetables, salads and fruits in season, giving delicious results. His breakfasts, too, are something rather special. Drinks and coffee are served in the book-filled lounge and The Bistro and bar serves light meals during the day. Dinner, room and breakfast per person from £46 (low season)/ £75 high season inc. VAT. Weekly from £259 low season and £434 high season. ≈≈≈≈ Highly Commended. **Bargain breaks:** Low season £44 pppn 2 nights inc. dinner, b&b; high season £70 pppn .

Glasgow 30, Edinburgh 40, Stirling 18, Oban 84, Perth 50, London 410.

F licence, 12 bedrooms, all with en suite bathroom, telephone and TV; room service; last orders for dinner 9.00 p.m.; bistro for lunches; special diets; children over 10 welcome; dogs by arrangement; golf, riding, shooting and fishing all nearby; hotel open all year; Visa and Mastercard welcome.

ARDEONAIG HOTEL
South Loch Tay, Killin, Perthshire FK21 8SU

Telephone: 01567 820400   *Fax: 01567 820282*

The Ardeonaig Hotel is none other than a pure haven for the visitor and sportsman alike. It is situated amongst the breathtaking scenery of this beautiful part of Scotland, amongst meadows and trees, where you will find the hotel's 9 hole golf course laid out beside Loch Tay. Within a 25 minute drive, there are more golf courses at Killin, Kenmore and Aberfeldy. This secluded 17th century inn has its own salmon fishing rights on the Loch, where the hotel's boats are moored in a small harbour, and a rod room and drying room are available. Guests can also fish for salmon on the River Tay, and excellent stalking can be arranged. The most hospitable owners, Eileen and Alan Malone, were finalists in the " 'Scottish Field' - Morrisons' Bowmore Restaurant of the Year 1993" and winners of the Perthshire Tourist Board/Glenturret Distillery Award for "The Most Enjoyable Restaurant Meal in Perthshire" 1994. They are continuing to build a fine reputation for both the food and wine in their restaurant. The tasty Scottish cuisine is created from the freshest of local produce, and is complemented by a good selection of international wines. The Ardeonaig boasts a cheery bar, which offers some of the best Scottish malts, a cosy sitting room, and a second floor library with wonderful views over Loch Tay and the hills of Ben Lawers. This delightful area is wonderful walking country, and has outstanding scenery with quiet roads for the discerning tourist. I can recommend a stay at the Ardeonaig either for the sporting facilities on hand, or purely for a spate of peace and relaxation. Room and breakfast from £43; dinner, room and breakfast from £62.50. Prices include VAT. **Perth 50, Stirling 50, Edinburgh 72, London 445.** *F licence; 16 en suite bedrooms (5 ground floor), all with tea/coffee making facilities; last orders for dinner 9. 00 p.m.; bar meals; special diets; dogs accepted; conferences max. 16; public telephone box in hotel; 9 hole golf course; own harbour and boats; shooting/fishing; riding nearby; limited service in the winter; only Switch credit card accepted.*

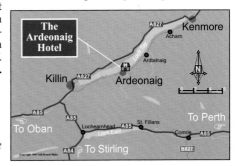

CROMLIX HOUSE
Kinbuck, By Dunblane, Nr. Stirling, Perthshire FK15 9JT

Telephone: 01786 822125   Fax: 01786 825450

Five minutes off the A9, in its own 3,000 acre estate, the calm and serenity of Cromlix House is a different world, with rolling parkland, an abundance of wildlife, miles of walks, and three trout lochs. The row of wellies at the front door and lack of a "reception", sets the feeling of entering David and Ailsa Assenti's home. It is immediately relaxing, welcoming and obviously well loved. An imposing exterior belies a wonderful interior, full of history, antique furniture, blazing log fires in all six public rooms (including the dining rooms), and a large conservatory - glorious for summer breakfast and afternoon tea. Masses of fresh flowers, together with a charming private chapel, make Cromlix the ultimate venue for an intimate wedding of 40 people. All the bedrooms, including the eight spacious suites are individual. No other house of this size can offer such a range of suites. Each is luxuriously furnished with care, and appointed with many personal and thoughtful extras. Half of the large bathrooms are original Edwardian, with huge baths, generous toiletries and bathrobes. Award winning cuisine is prepared with care and imagination, whilst all the staff are helpful, attentive and quietly professional. It is the lack of pretention, coupled with attention to detail, which lifts Cromlix into a class of its own. Room and breakfast from £95.00 single, £130 double, £175 suite inc VAT., Bargain breaks available October to March/April min. 2 nights from £75 midweek/£80 weekend, d,b&b. **Stirling 8, Perth 27, Glasgow 30, Edinburgh Airport 30, Glasgow Airport 38, Edinburgh 34, London 405.** *R & R licence; 14 en suite bedrooms (including 8 spacious suites), all with direct dial telephone and TV, room service, baby listening; limited night service, last orders for dinner 8.30p.m.; light lunches; special diets; children welcome; dogs allowed in bedrooms only; conferences max. 40; croquet; 3 trout lochs; 3,000 acre estate; tennis; riding and shooting by arrangement; golf 4 miles; own chapel for weddings; open all year; all major credit cards accepted.*

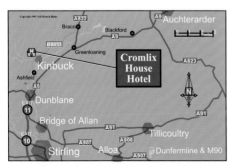

THE WOODSIDE HOTEL
High Street, Aberdour, Fife KY3 0SW

Telephone: 01383 860328   Fax: 01383 860920

The Woodside is an hotel which can claim personality, from the first warm welcome by Nancy and Peter Austen, the resident owners and their friendly staff. I enjoyed its character exemplified by its history and its facilities. It was built in 1873 by the Greig brothers, one of whom became a Russian admiral, and original oil paintings of them both hang in the foyer. As for the facilities: The Clipper Bar is one of the most unusual in Scotland featuring antique stained glass and panelling from the famous Orient line vessel *Orontes*. The style of the hotel persists into the elegant restaurant where Nancy's expertly prepared à la carte or table d'hôte menus range from Scottish through French to Chinese. The lovely bedrooms have been completely redecorated, each one individual in style and featuring a clan, and there is a superb suite as well . The village, dominated by its 14th Century castle is a gem offering the freshness of the seaside, the tranquillity of the country, a picturesque old harbour and the prettiest railway station in Britain - and there are many other attractions in the area. The personality of the Woodside, so perfectly matched by the character of the village, guarantees a most enjoyable stay. Single room with breakfast from £53. Double room including breakfast from £75.
Leisure Breaks: Reduced weekend rate of £53 per couple inc. breakfast. **Edinburgh 17 , Dunfermline 7½ , Kincardine 17 , Kinross 13, London 392 .** *Full licence. 20 en suite bedrooms with colour TV, direct-dial telephone, hairdryer, trouser press, laundry service, non-smoker bedrooms, tea/coffee making facilities. Last order for dinner 21.30 hrs. Special diets available. Golf free on local 18-hole course by prior arrangement. Sauna. Business services including meeting room with 25 guest capacity. Beauty salon adjacent. Car rental available. Car parking for 40 cars. Pets welcome. Open all year. Main credit cards accepted.*

THE MAITLAND HOTEL
33 Shandwick Place, Edinburgh, Lothian, EH2 4RG

Telephone: 0131-229 1467   Fax: 0131-229 7549

Quality and value for money and pride in delivering a personal and caring service take priority at this newly refurbished Townhouse Hotel. Guests can sleep in comfort, breakfast in style, then step right into the heart of Edinburgh. The hotel's spacious, individually designed luxurious bedrooms (including Executive and Family rooms) are styled for comfort and convenience. Entrance to them is by 'swipe card', ensuring a rapid check-in/check-out. Guests can start their day with a feast from the hotel's sumptuous breakfast buffet...and end it with a wee dram from the fine selection of Scotch whiskies. The hotel has no restaurant of its own but can supply a guide to recommended nearby eating places. Syndicate rooms are available for meetings. Enjoying a downtown location, the hotel is ideally situated for the city's financial district, the new International Conference Centre and Princes Street, the main shopping thoroughfare. Edinburgh remains one of Europe's cultural capitals and its historic monuments, castle, museums, concert halls and galleries are all within walking distance of the hotel. Single room with breakfast from £55; double £75; executive room £90. **Weekend short breaks** - £30 bed and breakfast per person available October '95 through April April '96.

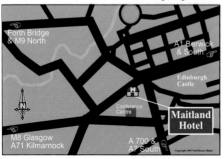

Stirling 36, Coldstream 48 , Glasgow 45 , Aberdeen 117 , London 375 .

R licence. 72 en suite bedrooms with satellite TV, radio and direct-dial telephone, hairdryer, laundry service, tea/coffee making facilities, music/radio/ alarm clock, safety deposit box Meeting room with capacity for 20 guests; secretarial services. Golf, massage, tennis and riding can be arranged nearby. Airport pick-up. Ample car parking. Open all year. Major credit cards accepted.

GREYWALLS HOTEL
Muirfield, Gullane, East Lothian, EH31 2EG

Telephone: 01620 842144   *Fax: 01620 842241*

This lovely hotel enjoys views over the Firth of Forth and Muirfield golf course. Its architecture, history, atmosphere and award-winning restaurant combine to make a stay at Greywalls a very pleasurable experience. The then holiday home was created by the Architect of New Delhi, Sir Edwin Lutyens, in 1901 and later the leading Scottish architect Sir Robert Lorimer added a wing, making Greywalls a unique co-operation between two eminent designers, as well as being the only remaining Lutyens' house in Scotland. The beautiful walled garden was designed by Gertrude Jekyll. One famous visitor was King Edward V11 and his outside lavatory is now transformed into a charming bedroom aptly named the King's Loo. Greywalls became a hotel in 1948 and the Weaver family which has now owned it for over seventy years continue to impart the atmosphere of a private house to their guests, which shows in the spacious, airy bedrooms and the wood panelled library with its open fire - probably one of the finest rooms in this home from home. The bar is cosy and the sun room a delight. Paul Baron has presided over the acclaimed restaurant for six years and built a reputation for modern British cooking with classical influence and local produce. The cool green dining-room overlooks Muirfield golf course. Greywalls is a perfectly enchanting place and the hotel's particular magic has few equals. Single room including breakfast from £95.00; double room with breakfast from £155.00. **Leisure Breaks:** Spring and autumn breaks available. **Edinburgh 18, Haddington 7¹/₂, Berwick-upon-Tweed 45, Glasgow 62 , London 377.**

Full licence. 22 en suite bedrooms with satellite TV, radio and direct-dial telephone, hairdryer, laundry service. Last order for dinner 21.15. Meeting room with capacity for 20 guests; secretarial services. Croquet, golf (local), tennis. Airport pick-up. Ample car parking. Open April-October. Major credit cards accepted.

THE MANOR HOUSE
Gallanach Road, Oban, Argyll PA34 4LS

Telephone: 01631 562087   *Fax: 01631 563053*

For peace and quiet within walking distance of the bustle of Oban, I recommend the elegant little Manor House Hotel. Built beside the sea on the tip of the bay, it enjoys unrivalled views over the harbour, the adjacent islands and the mountains beyond. The hotel is owned and supervised by Mr. and Mrs. J. Leroy who also own The Lake Hotel at Port of Menteith and Killiechronan House on the Isle of Mull, along with their manager, Gabriel Wijker. You can expect hospitality, service, comfort, good food and a very high standard of housekeeping. The house is furnished in keeping with its dignity and age, offering pretty, well appointed bedrooms and an elegant drawing room. The parlour and well furnished cocktail bar, with large windows overlooking the bay, make a pleasant spot for an aperitif or bar lunch. The pink dining room, which has an excellent reputation locally, glows with silver in the candlelight. Chef Neil O'Brien offers a tempting menu of Scottish and continental cuisine, specializing in local fish dishes and game in season. Oban is a good jumping off point for exploring the scenic West Coast, taking the car ferry to Mull or one of the smaller craft visiting other islands and places of interest, or planning a game fishing expedition. Dinner, room and breakfast per person from £42 (low season) - £66 (high season) inc. VAT. Weekly from £259 (low season) to £399 (high season). S.T.B. ⌐⌐⌐⌐ Highly Commended . AA Rosette for food. **Edinburgh 123, Dundee 116, Glasgow 96, Inverness 118, Fort William 50, London 489.**

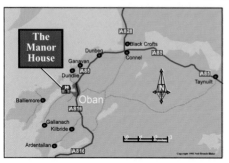

F licence; 11 en suite bedrooms, all with telephone, colour TV and full central heating; bar lunches; diets; dogs allowed; sea bathing; sailing and boating ¹/₂ mile; indoor heated swimming pool, sauna and solarium, golf, each within 2 mile radius; helipad; closed during January; Mastercard and Visa cards accepted.

THE CREGGANS INN
Strachur, Argyll PA27 8BX

Telephone: 01369 860279   *Fax: 01369 860637*

More than 400 years ago, Mary Queen of Scots landed at Creggans on her way through the Highlands. An inn with a tradition of hospitality, homely comfort and individual attention, The Creggans stands on a headland looking over Loch Fyne, to tremendous prospects of hill and sea. Sir Fitzroy MacLean, whose family has owned this delightful hotel since 1957, explained, "we have spent many years striving for excellence, and it is in that spirit that we are continuing to develop our facilities so we can be certain of providing the best for disceming guests" . The latest developments are the installation of yacht moormgs to allow guests to arrive at the hotel from Loch Fyne, and helicopter tours from the Inn. Inveraray Castle, home of the Clan Campbell, is 19 miles away, and you can also visit Inveraray Jail, Scotland's "living l9th century prison" . The Inn is an ideal base for holidays such as sailing, fishing, golfing, walking and touring, or just relaxing in front of an open fire. The Creggans has a well deserved reputation for excellent food; not surprising as Lady MacLean, who still supervises the kitchen, is the author of several famous cookery books. A warm welcome awaits you at The Creggans Inn by the General Managers, Alex and Shona Findlay. Room and breakfast from £40.00, dinner room and breakfast from £54.00 including VAT. **Special winter breaks** available 1st October 1995-31st May 1996 (exc. Xmas/New Year/Easter) £65.50 per person, min. 2 nights, 2 people sharing, inc, dinner, b & b.
Inveraray 19, Dunoon 19, Glasgow 59, Oban 69, Campbeltown 85, Edinburgh 101, London 447.

F licence; 19 bedrooms (1 for the disabled), 18 en suite and 1 with private bathroom, all with telephone and TV; room service until 11.30 p.m.; baby listening; last orders for dinner 9.00 p.m.; bar meals; special diets; children welcome; dogs accepted; conferences max. 85; pool table; sailing/boating; washing/drying facilities; sea bathing, shooting, fishing and tennis nearby; riding 10 miles; golf 15 miles; open all year; all major credit cards accepted.

STONEFIELD CASTLE HOTEL
Tarbert, Loch Fyne, Argyll PA29 6YJ

Telephone: 01880 820836   *Fax: 01880 820929*

Here is something unusual in the way of a holiday setting. Tastefully converted from a 19th century castle, once the home of the Campbells and overlooking Loch Fyne, Stonefield Castle is charmingly situated on a peninsula separating the Isles of Islay and Jura from Arran. It has panoramic views over the sea and its gardens are known for some of the finest rhododendrons in Britain, azaleas and other exotic shrubs that flourish in the mild west coast climate. Inside the castle, the rooms are spacious and comfortable. There is a large panelled cocktail bar, lounge-hall, library and drawing room. All the bedrooms are comfortably furnished, with those in the older part of the house being in traditional style, whilst a newer wing has rooms of a more contemporary style. There are also several luxurious master bedrooms. The dining room, which enjoys stunning views, offers interesting table d'hôte menus, using local produce where possible. The accompanying wine list satisfies every taste and pocket. A snooker room and sauna suite is located within the hotel, and there is an outdoor heated swimming pool, well sited to maximise the views over the gardens and sea. Most traditional outdoor pursuits are available nearby and ferry trips to Arran, Gigha (gardens to see), Islay, Mull and Iona, together with the Mull of Kintyre are all within reach. Dinner, bed and breakfast from £45-£75 per person, per night, depending on room and season. **Bargain breaks:**Very special offers of up to 30% off normal tariff available at certain times throughout the year.
Lochgilphead 12, Inveraray 38, Campbeltown 38, Oban 51, Glasgow 95, London 500.
F licence; 33 bedrooms (32 en suite), all with direct dial telephone and TV; room service; lift; bar meals from 12.15 p.m. to 2.00p.m. and last orders for dinner 9.00p.m.; special diets; children welcome; dogs accepted; conferences max. 100; snooker/billiards; outdoor heated swimming pool; sauna; solarium; sea bathing; sailing/boating; clay shooting, golf, riding nearby; fishing; open all year; all major credit cards accepted.

THE CLACHAN COTTAGE HOTEL
Lochside, Lochearnhead, Perthshire, Scotland FK19 8PU

Telephone: 01567 830247   *Fax: 01567 830300*

Situated in an area of Outstanding Natural Beauty with a magnificent view overlooking Loch Earn, the privately owned Clachan Cottage Hotel has all the genuinely Scottish ambience you could wish for in a hotel which is on the dividing line between the Highlands and Lowlands. Clachan's 300 years origins are still to be found in the building since it was converted from old tradesmen's cottages. The rooms are comfortably furnished and the lounge is welcoming whilst the cosy bar with its original open fire has a fine selection of malt whiskies. The separate Pub is popular for live entertainment. It is the restaurant with a Taste of Scotland award which provides the most truly Scottish feature with traditional cuisine made from fresh local fish and meat produce and the delicious four course table d'hôte menu is changed nightly. The Clachan Cottage is ideally situated for day trips, visits to distilleries and numerous sporting activities including being an excellent area for hill-walking. It is is the sort of delightful small hotel in a breathtaking setting which requires at least a week to savour . Single room including breakfast from £27; double room with breakfast from £54.

Leisure Breaks: 3 night break £114/ extra nights £38; 7 night break £256/extra nights £36.50. Golf Breaks: 6 nights d,b&b plus free golf from £255.00 pp sharing. **Stirling 30 miles, Perth 37, Fort William 64, Glasgow 56, Edinburgh 65, London 427.**

Full licence. 21 en suite bedrooms with tea/coffee making facilities; safety deposit box. Last orders for dinner 21.00 hrs. Special diets available. Fishing, watersports nearby. Golf, riding 7/10 miles. Two conference rooms with capacity for 40/40. Hairdresser. Airport pick-up. Car parking for 60 cars. Open March - December..

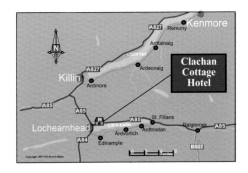

GREEN PARK HOTEL
Pitlochry, Tayside PH16 5JY

Telephone: 01796 473248   *Fax: 01796 473520*

After a long journey, it is a delight to stay in the Green Park Hotel with its breathtaking panoramic views of Loch Faskally and the surrounding green hills. The hotel is accessible both by car and by British Rail. You can be sure of a warm welcome from the staff, and this attitude pervades throughout. There are bright and spacious lounges, and the Sun Lounge overlooks the loch. The equally attractive bedrooms are comfortable and well equipped as you would expect in such a well run hotel. Bar lunches and bar dinners are available daily from 12-2.00 p.m. and 6-8.30 p.m. A popular feature is the cold buffet served for Sunday dinner. Guests attending the Pitlochry Festival Theatre will appreciate meals being served from 6.30 p .m., with the restaurant closing at 8.30 p.m. With Pitlochry centre only five minutes' walk away, you can find a variety of pastimes to make your holiday complete. Bed and breakfast from £38.00, inclusive of VAT. Spring and Autumn **Bargain Breaks** available from £40 per person per night, dinner, bed & breakfast and Curling Weekends in October - prices on application. Closed from the end of October to the end of March, but the office is open for enquiries. **Edinburgh 68, Glasgow 83, Braemar 41, Invemess 69, Kingussie 45, Kinloch Rannoch 21, Perth 28, London 444.**

F licence; 37 en suite bedrooms (10 on ground floor), all with telephone, tea/coffee making facilities; colour TV; children welcome; conferences; chess; cards; table tennis; 9 hole putting; swings; sailing and surfing on the loch; pony trekking, golf and fishing by arrangement.

DALMUNZIE HOUSE HOTEL
Spittal O'Glenshee, Blairgowrie, Perthshire PH10 7QG

Telephone: 01250 885224   Fax: 01250 885225

If you are looking for perfect peace and quiet or for a sporting holiday, this impressive country house, hidden away in the hills, is an excellent venue. Dalmunzie has been in the Winton family for many years, and is now looked after by Simon and Alexandra, whose care and attention result in a well run house, personal service, and a happy atmosphere. The sitting rooms, cosy cocktail bar and spacious bedrooms are all in excellent decorative order, well furnished and comfortable, and log fires and central heating ensure warmth in every season. Good old fashioned service is available for your requirements -tea trays are still brought to your room! In the dining room, the varied table d'hôte dishes are well cooked and feature traditional Scottish fare, which is accompanied by a carefully chosen wine list. This family owned sporting estate can organise almost any shooting holiday, whilst other field sports, trout fishing, walking and climbing also await you here. Dalmunzie have their own 9 hole golf course available for guests. Nearby Glenshee offers well organised skiing for all abilities, and for those wishing to explore on wheels, there are quiet roads and much to see. Room and breakfast from £36 per person, weekly rates from £368 per person, full board. During the ski season, dinner, bed and breakfast from £40-£47.

Bargain breaks: From Jan-April 2 nights from £80 & 5 nights from £190. From April-October 3 nights from £156. **Perth 35, Dundee 37, Braemar 15, Blairgowrie 20, Edinburgh 78, London 453.**

F licence, 18 bedrooms (1 for the disabled, 16 en suite), lift, last orders for dinner 8.30 p.m.; light bar lunches; special diets on request, children welcome; dogs accepted; conferences max. 20; games room; bar billiards; 9 hole golf course; tennis; shooting/fishing (trout/salmon, own rainbow trout stocked loch); skiing in Glenshee; riding 15 miles; closed November and December; Mastercard and Visa accepted.

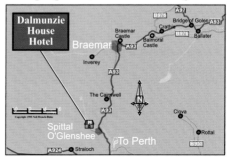

■ Histonc Houses, Gardens & Parks

GRAMPIAN
Castle Fraser & Garden, 4m N of Dunecht
Crathes Castle & Garden, Nr. Banchory
Cruickshank Botanic Gardens, Aberdeen University
Darnside Garden Herbs, Benholm by Johnshaven
Drum Castle & Garden, By Banchory
Duff House, Banff
Duthie Park & Winter Gardens, Aberdeen
Fasque, Fettercain
Fyvie Castle
Haddo House, Tarves
James Cocker & Sons, Rosegrowers, Aberdeen
Leith Hall & Garden, Kennethmont, Huntly
Monymusk Walled Garden
Pitmedden Garden & Museum of Farming by Ellon

HIGHLAND
The Achiltibuie Hydroponicum
Balmacara Estate & Lochalsh Woodland Garden, Kyle of Lochalsh
Brodie Castle, 4m W of Forres
Dunrobin Castle, Gardens & Museum, Golspie
Inverewe Garden, by Poolewe
Oldwick Castle, Wick

ISLE OF MULL
Torosay Castle & Gardens, 11/2m SSE of Craignure

ISLE OF SKYE
Dunvegan Castle

■ Walks & Nature Trails.

GRAMPIAN
Aden Coumtry Park, Mintlaw
Braeloine Visitor Centre, Glan Tanar, By Aboyne
Bullers of Buchan, Cruden Bay
Forview Nature Reserve, Newburgh

HIGHLAND
Abriachan Garden Nursery Walk, Loch Ness
Aultfearn Local Walk, Kiltarlity
Falls of Foyers Woodland Walks
Farigaig Forest Trails
Glen Affric Forest Walks
Plodda Falls Scenic Walk
Reelig Forest Walks, W of Inverness

ISLE OF MULL
Carsaig Arches, on shore 3m W of Carsaig

ISLE OF SKYE
Dalabil Glen, between Tarskavaig and Ostair
Forestry Walk - between Ardvasar and Aird of Sleat
The Trotternish Ridge

■ Historical Sites & Museums

GRAMPIAN
Aberdeen Maritime Museum - Provost Ross's House
Ballindalloch Castle, Ballindaloch
Balmoral Castle, Crathie
Braemar Highland Heritage Centre
Brodie Castle, Forres
Castle Fraser, Nr Inverurie
Dallas Dhu Distillery, Forres
Colgarff Castle, Strathdon

Crathie Church, Crathie
Elgin Cathedral
Kings College Chapel & Visitor Centre, Aberdeen
Provost Skene's House, Aberdeen
St Machar's Cathedral, Old Aberdeen

HIGHLAND
Cawdor Castle, 5m N of Nairn
Culloden Battlefield, 5m E of Inverness
Dornoch Cathedral
Durness Visitor Centre
Eilean Donan Castle, 9m E of Kyle of Lochalsh
Fort George, 10m W of Nairn
Glen Coe Visitor Centre, 17m S of Fort William
Glenfinnan Monument, Lochaber, 18m W of Fort William
Hugh Miller's Cottage, Cromarty, 22m NE of Inveness
Leckmelm Shrubbery & Arboretum, Nr. Ullapool
Lochinver Visitor Centre
Urquart Castle on Loch Ness, Nr. Drumnadrochit

ISLE OF MULL
Duart Castle, on E point of Mull
The Old Byrem, Dervaig

ISLE OF SKYE
Colbost Folk Museum
Giant MacAskill Museum, Dunvegan
Piping Centre, Borreraig
Skye Museum of Island Life, Kilmuir

■ Entertainment Venues

GRAMPIAN
Alford Valley Railway, Alford
Castle Grant, Grantown-on-Spey
Fowlsheugh RSPB Seabird Colony
Glenshee Ski Centre, Cairnwell, by Braemar
Honyneuk Bird Park, Nr. Macduff
Loch Muick & Lochnagar Wildlife Reserve, Crimond
North East Falconry Centre, Cairnie, By Huntley
Peterhead Fish Market
Royal Lochnagar Distillery, Crathie
St Cyrus National Nature Reserve, By Montrose
Speyside Heather Centre, Grantown
Storybook Glen, Maryculter
The Malt Whisky Trail, Speyside
Ugie Fish House, Peterhead

HIGHLAND
Aviemore Centre
Dulsie Bridge
Glen Ord Distillery, Muir of Ord
Highland Folk Museum, Kingussie
Loch Ness Centre, Drumnadrochit
Made in Scotland Exhibition of Crafts, Beauly
RothiemurchasEstate Nr Aviemore
Strathspey Steam Railway, Nr. Aviemore
Torridon Countryside Centre, 9m SW of Aberdeen

ISLE OF MULL
Isle of Mull Wine Company, Bunessan
Mull Railway, Craignure
Mull Little Theatre, Dervaig
Tobermory Distillery Visitor Centre

ISLE OF SKYE
The Clan Donald Visitor Centre at Armadale Castle
Talisker Distillery, Loch Harport
Skye Oysters, Loch Harport

January 20-21	SPILLERS BONIO SIBERIAN HUSKY OG GB SLED DOG RACE
	Glenmore Forest Park, Nr. Aviemore, Highland
March 20-24	ILE OF MULL DRAMA FESTIVAL
	Aros Hall, Tobermory
April 16	CULLODEN COMMEMORATION SERVICE
	Culloden, Nr. Inverness, Highland
April 25-	PITLOCHRY FESTIVAL THEATRE PROGRAMME
October 5	Pitlochry, Tayside
April 28-30	ISLE OF MULL MUSIC FESTIVAL
	Tobermory
June 9-10	SKYELIVE
	Various events, Isle of Skye
June 10-23	SKYE AND LOCHALSH FEIS
	Isle of Skye
June 11	KILDRUMMY CASTLE RALLY
	Kildrummy, By Alford, Grampian
June 15	OLD MELDRUM SPORTS & HIGHLAND GAMES
	Old Meldrum, Aberdeenshire
June 20-30	HIGLAND TRADITIONAL MUSIC FESTIVAL
	Dingwall, Highland
July 3	NATIONAL ARCHERY TOURNAMENT
	Armadale, Sleat, Isle of Skye
July 11	ELGIN HIGHLAND GAMES
	Elgin, Grampian
July 22	INVERNESS HIGHLAND GAMES
	Inverness
July 24-29	SKYE FOLK FESTIVAL
	Portree, Isle of Skye
July 24-29	INVERNESS TATTOO
	Inverness
July 31-August 10	ABERDEEN INT'L YOUTH FESTIVAL
	Various venues, Aberdeen
August 3	159th BLACK ISLE SHOW
	Muir of Ord, Highland
August 5-6	TURRIFF SHOW
	Turriff, Aberdeenshire
August 10	SALEN SHOW
	Glenaros, Isle of Mull
August 17	NAIRN HIGHLAND GAMES
	Nairn, Inverness-shire, Highland
September 7	BRAEMAR ROYAL HIGHLAND GATHERING
	Braemar, Grampian
October 13-15	2300 CLUB CAR RALLY
	Tobermory, Isle of Mull ˙
November 2	DUNVEGAN CASTLE FIREWORK DISPLAY
	Dunvegan, Isle of Skye

For further information contact the nearest Regional Tourist Board, Tourist Information Centre or

The Scottish Tourist Board
23 Ravelston Terrace
Edinburgh EH4 3EU
Tel: 0131 332 2433

THE MARCLIFFE AT PITFODELS
North Deeside Road, Aberdeen, Grampian ABl 9YA

Telephone: 01224 861000   Fax: 01224 868860

Here is an hotel of exceptional quality, owned and run by Stewart and Sheila Spence, whose hospitality is renowned. Set in eight acres of woodland garden, it is but a few minutes from the centre of Aberdeen and within 15 minutes of two golf courses, and some of Scotland's finest scenery. The personal service and the ambience is that of a country house, whilst offering discreet and flexible arrangements for entertaining and business meetings. Five foot double king size or Zip Link twin beds are provided in all the spacious bedrooms, where you will find added extras such as towelling bathrobes, hairdryers and refrigerated mini bars. The luxurious suites are graciously adorned with period furniture, flowers, fruit, and again, many other creature comforts. There are two restaurants, The Conservatory, which serves the most delicious lunches and dinners, and the more formal Invery Room, where in addition to the outstanding cuisine, one may draw on a cellar of 300 wines. Both restaurants maintain the highest levels of presentation and quality. The Marcliffe is an ideal base for touring the nearby attractions such as art galleries and museums, and both castle and distillery tours are available. For the sportsman, shooting, salmon fishing, stalking and golf at Royal Aberdeen can all be arranged by the hotel. The Marcliffe is situated on the A93 between Cults and the city centre, and it is where you will experience first class standards in every aspect. Room and breakfast from £90, dinner, room and breakfast from £115. Prices include VAT. A member of

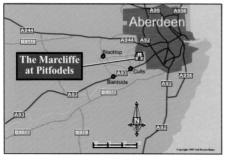

Small Luxury Hotels of the World. Open all year. **Bargain breaks:** All year dinner, b&b Fri,Sat,Sun night from £59.50 per person sharing twin/double . ☙☙☙☙☙ Highly Commended. Proprietors: Stewart & Sheila Spence. **Balmoral 53, St. Andrews 82, Edinburgh 106, Glasgow 146, London 481.** *F licence; 42 en suite bedrooms (1 for the disabled), all with telephone & TV; room service; baby listening; night service; lift; last dinner orders 10 p.m.; special diets; children welcome; conferences max. 400; games room; snooker/billiards; golf 1 mile; riding 2 miles; tennis & squash 3 miles; shooting/fishing by arrangement; all major credit cards accepted.*

CULDUTHEL LODGE
14, Culduthel Road, Inverness IV2 4AG

Telephone/Fax: 01463 240089

This beautifully appointed small hotel is owned and run by David and Marion Bonsor, who provide a welcoming atmosphere, high standards of housekeeping and good food. Set in a quiet residential area, a ten minute walk from the centre of Inverness, it is an ideal location for shopping, theatre going, sightseeing, touring and golf . Inverness is compact and a few minutes' drive will take you out into a variety of stunning countryside. However you spend your day, it is pleasant to return to the homely atmosphere created at Culduthel Lodge and to sample Marion Bonsor's delicious, freshly cooked food. Her table d'hôte menu changes daily, using the best of local produce. There is also a small, carefully chosen wine list. This comfortable hotel has restful colour schemes throughout, and antique and reproduction furnishings complement the Georgian house. A bowl of fruit, decanter of sherry and flowers in your room as a welcome, and a complimentary newspaper in the mornings, all add to the relaxing ambience of this hotel. Once in Inverness, follow the ring road and pick up the sign for Culduthel. Head for Culduthel Road and the hotel is on the right hand side. Room and breakfast from £33.00 per person, dinner, bed and breakfast from £49.00. **Bargain breaks:** From November 1995-March 1996 -3 days dinner, b & b £139 per person sharing. **Edinburgh 158, Aberdeen 108, Glasgow 170, Loch Ness 7, Inverness Airpon 7, West Coast 1 hour, London 533.**

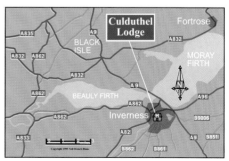

R licence; 12 en suite bedrooms, all with direct dial telephone, cassette/CD player, umbrella and TV, last orders for dinner 8.00 p.m.; vegetarian diets; dogs accepted, tennis ¹/₂ mile, golf 1 mile; shooting and fishing ¹/₂ mile, by arrangement; riding ten miles; open all year; Visa and Mastercard accepted.

LOCHALSH HOTEL
Kyle Of Lochalsh, Highland IV40 8AF

Telephone: 01599 534202   *Fax: 01599 534881*

Built in the days of rail travel, the Lochalsh Hotel retains an aura of the 30's, enhanced by the high standards of service and hospitality dispensed by Mr. Woodtli, the General Manager, and his staff. It is still possible to arrive in Lochalsh by rail, and cross over to the Isle of Skye on the newly opened bridge. The view from the grounds and most of the windows in the hotel, is one of the most beautiful in Britain. The Lochalsh is warm, comfortable and well ordered, with soft decorative schemes. The bedrooms are spacious and well equipped, and the bar in the cocktail lounge offers, amongst a variety of drinks, a wide selection of malts. In the dining room, there is a good choice of dishes available from the menu, all of which are beautifully presented and efficiently served, local seafood is a speciality. Lochalsh is an ideal centre for exploring the wild beauty of the west coast. Two hours will see you into Inverness after a delightful drive via Loch Ness, and few can resist the lure of Skye. To locate the hotel, simply follow the signs for the ferry. Room and breakfast from £65.00 single, and £85.00 double for 2 people. **Lochalsh breaks**: 2 night break from £120 inc. accommodation, Highland breakfast, table d'hôte dinner and VAT.

Plockton 5, Achnasheen 40, Inverness 86, Glasgow 194, Edinburgh 207, London 561.

F licence, 40 en suite bedrooms, all with direct dial telephone and TV; room service; baby listening; night service; lift; last orders for dinner 9. 30p.m .; light lunches; special diets; children welcome; dogs accepted; conferences max. 40; shooting/fishing; all major credit cards accepted.

EDDRACHILLES HOTEL
Badcall Bay, Scourie, Sutherland IV27 4TH

Telephone: 01971 502080   Fax: 01971 502477

The Eddrachilles commands a fine position, overlooking the sea with mountains behind it. Inside, the hotel is clean, bright and comfortable, with many of the windows having a sea view, thanks to the foresight of Mr. and Mrs. Alasdair Wood, who have restored and extended this old building, and are kind and hospitable hosts. The logistics of providing food and drink in these remote parts, makes the discovery of an à la carte and table d'hôte menu, together with an interesting wine list, a pleasant surprise. The emphasis is on home cooking, using fresh and seasonal ingredients. Hill lamb, venison and seafood are the local delicacies. The north of Scotland is unique; its remote and untouched beauty cannot be described in a few words. You can explore it from quiet, single-track roads, or, for the more energetic, there are numerous scenic walks and climbs. Nearby Handa Island, is famous as a bird sanctuary, and boat trips across the short stretch of water can be made from Tarbert. When returning to Eddrachilles after a tiring day of exploration, you can always be assured of warmth, comfort and good food. To find the hotel from Ullapool, take the A835 which joins the A837 and eventually the A894. Badcall Bay is on the left just before you reach Scourie. Room and breakfast from £32.00, dinner, room and breakfast from £43.00. Prices include VAT. **Bargain breaks** - reduced rates available on stays of 3, 6 or 10 days. **Ullapool 40, Thurso 95, Inverness 98, Edinburgh 245, Glasgow 266, London 620.**
F 1icence; 11 en suite bedrooms (4 on ground floor), all with direct dial telephone and TV; last orders for dinner 8. 00 p.m; bar lunches available; special diets by arrangement, children of 3 years and over welcome; sailing/boating; fishing; hotel closed Nov.-Feb. inclusive; Mastercard and Visa credit cards accepted.

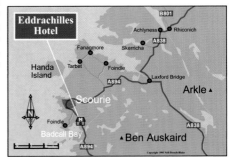

THE HOTEL
Isle of Colonsay, Argyll PA61 7YP

Telephone: 01951 200316   Fax: 01951 200353

If you are looking for somewhere romantic you should just take off to what is thought to be the most beautifully remote hotel in Great Britain. It was built in 1750 and is a listed historic building but the modern amenities which belie both the antiquity and its isolation ensure that today's guests are warmly welcomed. Most of the bedrooms are en suite and well appointed; there are larger family rooms, family bungalow and adjoining self-catering chalets. The hotel has ample public areas - dining room, lounge, sunroom and a pleasant and secluded garden. There are two bars and a separate building incorporating a bookshop and a café where a glass of wine, oysters and home-made bread are on offer. The dining room cuisine is table d'hôte based on fresh local produce and widely acclaimed. Colonsay is a paradise for naturalists with 200 species of bird including Golden Eagles, Atlantic Grey Seals; also abundant flora with a magnificent rhododendron collection. Archeologists come too, for the island was important even before the influential Viking period. Whatever your interest the mild winters and long light summers add to the perfection of this tranquil island and the local knowledge of your hosts Kevin and Christa Byrne ensures maximum enjoyment of Colonsay's many attractions. Single

room including breakfast from £35.00. Double room with breakfast from £70.00. **Leisure Breaks:** Bargain rates available for last minute bookings. **Mull 15 , Argyll mainland 25, Oban - Colonsay by boat 2½ hours. Edinburgh 145.**

Full licence. 8 en suite bedrooms - and three singles - with colour TV; hairdryer, trouser press, laundry service, tea/coffee making facilities. Last orders for dinner 19.30. Special diets available. Fishing, golf (18 holes), watersports, bicycle rental. Picnic cruises. Bookshop. Courtesy car pick-up. Car parking for 30 cars. Open March-October. Most credit cards accepted.

KILLIECHRONAN HOUSE
Aros, Isle Of Mull, Argyll PA72 6JU

Telephone: 01680 300403   *Fax: 01680 300463*

What more picturesque and quiet rural setting than at the head of Loch na Keal, on the west side of Mull? When I was there, a stag was leisurely cropping the grass in the garden, not the least worried by my photographing him. Killiechronan House is part of the beautiful 5000 acre Killiechronan Estate, with its own fishing and pony trekking facilities, and arrangements for stalking can easily be made. There are five miles of coastline along the north side of the Loch, and, of course miles of seldom used, single track roads. The hotel is easily accessible from the mainland, as it is only 14 miles from the ferry terminal at Craignure, and just a forty minute trip from Oban. The house was tastefully refurbished and redecorated in 1995, to the same standards as Mr. and Mrs. Leroy's other two hotels at Oban (page 222), and at Port of Menteith (page 216). The warm and cosy décor of both the lounge and drawing room is most welcoming, and during those colder days, open log fires are in full blaze. In overall charge, are Patrick and Margaret Freytag. Patrick, a very experienced chef, prepares the best of traditional Scottish cuisine, using fresh local produce. A special weekly rate is available allowing consecutive nights to be spent at two, or all three of the Leroy hotels, but at least two nights must be spent at Killiechronan. Dinner, room and breakfast from £46.00 per person. Minibreak (min. 2 nights) from £41 per person. STB ⌒⌒⌒⌒ Commended. AA ✿ for food. **Salen 2, Craignure 14, Tobermory 15, Iona 35, Edinburgh 130.** *R & R licence; 6 en suite bedrooms, all with direct dial telephone and radio; last dinner orders 8. 00 p.m, special diets; dogs accepted; sea bathing; sailing/ boating; pony trekking; shooting/fishing; stalking by arrangement; golf five miles; hotel closed from October 31st-1st March. Mastercard and Visa accepted.*

ROSEDALE HOTEL
Portree, Isle Of Skye IV51 9DB

Telephone: 01478 613131   Fax: 01478 612531

I was advised by friends in Uig to visit the Rosedale Hotel at Portree, and how glad I was to find this most attractive hotel, so well run by the proprietress, Mrs. Andrew and her son, Hugh. It is situated on the loch side facing the harbour and looking out across the Sound of Raasay to the Isle beyond. Mr. Andrew showed me round the hotel and I realised how much time and energy had been put into making this modernised, yet comfortably furnished and brightly decorated hotel so acceptable. The Andrew family have done a wonderful job. The bedrooms are very well appointed and the public rooms, including the cocktail bar, are attractive and comfortable, creating an atmosphere of peace and quiet. I enjoyed my meals in the AA Rosette award winning restaurant where meals are admirably cooked and well presented. Whilst you are assured of a great welcome at any time, the Andrews do recommend an early visit when the weather is at its best and the Island less busy. Room and breakfast from £33.00 per person inclusive of VAT. Other terms on application. Closed October to mid-May, but office open for enquiries and advance bookings.**Bargain breaks**: Skye Explorer holiday rates available for stays of 3 days or more including accommodation, breakfast, dinner and free admission into Dunvegan Castle, the Clan Donald Centre and the Museum of Island Life. Prices from £50 per day.

Edinburgh 237, Invermoriston 90, Fort Augustus 97, Kyle of Lochalsh 34, London 487.

F licence; 20 en suite bedrooms (7 ground floor) all with television, telephone, radio, tea/coffee making facilities, also 3 attractive twin bedded rooms with private bathrooms available in nearby Beaumont House; full central heating; boating; tennis and golf nearby; fishing by arrangement; good open air parking.

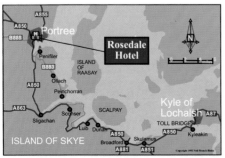

UIG HOTEL
Uig, Portree, Isle Of Skye IV51 9YE

Telephone: 01470 542205. Guests 542367   Fax: 01470 542308

The Uig Hotel is situated at the northern end of the lovely island of Skye looking down on the little bay and harbour of Uig. Grace Graham, who started in the hotel industry in 1946 and still plays an active role, and her son David Taylor, the owners, must be justly proud of their attractive and elegantly furnished hotel with its warm and cheerful atmosphere. The furniture, pictures and colour schemes are very pleasant. There are 11 pretty bedrooms in the hotel and at the rear, offering lovely seaviews, the old steading has been converted into 6 attractive bedrooms, one with a sitting room and all with their own bathroom. Next door, Primrose Cottage has been converted into 3 very comfortable self-catering apartments. The restaurant provides a varied table d'hôte menu, and the dishes are plentiful and skilfully cooked. The excellent wine list is sure to suit all tastes. For lunch there are interesting snacks with very good coffee. The cocktail bar has an open fire and comfortable arm chairs, fronted by a sun lounge that has sweeping views over the bay. You will enjoy your stay and the scenery and peace of the surrounding country, which has strong associations with Bonnie Prince Charlie and Flora MacDonald. Uig is now served by the roll on, roll off ferry, *The Hebridean Isles*. Room and breakfast from £30.00 per person inclusive of VAT. Other terms on application. Closed during the winter, but office open. **Bargain Breaks:** 3 and 7 day breaks May-September; also bridge weekends in April and birdwatching and wildlife holidays available. Prices on application. **Edinburgh 252, Portree 15, Kyle of Lochalsh 49, London 502.**

F licence; 17 en suite bedrooms, direct dial telephone, colour TV; late meals to order; diets by arrangement; drying room; children welcome; sea, river bathing; boating; fishing; shooting by arrangement; pony trekking; major credit cards accepted.

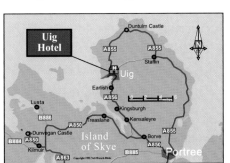

■ **Historic Houses, Gardens & Parks**

Castle Cornet & Maritime Museum, Castle Cornet
Saumarez Manor, St. Martins (venue for 'Le Viaer Marchi')
Specialist Gardens at Castle Cornet
Candie Gardens - St. Peter Port
Grande Marais Koi Farm, Vale
La Seigneurie, Island of Sark

La Valette Underground Military Museum, St. Peter Port
German Occupation Museum, St. Peter Port
Guernsey Aquarium, Havelet Bay
Guernsey Museum & Art Gallery, St Peter Port
National Trust of Guernsey Folk Museum,
   Saumarez Park
Fort Grey Shipwreck Museum, St. Saviours

■ **Walks & Nature Trails**

The Saumarez Nature Trail, starting at Cobo Bay
Le Catioroc Nature Trail & L'Eree Shingle Bank
Portinfer; Port Soif Nature Trail; Grandes Rocques
Saumarez Park Walk, starting at Cobo Bay
St Peter Port to St Martin's Point Walk

■ **Historical Sites & Museums**

■ **Entertainment Venues**

Guernsey Bird Gardens, St Andrews
Le Friquet Butterfly Centre, Castel
'Oatlands', Guernsey's Craft Centre, St Sampson's

GUERNSEY DIARY OF EVENTS 1996

January 20-28	GUERNSEY OPEN INDOOR BOWLS TOURNAMENT
March 1-16	GUERNSEY EISTEDDFOD
April 1-20	GUERNSEY FESTIVAL OF FOOD AND WINE
May 17-19	BRITISH BRIDGE LEAGUE CONGRESSS
June 16	HASH HOUSE HARRIERS HALF MARATHON
June 23-29	GUERNSEY SQUARE DANCE FESTIVAL
July 1	VIAER MARCHI (Traditional Evening)
July 13 or 14	ROUND TABLE HARBOUR CARNIVAL
July 27-August 3	ST. PETER PORT TOWN CARNIVAL
July/August*	GUERNSEY INTERNATIONAL FOLK FESTIVAL
August 3	ROCQUAINE REGATTA
August 7-8	SOUTH AGRICULTURAL SHOW
August 14-15	WEST AGRICULTURAL SHOW
September 7/14th*	KITE FLY '96
September 21-29	ENGLISH BRIDGE UNION CONGRESS
October 20-26	CHESS FESTIVAL

*dates to be confirmed

For further details contact:

States of Guernsey Department of Tourism and Recreation, PO Box 23, St. Peter Port, Guernsey, Channel Islands GY1 3AN. Tel: 01481 726611.

HOTEL BELLA LUCE
Moulin Huet, St. Martins, Guernsey GY4 6EB

Telephone: 01481 38764   *Fax: 01481 39561*

The Hotel Bella Luce is a former 12th century manor house that is attractive both inside and out. There is an abundance of flowers, from the sweet peas lining the swimming pool, to the wonderful hanging baskets on the walls. The pool, with its adjacent sauna/solarium room, is bounded on one side by a well manicured lawn. The Manager, Richard Cann, and his staff take great pride in running this hotel to ensure their guests' maximum contentment. All the public rooms are beautifully furnished and very comfortable. The lounge bar, with its oak beamed ceiling, has a warm and friendly atmosphere, and is the ideal place in which to enjoy either a drink or a dish chosen from the extensive bar lunch menu. The tastefully decorated bedrooms, three of which are on the ground floor, have the facilities expected in a quality hotel. The freshly prepared food served in the restaurant is excellent, with a delicious choice of dishes from either the table d'hôte or à la carte menus. To accompany these, there is a comprehensive wine list to suit all palates. During my recent visit, my overall impression was one of total peace and tranquillity, punctuated only by birdsong. The hotel is just two miles from the beautiful "capital" of Guernsey, St. Peter Port, and the island's magnificent cliffs and coastal scenery make breathtaking views. Room and breakfast from £48.00; dinner, room and breakfast from £72.00. **Bargain breaks** available 1st November-1st April, £24 pppn for b & b. *F licence; 31 en suite bedrooms (3 ground floor), all with direct dial telephone and TV; room service; baby listening; last orders for dinner 9.45p.m.; bar meals; special diets; children welcome; dogs accepted at management's discretion; conferences max. 20; outdoor heated swimming pool; sauna; solarium; open all year; major credit cards accepted.*

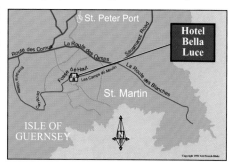

OLD GOVERNMENT HOUSE HOTEL
Ann's Place, St. Peter Port, Guernsey GY1 4AZ

Telephone: 01481 724921   *Fax: 01481 724429*

Within the heart of St. Peter Port, enjoying breathtaking views, the location of the OGH (as it is affectionately known) is the perfect setting for a holiday or business break on Guernsey. Once the official residence of the Island's Governors, the Hotel has served visitors since 1858 and is today a gracious blend of old and new, with all the well appointed bedrooms and private suites having colour schemes complementing the character of the hotel. The Regency restaurant is one of the island's finest with à la carte, table d'hôte and themed gourmet menus being offered, accompanied by Chateau and Estate bottled varieties of wine from an excellent wine list. The Centenary is one of three bars - each with their own personality - and light lunches can be taken there, if preferred to the relaxing poolside terrace outdoors. If night life is on your agenda, the Centenary Bar also hosts regular dancing as does the No 10 night club. The OGH is quite simply a very good hotel - to be recommended whatever the reason for your stay. Single room including breakfast from £49.00. Double room with breakfast from £98.00.

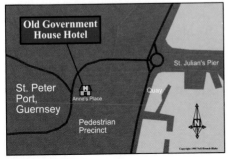

Full licence. 71 en suite bedrooms with satellite TV, direct-dial telephone; hairdryer, trouser press, laundry service. Last orders for dinner 21.30 hrs. Special diets available. Billiards/snooker, croquet, fishing, fitness centre, massage, golf, watersports, riding, sauna, squash, tennis all can be arranged nearby. Three conference rooms to capacity of 225 guests. AV equipment and full secretarial service. Car rental. Car parking for 25 cars. Open all year. All major credit cards accepted.

■ **Historic Houses, Gardens & Parks**

■ **Historical Sites & Museums**

Battle of Flowers Museum, St Ouen
Eric Young Orchid Foundation, Trinity
Elizabeth Castle, St Aubin's Bay
Fantastic Tropical Gardens, St. Peter's Valley
Faldouet Dolmen, Gorey
Howard David Park, St. Helier
German Underground Hospital, St. Lawrence
Jersey Flower Centre, St. Lawrence
Grosnez Castle & La Pinacle, Les Landes
Jersey Lavender Farm St. Brelade
Hamptonne Country Life Museunn, St. Lawrence
La Mare Vineyards, St. Mary
The Hermitage St Helier
Samares Manor, St Clement
La Hougue Bie, Grouville
St. Ouen's Manor Grounds, St Ouen
Island Fortree Occupation Museum, St. Helier
Sunset Carnation Nurseries, St. Ouen's Bay
Jersey Motor Museum
The Living Legend, St Peter
Mont Orgueil Castle, Gorey
The Pallot Heritage Steam Museum, Trinity

■**Walks & Nature Trails**
St. Peter's Bunker Museum, St. Peter

■ **Entertainment Venues**

Guided nature walks
Jersey's Coastal Walks:
Fort Regent Leisure Centre, St Helier
  i) Grosnez to Sorel
Jersey Butterfly Centre, St Mary
  ii) Sorel to Bouley Bay
Jersey Shire Horse Farm & Museum, St Ouen
  iii) Bouley Bay to St. Catherine's
Jersey Pottery, Gorey Village
Town Walk, St. Helier
Jersey Zoo, Trinity

JERSEY DIARY OF EVENTS 1996

April 28-31	JERSEY JAZZ FESTIVAL
April 26 to May 6	OFFICIAL E.B.U JERSEY FESTIVAL OF BRIDGE 1996
May 3-5	JERSEY INTERNATIONAL AIR RALLY
June 17-23	JERSEY IRISH FESTIVAL WEEK
July 15-20	JERSEY FLORAL ISLAND FESTIVAL
August 8	THE JERSEY BATTLE OF FLOWERS
September 12-14	INTERNATIONAL SALON CULINAIRE
September 20-23	THE 1996 JERSEY WORLD MUSIC FESTIVAL
September 21-Oct 6	JERSEY INTERNATIONAL FESTIVAL
October 2-5	ROYAL JERSEY PRO-AM GOLF TOURNAMENT
October 11-14	COUNTRY MUSIC WEEKEND

HORSE RACING AT LES LANDES RACECOURSE

*April 8th
*May 6th, 27th
*June 13th, 14th, 27th
*July 14th, 28th
*August 11th, 26th

*dates to be confirmed
For further information contact:
Jersey Tourism, Liberation Square, St. Helier, Jersey El lBB. Channel Islands. Tel: 01534 500700.

THE ATLANTIC HOTEL
St. Brelade, Jersey JE3 8HE

Telephone: 01534 44101   Fax: 01534 44102

With extensive refurbishments completed to the highest of standards, The Atlantic can now be recognised as a truly stylish and "international" hotel. Having been under local private ownership since 1970, great attention to detail in every aspect throughout, is paramount. From the imposing columned entrance, through to the reception hall and lounge areas, classic antique furniture, contemporary furnishings, and warm, inviting décor, all contribute towards a theme of understated luxury. Outstanding views across the gardens, the delightfully colourful, tropical outside pool area, and the coastline beyond, can be admired from both the lounge and the main restaurant. Innovative menus, a fine wine list, good presentation and attentive service in the elegant restaurant are all supervised by the most professional of restaurant managers. The Palm Club provides a romanesque feature indoor pool jacuzzi, solaria, sauna gymnasium, and an outside tennis court is also available for the use of guests. The bedrooms benefit from sea or golf course views, and are extremely well appointed with good facilities and high standards of décor and comfort throughout. Conferences can be catered for, and the many attractions and facilities to be enjoyed at The Atlantic Hotel, make it an ideal venue for any stay, be it for business or sheer self indulgence! The Atlantic is a first class hotel in a good location. Room and breakfast from £110.00. **St. Helier 5, Airport 2.**

F licence; 50 en suite bedrooms including Garden Studio Rooms, and two luxury suites, all with telephone, colour TV and radio; late meals to 9.30p.m.; lift; laundry service, conferences taken; diets available; children welcome; night service; sea bathing; golf nearby; health & leisure centre, tennis, indoor heated swimming pool; all major credit cards accepted.

THE ROYAL HOTEL
David Place, St. Helier, Jersey JE2 4TD

Telephone: 01534 26521   Fax: 01534 24035

The elegant Royal Hotel is a few minutes' walk from the centre of St. Helier and with its excellent combination of facilities and friendly service it is the ideal base for both family and business breaks on the island of Jersey. The décor in the bedrooms is individual in style and all rooms are appointed to a high standard with suites plus rooms with four poster beds also being available. The public rooms are classic and very comfortable. We enjoyed an excellent meal in the restaurant where both table d'hôte and à la carte menus as well as themed evening gourmet menus and local specialities are on offer. There is an extensive sheltered patio area which is an ideal sun-trap. The Royal Enclosure Bar is a lively venue for guests and locals alike who take part in the enter-tainment which is a regular feature of the hotel. The Royal is a delightful place with something for everybody and assuring a really comfortable stay. Single room including breakfast from £49.50. Double room with breakfast from £39.50 per person.
Leisure Breaks: Winter Weekend Breaks from 1st October 1995 to 31st March 1996 excluding Christmas/New Year period £170.00 pp sharing a twin/double room for a 2 night stay to include a Saturday night, plus d,b&b, car hire and return flight London-Gatwick.

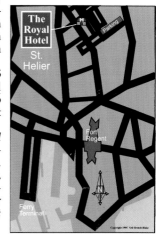

Full licence. 86 en suite bedrooms with radio, satellite TV, direct-dial telephone, hairdryer, trouser press, laundry service, tea/coffee mak-ing facilities. 24 hour room service. Last orders for dinner 21.30 hrs. Special diets available. Fishing, golf, watersports, riding, shooting, squash & tennis by arrangement nearby. Chemist, beauty salon, news-stand adjacent to hotel. Five meeting rooms with total capacity for 700 guests. Car rental. Car parking for 30 cars. Open all year. Credit cards accepted.

HOTEL PETIT CHAMP
Sark, Channel Islands GY9 0SF

Telephone: 01481 832046   Fax: 01481 832469

The island of Sark is truly unique. It retains a feudal constitution dating back to the reign of Elizabeth I, has its own government, no income tax and is home to just 550 residents. It is also a natural, car free and tranquil retreat for people who enjoy beautiful walks, breathtaking scenery and a refreshing break from the modern world. The Hotel Petit Champ is a reflection of all that with its secluded position and views to the sea. Here, under the expert supervision of the resident proprietors Chris and Caroline Robins, is a true gem of an hotel with a country house atmosphere and 16 cosy en suite bedrooms, some of which have balconies. There are three sun-lounges and a lounge with an extensive library which is a true haven of peace. Drinks before dinner are taken in the intimate bar and then guests repair to the candle-lit restaurant renowned for its good cuisine with local lobster and crab dishes which are specialities of the house. A solar heated swimming pool nestles in the natural setting of an old quarry and forms a perfect sun trap. The hotel Petit Champ, set in the island magic of Sark, is truly enchanting and the spell draws visitors back for holidays year after year. Single room including breakfast and dinner from £43.25. Double room with breakfast and dinner from £41.25.

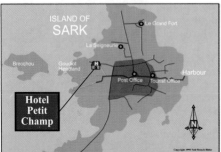

Full licence. 16 en suite bedrooms. Hairdryer available. Last orders for dinner 20.30 hrs. Putting green and solar heated outdoor swimming pool. Nearby sea fishing, tennis, billiards, badminton. All-inclusive holidays with travel available. Open Easter to October. Credit cards accepted.

Houses, Gardens & Parks

Andress House, Co Armagh
The Argory, Co Armagh
Castle Coole, Co Fermanagh
Castle Ward, Co Down
Downhill, Londonderry
Florence Court, Co Fermanagh
Gray's Printing Press, Strabane, Co Tyrone
Hezlett House, Co Londonderry
Mount Stewart House, Garden & Temple

Rowallane Garden, Saintfield, Co Down
Springhill, Moneymore, Co Londonderry

Templetown Mausoleum, Co Antrim
Wellbrook Beetling Mill, Cookstown, Co Tyrone

■ **Historical Sites & Museums**

Carrickfergus Castle, Carrickfergus, Co Antrim
City Hall, Belfast
Devenish Island, Lough Erne
Giant's Causeway, Nr Coleraine, Co Antrim
Glen of Glenariff, NE of Ballymena
Slieve Gullion, Newry, Co Down
Stormont Castle, Belfast
Ulster Museum, Belfast

NORTHERN IRELAND DIARY OF EVENTS 1996

January 6	MALLUSK INTERNATIONAL CROSS-COUNTRY
	World cross-country athletics, Belfast
March 2-9	OPERA NORTHERN IRELAND SPRING SEASON
	Grand Opera House, Belfast
March 12-14	TEMPLETON ANTIQUES & FINE ART FAIR
	6th year. Templepatrick, Co Antrim
March 17	ST PATRICK'S DAY CELEBRATIONS
	Armagh, Ballymena, Downpatrick, Newry
April 27-28	CITY OF BELFAST SPRING FLOWER FESTIVAL, Belfast
May 2-24	BELFAST CIVIC FESTIVAL
	inc. Lord mayor's Show (May 6) and American Festival, Belfast
May 6	BELFAST MARATHON & FUN RUN
15-17 May	ROYAL ULSTER AGRICULTURAL SOCIETY SHOW
	Balmoral, Belfast
May 19	NORTHERN IRELAND INTERNATIONAL AIR SHOW
	Londonderry
May 23-27	INTERNATIONAL JAZZ & BLUES FESTIVAL, Londonderry
June 14-22	PROMS '96
	Ulster Orchestra Symphony Concerts, Ulster Hall, Belfast
June 21-23	NORTHERN IRELAND GAME FAIR
	Shane's Castle, Antrim
July*	SENIOR BRITISH OPEN TOURNAMENT
	Royal Portrush Golf Club, Co Down
July 12	BATTLE OF THE BOYNE COMMEMORATIONS
	Belfast and other centres
July 13	ULSTER HARP LAGER DERBY
	Down Royal Racecourse, Maze, Lisburn
July 19-20*	500cc WORLD CHAMPIONSHIP IRISH MOTOCROSS GRAND PRIX
	Ballykelly, Co Londonderry
July 19-20	ULSTER TRACTION ENGINE RALLY
	Ballymena (prov. location)
August 24-26*	ANTIQUES & FINE ARTS FAIR
	Slieve Donard Hotel, Newcastle
August 26-27	OUL' LAMMAS FAIR
	Ireland's oldest traditional fair. Ballycastle
September 3-14	IDEAL HOME EXHIBITION, Belfast
September 5-29	ROYAL ULSTER ACADEMY OF ARTS EXHIBITION
	Ulster Museum, Belfast
October 29-31	ULSTER ANTIQUES & FINE ART FAIR
	Culloden Hotel, Belfast

* provisional dates. *For further information, contact:*
Northern Ireland Tourist Board, St Anne's Court, 59 North Street, Belfast. Tel: 01232 231221.

BEECH HILL HOUSE HOTEL
32, Ardmore Road, Londonderry BT47 3QP

Telephone: 01504 49279   *Fax: 01504 45366*

Every now and again there are hotels where you feel "comfortable" from the moment you cross the threshold and here is just such a place. Situated on the edge of the city in 32 acres of fine parkland with ponds, waterfalls and lovely trees, Beech Hill House has a well deserved name for friendliness, is a favourite venue for functions, and enjoys a reputation for its imaginative food. The public areas, including the lounge bar, are well proportioned rooms, some with ornate ceilings and furnished with easy chairs, and all encouraging a convivial, relaxed ambience. The cosy restaurant, overlooking the mature gardens and with its attractive display of china, conveys the same feeling of warmth, and people come from quite a distance to savour the classic cuisine. The bedrooms vary in size but all are individually furnished and smartly decorated. This small hotel is an ideal place to stay when visiting Londonderry, exploring the superb countryside in Donegal or the many treasures of Northern Ireland, or looking to play golf, fish or ride. Whatever your interest the staff at Beech Hill House are ever attentive and most knowledgeable with their advice. Single room £65; double £110; suite £130. **Bargain breaks**: weekends - 2 nights, b & b + dinner £90 per person; 3 nights £110 per person. **Belfast 70, Dublin 146.**

F licence. 17 en suite bedrooms with colour TV, direct-dial telephone, hairdryer, laundry/valet service, tea/coffee making facilities, trouser press; car rental; car parking; last dinner orders 9.45 pm; secretarial services; three meeting rooms - capacity up to 140; AV equipment available; closed 24-25 December; major credit cards accepted.

■ Historic Houses, Gardens & Parks

Annes Grove Gardens, Castletownroche
Ayesha Castle, Killiney, Co Dublin
Bantry House, Bantry, Co Cork
Birr Castle Demesne, Co Offaly
Blarney Castle & Blarney House, Blarney, Co Cork
Bunratty Castle & Folk Park, Bunratty, Co Clare
Carrigglass Manor, Longford, Co Longford
Castletown House, Cellbridge, Co Kildare
Cloghan Castle, Banagher, Co Clare
Colnalis House, Castlerea, Co Roscommon
Craggaunowen - The Living Past - Kilmurry, Co Clare
Cratlow Woods House, Cratloe, Co Down
Dunguaire Castle, Kinvara, Co Galway
Dunloe Castle Hotel Gardens, Beaufort, Killarney, Co Kerry
Emo Court, Portlaoise, Co Leix
Fernhill Garden, Sandyford, Co Dublin
Fota Wildlife Park, Fota Island, Carrigtwohill, Co Cork
Glin Castle, Glin, Co Limerick
GPA Bolton Library, Cashel, Co Tipperary
Japanese Garden, Tully, Co Kildare
Johnstown Castle Demesne, Wexford, Co Wexford
The James Joyce Tower, Sandycove, Co Dublin
The John F Kennedy Arboretum, New Ross, Co Wexford
Knappogue Castle, Quin, Co Clare
Kylemore Abbey, Kylemore, Connemara, Co Galway
Lismore Castle, Lismore, Co Waterford
Lissadell, Sligo
Lough Gur Visitor Centre, Lough Gur, Co Limerick
Lough Rynn Estate & Gardens, Mohill, Co Leitrim
Malahide Castle, Malahide, Co Dublin
Mount Congreve Gardens, Nr. Waterford
Mount Usher Gardens, Ashford, Co Wicklow
Muckross House & Gardens, Killarney, Co Kerry
National Botanic Gardens, Glasnevin, Dublin 9
Newbridge House, Donabate, Co Dublin
Phoenix Park, Dublin
Powerscourt Gardens & Waterfall, Enniskerry, Co Wicklow

Powerscourt Townhouse Centre, 59 South William St, Dublin 2
Riverstown House, Glanmire, Co Cork
Royal Hospital, Kilmainham, Co Dublin
Russborough, Blessington, Co Wicklow
Slane Castle, Slane, Co Meath
Strokestown Park House, Strokestown, Co Roscommon
Swiss Cottage, Chir, Co Tipperary
Thoor Ballylee, Gort, Co Galway
Timoleague Castle Gardens, Bandon, Co Cork
Tullynally Castle, Castlepollard, Co Westmeath

■ Historical Sites & Museums

Augustinian Priory (14thC), Kells, Co Kilkenny
Blarney Castle & Stone, Co Cork
Castle (State Apartments), Dublin
Christ Church Cathedral, Dublin
Cliffs of Moher & O'Brien's Tower, Lahinch, Co Clare
Glengarrif, 8m N of Bantry, Co Cork
Grianan of Eilach Fort, 18m NE of Letterkenny, Co Galway
Jerpoint Abbey ruins, 12m SE of Kilkenny, Co Kilkenny
Lough Corrib/Claregalway, Galway, Co Galway
Lough Gill/Lough Colgath, Sligo, Co Sligo
Lynch's Castle, Galway, Co Galway
Mellifont Abbey, Drogheda, Co Louth
Monasterboice, Drogheda, Co Louth
Monastic City/St Kervin's Church, Glendalough, Wicklow
Municipal Art Gallery/Hugh Lane Gallery, Dublin
Museum of Modern Art, Kilmainham, Dublin
National Gallery, Dublin
National Museum, Dublin
Ring of Kerry, Killarney, Co Kerry
St Ann's Shandon Church, Cork
St Canice's Cathedral, Kilkenny, Co Kilkenny
St Patrick's Rock (Rock of Cashel), Co Tipperary
Sheehans Pt, remains of Carhan House, Waterrville, Co Kerry
Timoleague Franciscan Abbey, Courtmacsherry, Co Cork
Trinity College Library, Dublin
Tulla Church, 10m E of Ennis, Co Clare
Writers' Museum, Dublin

Signpost Ireland inspectors Susie Wingfield (left) and Jackie Vivian (right), with Myrtle Allen, proprietor of Ballymaloe House, Shanagarry, Co. Cork.

January 20	IRISH RUGBY FOOTBALL UNION
	Ireland v Scotland, Landsdowne Road, Ballsbridge, Dublin 4
March 2	IRISH RUGBY FOOTBALL UNION
	Ireland v Wales, Lansdowne Road, Ballsbridge, Dublin
March 5-14	DUBLIN FILM FESTIVAL
	Various city cinemas in Dublin.
March 17	ST PATRICK'S DAY CELEBRATIONS
	Nationwide
March 26-31	BENSON & HEDGES IRISH MASTERS SNOOKER TOURNAMENT
	Kildare Paddocks, Kill, Co Kildare
May 2-5	CORK INTERNATIONAL CHORAL FESTIVAL
	City Hall, UCC, Triskel Arts Centre, Cork
May 15-17	SENIOR INTER-PROVINCIAL GOLF CHAMPIONSHIP
	Mount Juliet, Thomastown, Co Kilkenny
May 17-23	CO WICKLOW GARDENS FESTIVAL
	Throughout Co Wicklow, south Co Dublin, Co Carlow & N Co Wexford
May 24-26	A.I.M.S CHORAL FESTIVAL
	New Ross, Co Wexford
May 30-June 2	GARDEN FESTIVAL
	Royal Hospital, Kilmainham, Dublin
June 13-16	BLARNEY INTERNATIONAL 3-DAY HORSE TRIALS
	Blarney Castle Estate, Blarney, Co Cork
June 16*	BLOOMSDAY
	Variety of events in Dublin marking the day Ulysses was set in 1904
June 21-22	CURTIS GOLF CUP, Killarney, Co Kerry
June 21-23*	CASHEL HERITAGE FESTIVAL
	Cashel, Co Tipperary
July 4-7	MURPHYS IRISH OPEN GOLF CHAMPIONSHIP
	Portmarnock, Co Dublin
July 10-21	GALWAY ARTS FESTIVAL, Galway City, Galway
August 8*	DUBLIN HORSE SHOW
	Ros Showground, Ballsbridge, Dublin
August 17-25	KILKENNY ARTS WEEK
	St Canices Cathedral, Watergate & Cleeres Theatre, Kilkenny
August 23-29	ROSE OF TRALEE INTERNATIONAL FESTIVAL
	Tralee, Co Kerry
August 24-25	LIMERICK AGRICULTURAL SHOW
	Greenpark Racecourse S C Road, Limerick
September 14-21	CARRICK-ON-SHANNON ANGLING & TOURISM ASSOCN FESTIVAL
	River Shannon and Lakes in Carrick-on-Shannon, Co Leitrim
September 15	ALL IRELAND FOOTBALL FINAL. Croke Park, Dublin 3
September 19-21	CUPS & SHIELDS GOLF (NATIONAL FINALS)
	Tramore, Co Waterford
September 21- October 6	WATERFORD INTERNATIONAL FESTIVAL OF LIGHT OPERA Theatre Royal, Waterford
October 3-6	20TH INTERNATIONAL GOURMET FESTIVAL
	Kinsale, Co Cork
October 6-13*	CORK INTERNATIONAL FILM FESTIVAL
	Cork Opera House, Triskel Arts, Cork City
October 7-19	DUBLIN THEATRE FESTIVAL. Various theatres all over Dublin
October 17-Nov 3	WEXFORD FESTIVAL OPERA, Theatre Royal, Wexford
October 24-28	IDEAL HOMES EXHIBITION
	RDS, Simonscourt, Ballsbridge, Dublin
October 25-28	CORK JAZZ FESTIVAL AUTUMN HOLIDAY WEEKEND
	Kinsale, Co Cork
November 18-19	ROSSMORE DRAMA FESTIVAL
	Cloankilty, West Cork

*Provisional dates. *For further information, contact:*
Bord Fáilte (Irish Tourist Board), Baggot Street Bridge, Dublin 2. Telephone: 1 676 5871.

DROMOLAND CASTLE
Newmarket-on-Fergus, Co. Clare

Telephone: 061 368144   Fax: 061 363355

There are several reasons not to feel intimidated by Dromoland, which is after all one of the most famous baronial castles in Ireland, once the ancestral home of the O'Briens, set in 370 acres of parkland, and naturally imposing - yet it conveys the feel of the well run hotel. Attentive staff quickly dispel the formality, and the public rooms with open log fires, comfortable furniture, antiques and family portraits are warm and relaxing. The bedrooms are spacious and beautifully decorated with fine views over the lake or the grounds, and they offer every conceivable luxury. You dine in fine style in the dining room with its high ceilings, chandeliers and fine china. The quality classical cuisine offered through a whole variety of menus includes delicious Taste of Ireland fare. The hotel has every leisure facility including an 18 hole golf course, fishing and boating, delightful walled garden and 370 acres of parkland. Dromoland has excellent conference facilities and is well placed for excursions to local places of interest such as Bunratty Folk Park. Prices from £114 to £414. **Bargain breaks**: £195.00 pp sharing includes 2 nights with breakfast and dinner Nov. 1st. - March 31st.

Shannon Airport 8 miles, Ennis 8, Limerick 15, Dublin 136.

F licence. 73 en suite bedrooms with radio & satellite TV; direct-dial telephone; hairdryer, trouser press, laundry service, safety deposit box. Non-smoker bedrooms. Last orders for dinner at 21.30. Special diets available. Billiards/snooker; fitness centre, indoor games room, massage. Fishing, golf, riding, tennis, shooting - all by arrangement. Full business services and four conference rooms with total capacity for 400 delegates. Newsstand; hairdresser, beauty salon. Facilities for disabled. Car parking for 400 cars. Open all year. Credit cards accepted.

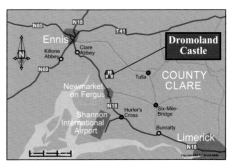

BALLYMALOE HOUSE
Shanagarry, Co. Cork
Telephone 021 652531   Fax 021 652021

There is no shortage of character in this wonderful example of a good family-run hotel for its 14th century keep belies its roots as a castle and the farmhouse role is still played out in the 400 acres of its own land. To stay here is to savour all the charm of Irish countryside living at its best, exemplified by the spacious public rooms graced by modern Irish paintings and in particular the large comfortable drawing room where you can relax for ever in front of that roaring open fire. The bedrooms are full of character and are cosy, traditionally furnished or more modern depending upon whether they are situated in the main "home" or in one of the nearby buildings. The Allen family is a legendary name in Irish cooking and the restaurant predictably serves as superb a cuisine as you will find anywhere in the country. Vegetables are home-grown on the farm and meat and fish fresh from the local fishing village, Ballycotton. Nor should you miss the most genuine Irish breakfast I have ever sampled. There is beautiful country to explore nearby: sandy coves, hills to climb and two excellent golf courses - but Ballymaloe House is the jewel in the crown of this lovely region with the warmth and wel-come of a home creating a carefree, smiling ho-tel. Single room inc. breakfast from £65; double room from £50.

Bargain breaks: November to March, 2 nights dinner, b & b from £150 per person.

Cork 25, Waterford 64, Dublin 163 .

F licence. 30 en suite bedrooms, direct-dial tel-ephone, hairdryer, laundry/valet service, trouser press; car parking; last dinner orders 9.30 pm; secretarial services; meeting rooms - capacity up to 15; AV equipment available; closed 24-26 Decem-ber; major credit cards accepted.

INNISHANNON HOUSE HOTEL
Inishannon, Co. Cork

Telephone: 021 775121   Fax: 021 775609

Back in 1720 when a wealthy farmer had his home built half a mile from the village of Inishannon, he could hardly have imagined that over two and a half centuries later it would be a delightful country house hotel offering hospitality to the world. Innishannon House Hotel is only 30 minutes from Cork airport but the setting is as romantic as you could wish, with gardens running down to the River Bandon where salmon and trout fishing as well as boating are available free to guests. All the bedrooms overlook this rural idyll and they in turn are full of personality being individually decorated and furnished with antiques. They vary in size, from smaller attic rooms to spacious ones on the first floor and the vast suite with its period bathroom. My walk round the public rooms was also an experience. A pleasant sunny drawing-room with a corner bar gives on to a separate 'snug' and the whole is decorated with verve using idiosyncratic modern paintings juxtaposed with traditional Irish landscapes. As to dining, suffice to say that the restaurant has won several awards and, to judge from my meal, there should be more on the way! The Innishannon is a hotel to be savoured for its character and the quality of its hospitality. Single room including breakfast from £65; double room with breakfast from £95.

Leisure Breaks: Any two nights b&b plus 1 table d'hôte dinner from £75 pp sharing; Jan-Mar, November and sometimes April, May, Oct. Dec. **Cork 14, Killarney 46, Bandon 4¹/₂, Dublin 175.** *Full licence. 14 en suite bedrooms with radio and colour TV; direct-dial telephone, hairdryer, laundry service; non-smoker rooms; facilities for disabled. Last dinner orders 21.30. Fishing, golf, boating, riding, shooting, squash and tennis all nearby. One meeting room with 150 capacity; AV equipment & secretarial services. Safe deposit box. Car parking 100 cars. Open all year. All major credit cards accepted.*

SHANDON HOTEL
Marble Hill Strand, Sheephaven Bay, Via Letterkenny, Co. Donegal

Telephone: 074 36137   Fax: 074 36430

Whilst exploring the spectacular north-west coast of Donegal, I came upon Sheephaven Bay with its dramatic scenery where wildlife and flora thrive. Marble Hill Strand is a sheltered beach which holds the coveted Blue Flag, is warmed by the Gulf Stream and is an ideal place "to build sand castles", windsurf or sail a small boat. Perched up above it is the family run Shandon Hotel where Dermot and Catherine McGlade will welcome you warmly and do everything to make your stay comfortable. Most of the rooms have glorious views over the Bay. Facilities for youngsters include the excellent 'children's activity centre', and, should it rain, you can enjoy the extensive leisure centre with its excellent indoor heated pool. This hotel also welcomes the elderly, has built a special access ramp for the disabled and lifts to the upper floors. The menu was inviting and I looked into McGlades relaxing bar lounge and coffee shop before leaving this friendly place with some reluctance - albeit to continue exploring the lovely area - with the memory of a sea holly hedge entwined with a red rose. Single room including breakfast from £42. Double room rate for two people sharing £70. **Leisure Breaks**: Special Sunday-Friday rates from IR£245.00 pp. Over 60's 10% reduction in May, June & September. Weekend from IR£90.00 (2 b&b+1 dinner) pp. Weekly from IR£329.00 (7 b&b+7 dinners) pp. **Dublin 180, Galway 190, Belfast 120, Londonderry 43, Letterkenny 21.**

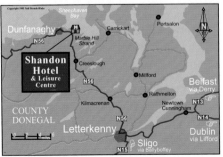

Full licence. 55 en suite bedrooms with radio, colour TV, video, direct-dial telephone; hairdryer, laundry service; non-smoker bedrooms, facilities for the disabled. Last orders for dinner 21.00. Special diets available. Indoor games room; sauna, whirlpool. Fishing, golf, tennis, watersports, riding, walking all available nearby by arrangement. Safety deposit box by reception. Airport pick-up by arrangement. Car parking for 80 cars. Open April to October. Major credit cards accepted. &

SAND HOUSE HOTEL
Rossnowlagh, Donegal Bay, Co. Donegal

Telephone: 072 51777   Fax: 072 52100

The Sand House is one of Ireland's treasures. Built as a hunting lodge, it has been converted into a hotel of high standards. It is both comfortable to the point of de luxe and also boasts a superb cuisine - which is able to serve wonderful fresh local produce - and what greater joy is there than to eat fish so fresh that it literally melts in the mouth, and oysters direct from the nearby beds! This hotel soon had me enveloped in its charm and not least because of that one remarkable feature, the Conservatory on the first floor that made me feel as if I was "floating on an island of sea". I loved the rooms too and their décor with some individually furnished with antiques and many had splendid views. The Sand House is in a magnificent position right on the edge of Donegal Bay, overlooking the Atlantic and standing beside miles of superb sandy beach renowned for its surfing. Paul Diver is a friendly, helpful manager who places above all else the services to his guests, and this caring touch practised by the staff ensures that every need is met. Only ten minutes from Donegal town and well placed for golf and riding, this happy hotel is a haven to return to - to be welcomed by fresh flowers, smiling faces and good food. Single room with break-fast from £45.00. Double room incl. breakfast from £90.00.

Ballyshannon 4, Donegal 9, Sligo 33, Dublin 157. *Full licence. 50 en suite bedrooms with direct-dial telephone; hairdryer, safety deposit box; non-smoker bedrooms. Last orders for dinner 20.45 hrs. Special diets available. Indoor games room, Billiards/ snooker, croquet. Watersports, tennis, fishing, golf, riding 6-8 miles. Business services include three meeting rooms to total capacity of 80. AV equipment on request. Car parking. Open Easter to end October. Access, Amex accepted.*

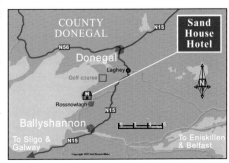

MERRION HALL
54/56 Merrion Road Ballsbridge Dublin 4

Telephone: 01 668 1426/1825   *Fax: 01 668 4280*

When awards are given there is always a lurking danger of complacency setting in - but in so far as Merrion Hall, the 1994 Guest House of the Year, is concerned, the reverse applies. This impeccably maintained family-run guest-house is situated south of the city centre on the main ferry road, and specialises in providing an exceptionally warm and welcoming ambiance where nothing is too much trouble for the proprietress Mrs. Sheeran. Here too you have all the facilities of a superbly run hotel: the place is spotless, the en suite bedrooms attractive

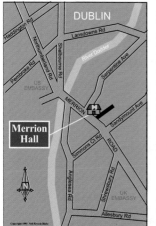

and well equipped, and the dining room overlooking a pretty garden is bright and airy. Yet my favourite room was the larger of the two sitting rooms which is naturally homely and nicely furnished with the family harp providing an original centrepiece. At Merrion Hall you start your day fully refreshed for it has won awards for its breakfasts too. The menu is a full page of fresh and home-made fare and, to do full justice to it and to this charming guest house, you will need to stay for quite a few days - and that in turn would be a very happy experience. Single room including breakfast from £40.00; double room with breakfast from £60.00.

Leisure Breaks: Winter weekends - 2 nights from £50.00 pp with breakfast.

14 en suite bedrooms with satellite TV; direct-dial telephone, hairdryer, laundry service; tea/coffee making facilities. Breakfast only, but several good restaurants nearby. Airport pick-up. Car parking 12 cars. Closed 17/12 - 2/1. Credit cards accepted.

THE SHELBOURNE HOTEL
27 St. Stephens Green, Dublin 2.

Telephone 01 676 6471   Fax 01 661 6006

The Shelbourne has probably the most distinguished address in Ireland, for it is part of the country's history synonymous with Dublin, and is located in the heart of the city with superb views of St. Stephens Green - Europe's largest garden square. The Irish Constitution was drafted here and both Thackery and James Joyce wrote of its grandeur as still expressed in its marbled hall and spacious lounge where people gather to gossip over tea or coffee. Hence its other reputation as a fashionable place to meet and measure the business of the world, in the famous Horseshoe Bar or the Shelbourne. For this elegant Georgian hotel has been at the centre of Dublin life since 1824. Another tradition which remains is its standing as a superbly comfortable hotel with a welcoming demeanour. The bedrooms are generally large and stylish in their décor with the suites having lovely more traditional furniture, and all rooms being well appointed. Following refurbishment, the Shelbourne is an even finer hotel than it was, yet it has lost nothing of the charm and personality which has given it such a distinctive place in history. I would stay there as much for those characteristics as for the sheer enjoyment of experiencing the qualities of a first class hotel. Single room including breakfast from IR£164. Double room with breakfast from IR£200. *Full licence. 164 en suite bedrooms with radio, colour TV & direct-dial telephone; Hairdryer, laundry service, mini-bar; non-smoker bedrooms; 24-hour room service. Safety deposit box, trouser press available. Last orders for dinner 22.30 hrs. Special diets available. Facilities for disabled. Massage. Golf - 8 miles. Full business services including 11 meeting rooms to total capacity 500; AV equipment available. Barber shop; beauty salon; news stand. Car parking for 44 cars. Open all year. Major credit cards accepted.*

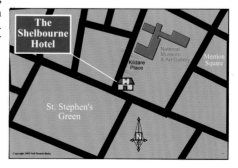

ARDAGH HOTEL AND RESTAURANT
Ballyconneely Road, Clifden, Co. Galway

Telephone 095 21384   Fax 095 21314

Stephane and Monique Bauvet add gallic flair to this simple family run hotel which is situated beside the road, close to lovely, sandy beaches and the excellent Connemara Golf Club. It is a quiet place and unpretentious but with two features of remarkable quality in its restaurant and the bedrooms. The first floor dining room enjoys beautiful views over Ardbear Bay and Monique creates the most delicious fare from local produce with lobster and seafood generally being a speciality, complemented by locally grown vegetables. The wine list is good as well. In addition there's a comfortable bar downstairs where pub lunches are served and the home-made soup is lovely. The Ardagh has two pleasant lounge areas for relaxation but it was the family rooms which impressed me as being amongst the best I have ever seen. Twin beds for the children are set aside in an alcove slightly separated from the rest of the room. There is plenty of space for them to play too - and colour TV and sea views. The rooms reflect the whole ambience of the Ardagh as being clean, comfortable and friendly. It is a charming hotel for a leisurely holiday. Double room for 2 persons from £75.00.

Oughterard 32, Galway 49,Ballyconeely 5, Westport 43 , Dublin 168 .

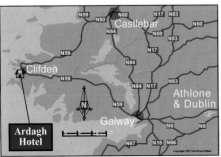

Licence. 21 en suite bedrooms with TV. Billiards/ snooker. Squash one mile. Watersports three miles. Riding five miles. Golf (10 miles) by arrangement with hotel. Open end march - November. All major credit cards accepted.

THE KILLARNEY PARK HOTEL
Kenmare Place, Killarney, Co. Kerry

Telephone: 064 35555   Fax: 064 35266

Four years ago The Killarney Park was high on the awards list of Best Hotel Newcomer and I enjoyed my visit there because it is quite simply still a lovely place. Initially it is made so by its public rooms, for there is lots of comfortable seating in the large airy reception lounge, and a consistently attractive décor in the bar, the library and an area set aside for television. If you are made to feel welcome here, the bedrooms are just as inviting, for although they tend to vary in shape, size and colour, all are very spacious, well appointed distinguished by marble bathrooms and ideal for families. There is a good contrast of food which is excellent in the bar, with more sophisticated international fare being offered from the main restaurant. To comlete the picture of the hotel, it has modern conference facilities and a leisure centre with an indoor pool. The Killarney Park is busy and popular as you would expect of an hotel of this standard in a town centre location - yet it is set back from the main street and situated in attractive gardens, giving it a relaxed, unhustled atmosphere. Single room with breakfast from IR£80.00. Double room with breakfast from IR£ 110.00. **Tralee 15 , Cork 50 , Limerick 69, Kenmare 24, Shannon 80, Dublin 189.**

Full licence. 66 en suite bedrooms with satellite TV, direct-dial telephone, laundry service, non-smoker bedrooms, tea/coffee making facilities, trouser press, safety deposit box; 24-hour room service; last orders for dinner 21.15 hrs. Special diets available. Indoor pool, massage on request; steam room. Fishing, golf, riding, shooting, squash, tennis - all by arrangement nearby. Watersports - 20 miles. Full business services with 2 conference rooms and AV equipment. News stand. Airport pick-up. Facilities for disabled. Car rental. Car parking for 80 cars. Open all year. Credit cards accepted. ♿

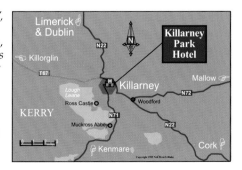

PARKNASILLA GREAT SOUTHERN HOTEL
Sneem, Co. Kerry
Telephone 353 64 45122   Fax 353 64 45323

When I last stayed in this remote hotel it was a good experience so I was pleased to find it even more inviting under new owners. It is the view that makes it really special. The luxurious Victorian Great Southern Hotel overlooks Kenmare Bay and stands in 300 acres of sub-tropical gardens. The setting is majestic and it blends easily with its parkland surroundings which offer a nine-hole golf course, horse-riding, and much else. The interior is impressive: - lots of public rooms and an especially fine upper conservatory corridor in glass with comfortable seats and splendid views over the bay. The stylish Pygmalion Restaurant, which George Bernard Shaw patronised, enjoys the same outlook whilst the library, the billiard room and the Doolittle bar are a quiet contrast to the bustling main lounge. The roomy bedrooms have sparkling bathrooms and all modern facilities. The hotel is celebrating its centenary and the doorman has been there for 43 of those years, so he can tell you of the spectacular mountains, and the villages of West Cork, the Ring of Kerry and the Killarney National Park. The Parknasilla is the perfect base to explore the beauties of south-west Ireland. Single room with breakfast from IR£90.50; Double room from IR£73.50 per person. **Bargain breaks**: 2 nights, 1 dinner low season IR£103; high - IR£135 per person. **Kenmare 16, Cork 80, Limerick 100, Dublin 216.**

Full licence. 83 en suite bedrooms with satellite TV, direct-dial telephone, hairdryer, trouser press, laundry service; non-smoker bedrooms. 24-hour room service. Last orders for dinner 20.45 hrs. Special diets available. Billiard/snooker; indoor games room; jacuzzi, sauna; indoor swimming pool; jogging track; watersports, riding, fishing, shooting, tennis, 9-hole golf course. Full business services and 2 conference rooms with capacity for 50 guests;. AV equipment. Airport pick-up. Car parking for 75 cars. Closed Jan/Feb; Major credit cards accepted.

BUTLER ARMS HOTEL
Waterville, Co. Kerry

Telephone 66 74144   Fax 66 74520

The Butler Arms, facing the Gulf Stream, is one of the best known hotels in the West of Ireland and has been owned by the Huggard family for over three generations. The hotel offers an intimate homely atmosphere with two comfortably furnished lounges, a sun lounge and cocktail bar, as well as the olde worlde Fisherman's Bar. The restaurant specialises in locally caught seafood and also has an excellent wine list. Waterville's Lough Currane has a world-wide reputation for its free salmon and sea trout fishing. In addition the hotel's four privately owned lakes offer additional seatrout fishing. Ghillies and boats, deep sea fishing and tackle hire can be arranged. The botanist, the photographer, the bird watcher and the rambler will find a wealth of surprises and sub aqua diving, cycling and horse riding are available near at hand. Waterville is an ideal centre for touring the south west region with scenery that is difficult to equal. The archeological remains of Staigue Fort, Church Island on Lough Currane and the 8-mile offshore Skelligs monastic settlement are nearby. Kerry is also a mecca for golfers with Ballybunion, Tralee, Killarney and Waterville's own championship 18-hole links close at hand. Single room and breakfast from IR£60; double from IR£80.

Killarney 48, Dublin 238.

Full licence. 30 en suite bedrooms with colour TV, direct-dial telephone, hairdryer, laundry service; Last orders for dinner 21.00 hrs. Special diets available. Billiards/snooker; tennis, riding one mile, golf one mile, fishing, game shooting, watersports six miles, Visa, Mastercard, Amex cards accepted. Hotel open mid-April to mid-October.

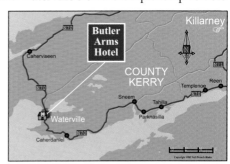

THE KILDARE HOTEL & COUNTRY CLUB
Straffan, Co. Kildare

Telephone: (353-1) 627 3333   Fax: (353-1) 627 3312

Opulent is the word often used to describe The Kildare Hotel & Country Club and it lives up to its reputation as a superlative country house hotel. The elegant 19th Century manor house is set in 330 acres of landscaped countryside, with a mile of the river Liffey offering trout and salmon fishing to guests. The public areas are stylish with hand-painted drawing room and cocktail bar, period antiques and sumptuous furnishings set among the marble fireplaces and a marvellous fine art collection. The spacious bedrooms are luxurious, individually designed and richly furnished offering every indulgence - and with palatial bathrooms. "The K Club" also has self-contained courtyard suites and a fine three bedroom lodge in the grounds. The Byerley Turk restaurant delivers a superb standard of table d'hôte and à la carte cuisine; and finally the sporting facilities, including the Arnold Palmer designed golf course (home to the Smurfit European Open), are totally comprehensive."The K Club" is one of the most complete places I have visited and it is an experience in itself to stay there. Single room including breakfast from £203.50. Double room with breakfast from £273. **Leisure Breaks**: Nov 1st - March 31st 1996. *Package A*: 2 nights' acommodation, 2 full breakfasts, 1 dinner and a

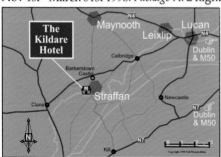

choice of one leisure activity - at £250 pp sharing. *Package B*: 3 nights, 3 breakfasts, 2 dinners plus 2 choices of leisure activity at £369 pp sharing, subject to availability. **Naas 7, Dublin City Centre 17.**

Full licence. 45 en suite bedrooms with radio, satellite TV, direct-dial telephone; hairdryer, laundry service; minibar, 24 hour room service. Facilities for disabled. Last dinner orders 21.45 hrs. Full business services provided including 3 conference rooms for 10-120 guests. AV equipment. Hairdresser; beauty salon; safety deposit box. Car rental. Transfers arranged. Open all year. Credit cards accepted.

ASHFORD CASTLE
Cong, Co Mayo
Telephone: 092 46003   Fax: 092 46260

This splendid place is situated in acres of gardens and parkland on the shores of Lough Corrib, and to come here is to visit a stately home with the suits of armour, fine furnishings, and beautiful paintings set amidst rooms decorated by rich panelling and graced by chandeliers. Here too you relax in the conservatory or the Dungeon Bar, where you will be entertained in the evening by harpist, pianist or folk singer. There are two elegant restaurants in character with the hotel - the main George V Room and the intimate à la carte Connaught Room. The food is superb as you would expect, with ample use of the local produce of fish and lamb. The bedrooms, including several suites, and the bathrooms are both very large - they have been refurbished to a de luxe standard having all luxuries and facilities - plus lovely views over the lake. Ashford Castle offers countless leisure activities including its 9 hole golf course and there is a fully equipped gym. Nothing has been overlooked in the efforts to please the guests - it is the sort of place which exists in dreams but it is a reality and to stay there is a very pleasurable experience. Single room with breakfast from IR£130; double room including breakfast from IR£145. **Bargain breaks**: £195 pp sharing - 2 nights dinner/bed/ breakfast from 1/1 - 22/12/95 & 2/1 - 31/3/96. **Headford 10 , Galway 28 , Ballina 49, Dublin 160.** *Full licence. 83 en suite bedrooms with satellite TV, direct-dial telephone, hairdryer, trouser press, laundry service, 24-hour room service; safety deposit box. Special diets available. Billiards/snooker; fitness centre, jacuzzi, jogging track, massage, sauna. Golf, fishing , riding, clay shooting, tennis, cruising, archery all by arrangement. Full business service; conference room with 110 capacity. AV equipment available. Open all year. All major credit cards accepted.*

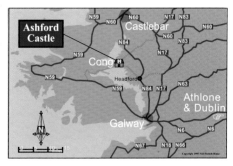

RICHMOND HOUSE
Cappoquin, Co. Waterford

Telephone: 058 54278   Fax: 058 54988

This elegant 18th Century Georgian house stands in timbered parkland in the undiscovered Blackwater valley close to the picturesque town of Cappoquin. Managed personally by Jean Deevy, Richmond House has all the old world charm and character of the family home which it is, yet with the facilities to be found in any good hotel, ensuring a high quality of comfort throughout. The public rooms are as cosy and warm as the attention given to guests, with the main drawing-room leading to a conservatory overlooking the garden where you can have a quiet drink before dinner. Pride of place should be given to the spacious restaurant with one of its three rooms set aside as 'honeymooners' corner.' The son of the house, Swiss-trained Paul and his wife, Claire, preside over a menu which is not only popular locally - using as it does fresh local produce such as the famous Blackwater salmon - but also enjoys international recognition being featured in many guide books. The beauties of Co. Waterford are on the doorstep of Richmond House and can be enjoyed peacefully or more actively since it is an ideal centre for fishing, golfing, horse-riding and mountain walking. Single room including breakfast from £30.00 Double room with breakfast from £50.00.

Cork 31, Rosslare 90 , Waterford 40 , Dublin 136.

10 en suite bedrooms with colour TV; direct-dial telephone; hairdryer, trouser press, tea/coffee making facilities. Last orders for dinner 21.00 hrs. Special diets available. Fishing, golf, riding, tennis nearby. Car parking for 15 cars. Open 1st February - 23rd December. Visa/Access accepted.

Ten exclusive Westcountry Hotels.
Just a phone call away.

Brend Hotels

The Great Little Hotels Of Britain

For your Holidays, Short Breaks or Business Travel

A full colour brochure of OVER 200 proprietor-run hotels throughout Great Britain is available from:

MINOTELS GREAT BRITAIN LTD

37, Springfield Road, Blackpool FY1 1PZ

Tel: (01253) 292000   Fax: (01253) 291111

SPORTING AND CONFERENCE FACILITIES

Sporting and conference facilities to be found at *Signpost* hotels are tabulated on the following pages. This section is arranged by regions within England, Wales, Scotland, the Channel Islands and Ireland and by counties or regions within each country.

KEY

●   Facilities available at hotel

○   Facilities available within five miles of the hotel

✪   Special arrangements can be made by the hotel

Page	Other	Watersports	Tennis	Swimming pool	Squash/badminton	Shooting	Sea/river bathing	Sauna/solarium	Sailing/boating	Riding	Massage	Jogging track	Jacuzzi/whirlpool	Indoor games	Golf	Gym/fitness centre	Fishing	Croquet	Conferences	Billiards/snooker
ENGLAND																				
CORNWALL																				
4 Treglos Hotel, Constantine Bay	Surfing		✪	●			●		●	○			●		✪		●		●	●
5 Falmouth Beach Resort		✪	✪	●	●	○	●	●		✪	●	●	●	●	○	●	✪		●	●
6 Royal Duchy Hotel, Falmouth				●		○	●	●	○	○					✪		○			●
7 Cormorant Hotel, Golant				●																
8 Marina Hotel, Fowey			○			○	●		●	○					○		○			
9 Polurrian Hotel, Lizard Peninsula			●	●	●	○	●	●	○				●	●	○	●	○		●	●
10 The Headland Hotel, Newquay		✪	✪	●	○	○				○				●	✪		✪	●	●	●
11 Carlyon Bay Hotel, St Austell		●		●		○	●	●	○	○			●		●		○		●	●
12 Boskerris Hotel, St Ives	Putting green		○	●			○		○						○					
13 The Garrack Hotel, St Ives		○	○	○	○	○		●		○			●		○	●	○		●	
14 Tregenna Castle, St Ives			●	●	●			●							●			●	●	●
15 Idle Rocks Hotel. St Mawes							●		●						○		●			
DEVON																				
17 Blagdon Manor Country House, Ashwater	**Golf practice ground**					✪				○					○		○	●	●	●
18 Downrew House, Nr. Barnstaple			●	●	○			●		○				●	●	○	○	●		●
19 The Edgemoor Hotel, Bovey Tracey			○			○				○					○				●	
20 The Berry Head Hotel, Brixham	Boules		○	○	○	○	●		○	○					○		○		●	
21 Kittiwell House Hotel, Croyde	Cycling		○			✪				○					○		○			
22 Langstone Cliff Hotel, Dawlish			●								●			●	○				●	●
23 Combe House Hotel, Nr. Honiton			○												✪		●	●	●	
24 The Cottage Hotel, Hope Cove							●		●					●	○				●	
25 Ilsington Country Hotel, Dartmoor	Bowls	○		●		○		●		○			●	●	○	●	○	●		
26 Buckland-tout-Saints Hotel, Kingsbridge	Putting green														○			●	●	
27 Maypool Park Hotel, Nr. Kingswearmouth							○		○	○					○		○		●	
28 Manor House Hotel, Moretonhampstead	Ballooning						●			○					●		●	●	●	●
29 Bolt Head Hotel, Salcombe	Private moorings		○	●					●								●			
30 Tides Reach Hotel, Salcombe		●	○	●	●		●	●	●	○	●				○	●	●			●
31 Heron House Hotel, Thurlestone Sands			○	●			●	●	○	○					✪	○	○		●	
32 Saunton Sands Hotel, Saunton Sands			●	●	●	●	●	●	●	●					○		●		●	●

	Surfing	Putting	Surfing	Short mat bowls, yacht		Putting green			Windsurfing		Indoor bowls							Bike hire, beautician	
	✪			✪		○					○				○					
33 Royal Glen Hotel, Sidmouth	○	●	●	○		○	●		●	●	○	●			✪	○	●	●	○	○
34 Victoria Hotel, Sidmouth	●	●	●	●	●	●		●	●	○	●		●	●		●	●			●
35 Gabriel Court Hotel, Stoke Gabriel	○		●			●					●	●			✪	○	○	○	●	○
36 Watersmeet Hotel, Woolacombe		○	○			✪			○							○			○	
37 Woolacombe Bay Hotel, Woolacombe	●	●	●	●	●		●	○		●	○	●			●				●	
39 Balcombe House, Exmouth	●		●		●	●		●	●		●	●		●		●		●	●	●
41 Torbay Holiday Motel, Paignton	●	○	●			○		○		○	○	●			○				✪	
42 Anchor Inn, Seaton	○	○	○	○	✪	✪		○	○	○	○	●	○	○	✪	✪	○	○	○	○
DORSET										○		●								
44 Queen's Hotel, Bournemouth											●									
45 Manor Hotel, Dorchester	●			●				●			●				●		●		●	
46 Devon Hotel, Lyme Regis		●		●					●		●									
47 The Haven Hotel, Sandbanks	○	○	○	●	✪	✪		○	○	○	○	○	●	○	○	●	✪	○	○	○	○
48 The Eastbury, Sherborne		●		●		●		●		●	●	●			○		●	●		●	●
49 Manor House Hotel, Studland Bay	✪	●	○	○	✪	✪		○	●	○		○	○		✪		○	○		●	○
50 Knoll House Hotel, Studland Bay		●						○					●			●	●	●			
52 Plumber Manor, Sturminster Newton	●		●			●	●	●	●	●		●		●	●	●		●	●	●
53 Springfield Country House, Wareham	●		●					●			●	●			●		●			
54 Moonfleet Manor Hotel, Nr. Weymouth																				

Facility	83	84	85	86	87	88	89	90	93	95	96	97	98	99	102	104	110
Other						Hot air ballooning										Putting green	
Watersports	○	○									✪	✪					
Tennis	●	○	●	○	●	●	○	○	✪		✪	✪	○	●	✪		●
Swimming pool	●		●	●	●	●			●				○	●	●	●	○
Squash/badminton		○		○	○						✪	✪	○	●			
Shooting				○	○	✪				○	○	✪		○	✪		✪
Sea/river bathing			○	○	○												
Sauna/solarium			●		●	●			●					●	●	●	
Sailing/boating			○	○	○												
Riding	○	○	○	○	○	●				○	✪	○	○	○	✪		
Massage									●					●	●		
Jogging track	●										●			●			
Jacuzzi/whirlpool						●			●		●			●	●	●	
Indoor games			●												○		
Golf	○	○	○	○	●	●			○	○	✪	○	○	●	○	●	○
Gym/fitness centre			●		●	●							○	●	●	●	
Fishing		○		○	○				○					○	✪		✪
Croquet	●		●							●		●		●	●		
Conferences	●					●	●	●	●				●	●	●	●	●
Billiards/snooker	●					●								●	●		

BUCKINGHAMSHIRE
83 Danesfield House, Marlow

HAMPSHIRE
84 Cockle Warren Cottage, Hayling Island
85 Passford House Hotel, Nr. Lymington
86 South Lawn Hotel, Milford-on-Sea
87 Chewton Glen Hotel, New Milton

HERTFORDSHIRE
88 Stocks Hotel, Golf & Country Club
89 Redcoats Farmhouse Hotel, Nr. Hitchin
90 St Michaels Manor, St Albans

KENT
93 Rowhill Grange Country House Hotel, Hextable

OXFORDSHIRE
95 The Bay Tree Hotel, Burford
96 The Plough at Clanfield
97 Studley Priory, Horton-cum-Studley

SURREY
98 Chase Lodge, Kingston-upon-Thames
99 Selsdon Park Hotel, Sanderstead

EAST SUSSEX
102 Flackley Ash Hotel, Peasmarsh
104 Dale Hill Hotel, Golf & Country Club

DERBYSHIRE
110 Riber Hall, Matlock

	Falconry	Boules, water-ski-ing						Ballooning/aerial trips	Rock-climbing/abseiling				Ballooning		Helipad	Pitch & putt
111 The Peacock Hotel, Rowsley									○		✪ ✪		○			
LEICESTERSHIRE																
112 Stapleford Park, Nr. Melton Mowbray	○	○	○	●				○		○ ○ ● ✪ ○			✪	●		●
LINCOLNSHIRE																
113 Washingborough Hall Country House Hotel		●	● ●			●						●		●		●
NORFOLK																
114 The Blakeney Hotel, Nr. Holt		○							○	● ○ ○						
115 South Walsham Hall, Nr Norwich	●		○		○	✪	✪					○	○	✪		✪
NOTTINGHAMSHIRE																
116 Langar Hall, Langar		○														
117 The Old England. Nr. Newark		●			●			●			●		●			
SUFFOLK																
118 Chippenhall Hall. Nr Eye		○ ○														
GLOUCESTERSHIRE																
123 Bibury Court, Bibury	●	○	●		✪	✪ ○ ✪		○ ○	✪ ✪ ○ ✪ ○		✪	○		✪		
124 Hotel on the Park, Cheltenham	●								○							
125 Tudor Farmhouse Hotel, Clearwell	●		●		●			● ●	●							
126 Manor House Hotel, Moreton-in-Marsh		●														
127 Orchard House, Nr. Newent		○	○	○ ○	✪			○ ○	✪ ✪ ○ ✪ ○		○	●				
128 Stonehouse Court Hotel, Stonehouse		○	●						●							
129 The Grapevine, Stow-om-the-Wold	●	○	●	○	● ○			●	○ ✪ ✪ ✪		○	○				✪
130 Hare & Hounds, Westonbirt	●			●		○			●		●		●		● ●	
131 The Snooty Fox, Tetbury		●	● ●	● ●	●		●	● ● ●	●		●		●		● ●	
132 Hatton Court Hotel, Upton St Leonards					●			●			●		●			
HEREFORD & WORCESTER																
135 The Swan at Hay Hotel, Hay-on-Wye																
SHROPSHIRE																
137 Hawkestone Park, Weston-under-Redcastle																
WARWICKSHIRE																
138 Nuthurst Grange, Hockley Heath																
139 Billesley Manor, Nr. Stratford-upon-Avon																

Hotel key (Page No / column number):

CHESHIRE
- 144 Broxton Hall Country House Hotel
- 145 Rowton Hall Hotel, Chester
- 146 Sutton Hall Hotel, Nr. Macclesfield

CUMBRIA
- 148 Kirkstone Foot Country House Hotel
- 149 Rothay Manor Hotel, Ambleside
- 150 Wateredge Hotel, Ambleside
- 151 Appleby Manor Country House Hotel
- 152 The Pheasant Inn, Bassenthwaite Lake
- 153 Graythwaite Manor Hotel, Grange-o-Sands
- 154 Netherwood Hotel, Grange-over-Sands
- 155 Aynsome Manor Hotel, Grange-over-Sands
- 156 The Wordsworth Hotel, Grasmere
- 157 Dale Head Hall Lakeside Hotel, Keswick
- 158 Lyzzick Hall Hotel, Nr. Keswick
- 159 Stakis Keswick Lodore Swiss Hotel, Keswick
- 160 Underscar Manor, Nr. Keswick
- 161 Scafell Hotel, Nr. Keswick
- 162 The Mill, Mungrisdale, Penrith
- 163 The Swan Hotel, Newby Bridge
- 164 Sharrow Bay Contry House Hotel, Ullswater
- 165 Cedar Manor Hotel, Windermere
- 166 Fayrer Garden House Hotel, Windermere
- 167 Linthwaite House Hotel, Windermere
- 168 The Mortal Man Hotel, Windermere
- 169 Old Vicarage Country House Hotel, Witherslack

LANCASHIRE
- 170 The Georgian House Hotel, Bolton
- 171 Chadwick Hotel, Lytham St Annes

(Hotels not listed have not informed us of sporting/conference facilities)

Legend: ● = yes, ○ = available, ✪ = special (Marina / Hot air ballooning / Golf practice hole, par 3)

Facility	144	145	146	148	149	150	151	152	153	154	155	156	157	158	159	160	161	162	163	164	165	166	167	168	169	170	171
Other																		Marina	Marina			Hot air ball.	Golf prac. hole				
Watersports																				○							
Tennis	●	○		○	○			●	○	○		●		●		✪			○				●				○
Swimming pool	○	●						●	○	●	●	●		●	●						○	○				●	●
Squash/badminton	○				○		○			○	○	○		●			●				○		○	○			○
Shooting	○								○			●	○				●			✪	✪		○				
Sea/river bathing					●				●						○		●	●			○						
Sauna/solarium	●							●			●		●		●						○	○				●	●
Sailing/boating					○	○	●		●	○		●	○	○			○		●	●	○	○		○			○
Riding	○	○	○		○		○	○	○	○	○	○		○	○	○	●	●	○	○	○	○	○	○	○		○
Massage																											
Jogging track																											
Jacuzzi/whirlpool						●					●																●
Indoor games						●											●										●
Golf	○		○		○			○	○	○		✪	○	○	○	○	○	✪	○		○	✪	○	○	○		○
Gym/fitness centre	●				○	○	●		●		●	○		●							○	○		○		●	●
Fishing	○	○		○	○	●	○	○		○		●	○	✪	○	○	○	●	●	○	✪	●	●	○			●
Croquet	●																										
Conferences	●	●	●	●	●	●		●	●		●	●		●	●				●	●	●	●	●			●	●
Billiards/snooker						●			●								●										●

Column headings (left to right, most unlabelled):

- Pitch & putt, birdwatching
- Gliding, grass ski-ing
- Windsurfing, pitch & putt, birdwatching

GREATER MANCHESTER
172 Victoria & Albert Hotel, Manchester

CO DURHAM
177 Royal County Hotel, Durham

NORTHUMBERLAND
178 Waren House Hotel, Bamburgh
179 Kings Arms Hotel, Berwick-on-Tweed
180 Warkworth House Hotel, Warkworth

YORKSHIRE
180 Appleton Hall Hotel, Appleton-le-Moors
181 George & Dragon Hotel, Kirkbymoorside
181 Aldwark Manor Golf Hotel, Nr. York
182 Milburn Arms Hotel, Pickering
182 Park Hall Hotel, Nr. Sheffield
183 Devonshire Arms Hotel, Bolton Abbey
184 Balmoral Hotel, Harrogate
185 Kimberley Hotel, Harrogate
186 Feversham Arms Hotel, Helmsley
187 The Pheasant, Nr. Helmsley
188 Ryedale Lodge, Nr Helmsley
189 Lastingham Grange Hotel, Kirkbymoorside
190 King's Arms Hotel, Nr. Leyburn
192 East Ayton Lodge Hotel, Nr. Scarborough
193 Wrea Head Country Hotel, Nr. Scarborough
194 Judges Lodging Hotel, York

WALES

GWENT
197 Llanwenarth House, Abergavenny
198 Glen-Yr-Afon House, Usk

GWYNEDD
199 Trefeddian Hotel, Aberdovey

Page No.	200 Borthwnog Hall, Nr. Dolgellau	201 Bontddu Hall Hotel, Nr. Dolgellau	**DYFED** 202 Warpool Court Hotel, St David's	**POWYS** 203 Gliffaes Country House Hotel, Nr. Crickhowell	204 Bodfach Hall Ciountry House Hotel, Llanfyllin	**SCOTLAND BORDERS** 210 Sunlaws House Hotel, Kelso	211 Cringletie House Hotel, Peebles	**DUMFRIES & GALLOWAY** 212 Cairndale Hotel & Leisure Club, Dumfries	213 Moffat House Hotel, Moffat	**CENTRAL** 216 The Lake Hotel, Port of Menteith	217 Ardeonaig Hotel, South Loch Tay	218 Cromlix House, Nr. Stirling	**FIFE** 219 The Woodside Hotel, Aberdour	**LOTHIAN** 220 The Maitland Hotel, Edinburgh	221 Greywalls Hotel, Gullane	**STRATHCLYDE** 222 The Manor House, Oban
Other	Art gallery			Hang gliding nearby		Health & beaty salon		Bicycles, beautician								
Watersports																
Tennis			●	●	○	●	●		○			●		●	●	
Swimming pool			●					●								○
Squash/badminton																
Shooting						●				○	●	✪				
Sea/river bathing		○	●													●
Sauna/solarium			●					●					●			○
Sailing/boating			○	○							●					○
Riding	○	○		○		●	○		○	○	○	✪		●		
Massage								●						●		
Jogging track																
Jacuzzi/whirlpool								●								
Indoor games																
Golf	○	○	○	○	○	○	○	○	○	○	●	○	○	●	○	○
Gym/fitness centre			●		○	●		●	○	○						○
Fishing				●		●	✪			○	●	●				
Croquet				●			●					●			●	
Conferences				●		●		●	●		●	●		●	●	
Billiards/snooker				●												

(Hotels not listed have not informed us of their sporting/conference facilities)

223 The Creggans Inn, Strachur		●		○								●		○	○			○		
224 Stonefield Castle Hotel, Tarbert		●		●		○					○	●	●		○		●			
TAYSIDE																				
225 Clachan Cottage Hotel, Lochearnhead		●		○		✪					✪								✪	
226 Green Park Hotel, Pitlochry		●		✪		✪	●				✪	●								Bar billiards,9-hole putting
227 Dalmunzie House Hotel, Spittal of Glenshee		●		●		●									●			●		Ski-ing nearby
GRAMPIAN																				
230 Marcliffe at Pitfodels, Aberdeen	●	●		✪		○					○				✪	○		○		
HIGHLAND																				
231 Culduthel Lodge, Inverness				✪		○									✪			○		
232 Lochalsh Hotel, Kyle of Lochalsh		●		●											●					
233 Eddrachilles Hotyel, Scourie				●								●								
STRATHCLYDE																				
234 The Hotel, Isle of Colonsay				○		○													○	Bicycles
235 Killiechronan House, Isle of Mull				●		○					●	●		●	●					Stalking by arrangement
236 Rosedale Hotel, Isle of Skye				✪		○						●		●				○		
237 Uig Hotel, Isle of Skye				○							○	○		○	✪					
CHANNEL ISLANDS																				
239 Hotel Bella Luce, Guernsey		●											●				●			
240 Old Government House Hotel, Guernsey	○	●	○	○	○	○				○	○		○			○	●	○	○	
242 The Atlantic Hotel, Jersey		●			●	○							●	○			●	●		
243 The Royal Hotel, Jersey		●		○		○					○				○	○		○	○	
244 Hotel Petit Champ, Sark	○			○			○										●	○		Putting green
IRELAND																				
249 Dromoland Castle, Co Clare	●	●		✪	●	✪	●		●	●	○				✪			✪		
251 Innishannon House, Co Cork		●		○		○					○	○			○	○		○		
252 Shandon Hotel, Co Donegal				○		○	●	●			○		●					✪	○	Walking
253 Sand House Hotel, Co Donegal	●	●	●	✪		✪	●				✪	○							✪	
255 Shelbourne, Dublin		●				✪				●						○				
256 Ardagh Hotel & Restaurant, Co Galway						✪					○					○			○	
257 KIllarney Park Hotel, Co Kerry		●		○	●	○				✪	○				✪	○	●	○	✪	
258 Parknasilla Gt Southern Hotel, Co Kerry	●	●		✪		✪	●	●	●		✪		●		✪		●	✪	✪	
259 Butler Arms Hotel. Co Kerry	●			●		○					○				○				✪	Cycling , birdwatching
260 Kildare Hotel & Country Club, Co Kildare	●	●	●	✪	●	✪		●		●	○		●		○	✪	●	✪	✪	
261 Ashford Castle, Co Mayo	●	●		✪	●	✪		●	●	●	✪		●		✪			✪		Cruising, archery
262 Richmond House, Co Waterford	●			○		○					○							○		

LOCATION INDEX
ENGLAND

THE WEST COUNTRY

(* Hotels whose names are printed in italics are Budget hotels or guest houses)

LONDON AND THE SOUTH

(* Hotels whose names are printed in italics are Budget hotels or guest houses)

HEART OF ENGLAND

(* Hotels whose names are printed in italics are Budget hotels or guest houses)

YORKSHIRE & THE NORTH EAST

WALES

(* Hotels whose names are printed in italics are Budget hotels or guest houses)

SCOTLAND

CHANNEL ISLANDS

IRELAND

Children
matter

The Children's Society is an independent organisation working with children, young people and their families throughout England and Wales. The range of work undertaken is enormous:

- Streetwork projects help young runaways at risk in cities.
- Family centres offer a safety valve to parents under pressure.
- Children with learning difficulties or disabilities are given respite care both as a benefit for them and so that their families can take a needed break.
- Advocacy work is undertaken for young people in care or involved in court proceedings.
- Research and policy development are undertaken and a wide range of publications produced.

Through a programme of national and local promotions Fiat and The Children's Society are working in partnership, to raise much needed funds for disadvantaged children and young people. The relationship is built on the shared philosophy of working closely within the local community.

TOGETHER WE'RE MAKING
The Children's Society
CHARITY REGISTRATION NO:221124
FIAT
LIVES WORTH LIVING

For further information about these or other aspects of our work please contact:
The Children's Society, Edward Rudolf House, Margery Street, London WC1X 0JL Tel: 0171 837 4299

If you have stayed in an hotel which is not yet featured in SIGNPOST and you think it merits an inspection for possible future inclusion, please send one of the forms below in confidence (no stamp necessary) to Signpost, Priory Publications Ltd, FREEPOST NH0504, Brackley, Northamptonshire NN13 5BR

GUEST RECOMMENDATION FORM

I would like to recommend the under-mentioned hotel for possible inclusion in the next edition of SIGNPOST - the premier hotel guide to the British Isles.

My name_____

My address_____

Name of hotel_____

_____

City/Town_____

_____

I certify that I have no connection of any sort with the management or owners of the above hotel.
Signed_____Date_____

GUEST RECOMMENDATION FORM

I would like to recommend the under-mentioned hotel for possible inclusion in the next edition of SIGNPOST - the premier hotel guide to the British Isles.

My name_____

My address_____

Name of hotel_____

_____

City/Town_____

_____

I certify that I have no connection of any sort with the management or owners of the above hotel.
Signed_____Date_____

GUEST REPORT FORM

Cut out and send the enclosed form (no stamp necessary) to Signpost, Priory Publications Ltd, FREEPOST NH0504, Brackley, Northamptonshire NN13 5BR

I have stayed in the below mentioned hotel, recommended by SIGNPOST, and would make the following comments: *(Continue overleaf if necessary)*

NAME OF HOTEL   TOWN

REPORT

I certify that I have no connection with the management or owners of the hotel and I understand that my report will be treated in the strictest condidence.

Name:...Date...

Address:.. SIG96/1

GUEST REPORT FORM

Cut out and send the enclosed form (no stamp necessary) to Signpost, Priory Publications Ltd, FREEPOST NH0504, Brackley, Northamptonshire NN13 5BR

I have stayed in the below mentioned hotel, recommended by SIGNPOST, and would make the following comments: *(Continue overleaf if necessary)*

NAME OF HOTEL   TOWN

REPORT

I certify that I have no connection with the management or owners of the hotel and I understand that my report will be treated in the strictest condidence.

Name:...Date...

Address:.. SIG96/2

PRICES
Please note that the prices quoted to us by establishments listed in this book date, in many cases, from mid-1995 and are liable to amendment by the hotels without prior notice.

TRADE DESCRIPTIONS ACT 1968
The facilities in italics in each hotel entry are submitted each year to us by hotels but the comments on each hotel are the personal opinion of a member of the Signpost team as he or she found it. Due to a number of factors such as changes in management or chefs, we are unable to guarantee that the visitor will find any particular hotel in the exact state that our inspectors found it or will have the same opinion of it. We are therefore not responsible for eventual disappointment but we try to include in the book a wide a range of hotels and we sincerely hope that guests will agree with our inspectors' choice. Please use the Report Forms on the previous page if you would like to make any particular comments.

SEND FOR YOUR <u>FREE</u> BROCHURES!

TO RECEIVE THE BROCHURE OF ANY HOTEL FEATURED
IN THIS 57TH EDITION, SIMPLY PUT THE APPROPRIATE
PAGE NUMBERS IN THE BOXES BELOW AND RETURN
THE CARD TO US

PLEASE LIST IN PAGE ORDER

NAME (Mr/Mrs/Miss)..(CAPITALS)

ADDRESS ....

....

....

....**POSTAL CODE**.......................

Business Reply Service
Licence no: **NH 0504**

SIGNPOST
PRIORY PUBLICATIONS LTD
PO BOX 24
BRACKLEY
NORTHAMPTONSHIRE NN13 5BR

SIGNPOST - COLOUR HOTEL GUIDE 1996
ORDER FORM

No. of Copies	Price	Total
	£9.95	
For Postage per copy to:		
U.K. Free of charge		FOC
Europe add £2.70		
Outside Europe Air mail add £5.50		
Outside Europe Surface (allow 12 weeks for delivery) add £2.25		
TOTAL (inc. carriage)		
Ref:		

TO SIGNPOST, PRIORY PUBLICATIONS LTD, SYRESHAM, BRACKLEY, NORTHANTS NN13 5HH (TEL: 01280 850603)

I enclose cheque/Eurocheque in the sum of £..........................
made payable to Signpost Ltd, or

VISA I wish to pay by Visa/Master Card/Amex; please charge to my account. My card number is (13 or 16 digits):

MasterCard.

Signature   Expiry date

Name (on card)

Address

Postcode

Please deliver to:

NAME..

ADDRESS ....

....

....POSTAL CODE.....................

SIGNPOST - COLOUR HOTEL GUIDE 1996
ORDER FORM

No. of Copies	Price	Total
	£9.95	
For Postage per copy to:		
U.K. Free of charge		FOC
Europe add £2.70		
Outside Europe Air mail add £5.50		
Outside Europe Surface (allow 12 weeks for delivery) add £2.25		
TOTAL (inc. carriage)		
Ref:		

TO SIGNPOST, PRIORY PUBLICATIONS LTD, SYRESHAM, BRACKLEY, NORTHANTS NN13 5HH (TEL: 01280 850603)

I enclose cheque/Eurocheque in the sum of £..........................
made payable to Signpost Ltd, or

VISA I wish to pay by Visa/Master Card/Amex; please charge to my account. My card number is (13 or 16 digits):

MasterCard

Signature   Expiry date

Name (on card)

Address

Postcode

Please deliver to:

NAME..

ADDRESS ....

....

....POSTAL CODE.....................

SIGNPOST
PRIORY PUBLICATIONS LTD
PO BOX 24
BRACKLEY
NORTHAMPTONSHIRE NN13 5BR

Business Reply Service
Licence no: **NH 0504**

SIGNPOST
PRIORY PUBLICATIONS LTD
PO BOX 24
BRACKLEY
NORTHAMPTONSHIRE NN13 5BR

MAPS

The following section contains road maps of the British Isles and a plan of Central London.

The names of principal towns are marked in green.

The locations of SIGNPOST hotels are marked in black on the maps and by name on the London plan.

Only major roads are shown and we therefore recommend that travellers also use a comprehensive road atlas when travelling "off the beaten track".

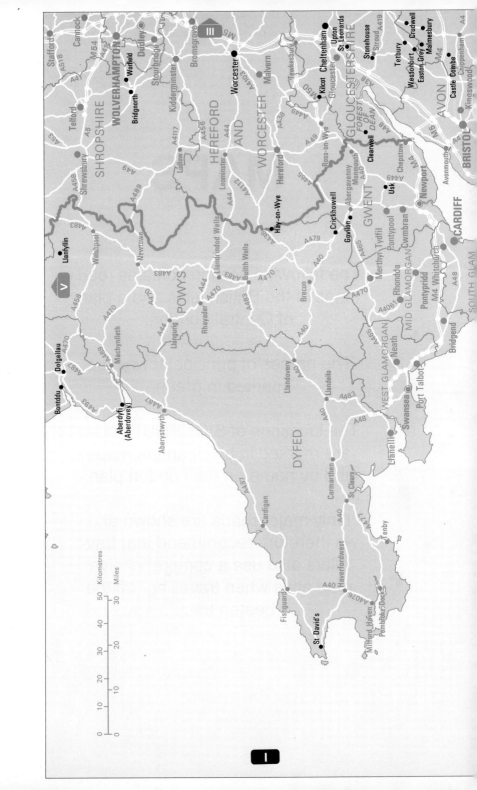

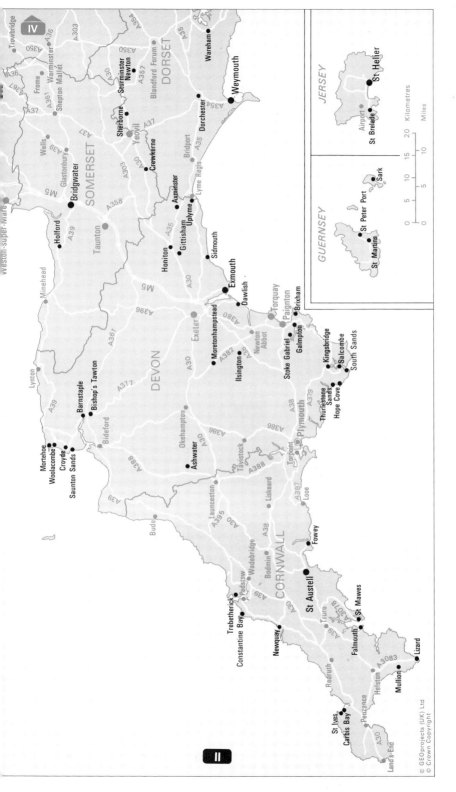

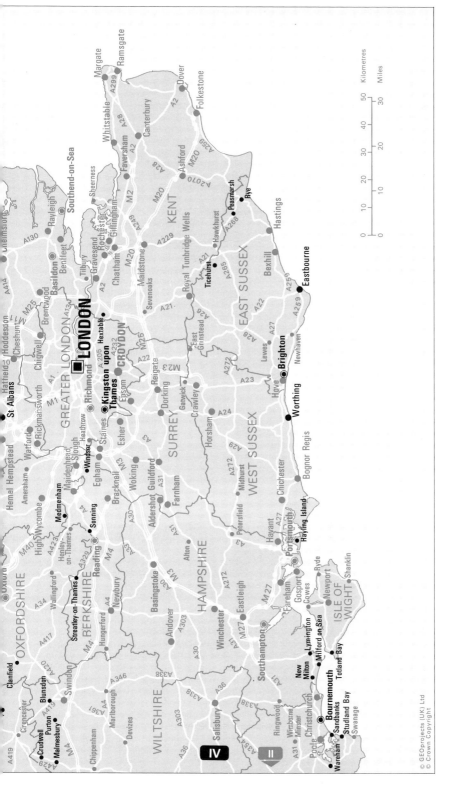

© GEOprojects (UK) Ltd
Crown Copyright

IX

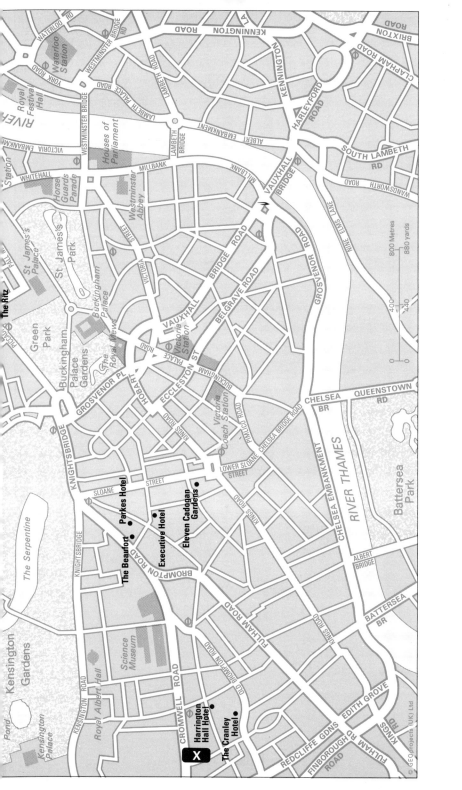

© GEOprojects (UK) Ltd
© Crown Copyright

XI